Subalternity and Representation

Post-Contemporary Interventions   Series Editors: Stanley Fish and Fredric Jameson

Subalternity and Representation

Arguments in Cultural Theory

John Beverley

Duke University Press   Durham and London 1999

Second printing, 2004
© 1999 Duke University Press
All rights reserved
Printed in the United States of America on acid-free paper ∞
Typeset in Quadraat by Keystone Typesetting, Inc.
Library of Congress Cataloging-in-Publication Data appear
on the last printed page of this book.

For Mili, in loving memory

Contents

Acknowledgments   ix
Introduction   1
1 Writing in Reverse: The Subaltern and the Limits of
   Academic Knowledge   25
2 Transculturation and Subalternity: The "Lettered City" and the
   Túpac Amaru Rebellion   41
3 Our Rigoberta? I, Rigoberta Menchú, Cultural Authority, and the
   Problem of Subaltern Agency   65
4 Hybrid or Binary? On the Category of "the People" in Subaltern
   and Cultural Studies   85
5 Civil Society, Hybridity, and the " 'Political' Aspect of Cultural
   Studies" (on Canclini)   115
6 Territoriality, Multiculturalism, and Hegemony: The Question
   of the Nation   133
   Notes   169
   Index   195

Acknowledgments

This book can be read as a conversation with Ranajit Guha, so my first acknowledgment is for the example of his work, and for the friendship and solidarity he has shown me and the Latin American Subaltern Studies Group. My personal introduction to subaltern studies came at a meeting of the South Asian Subaltern Studies Group that Gayatri Spivak organized when she was director of the cultural studies program at the University of Pittsburgh in the late 1980s. My debt to her in what follows, beginning with the question of representation announced in the title, is second only to my debt to Guha. Spivak's *A Critique of Postcolonial Reason: Towards a History of the Vanishing Present* (Cambridge: Harvard Univ. Press, 1999) came out as I was correcting the proofs. But at least some of its concerns are anticipated, and sometimes echoed, here. Perhaps because this book is *American*, and Spivak's more ambiguously so, however, there is a difference in our understanding of the political consequences of subaltern studies that will become evident, especially in the later chapters.

I am also indebted to the participants in my 1995 seminar on subaltern studies at the University of Pittsburgh, with whom I tried out many of these ideas for the first time, and, especially, to my graduate students in the Department of Hispanic Languages and Literatures, who have shared the concerns of this book (and taught me a great deal in the process) in their own work. Amy Smith's dedication on their and my behalf made this book possible. Doris Sommer and Roberto Fernández Retamar, each in their own way, helped me overcome my prejudice against the idea of multiculturalism and realize that it had to be a central concern here. My thanks also to Jean-François Chevrier and Brian Holmes of Dokumenta, to Manuel Borja-Villel and Noemi Cohen at the Fundació Tàpies in Barcelona, and Kathy Lehmann at the University of Auckland. It is nice to have an editor who is also a compañero. Without the support and good advice of Reynolds Smith at Duke University Press this book—and many others like it—would not have been possible.

There is no part of this book that does not involve in some way the hopes and passions, debates and disappointments of the Latin American Subaltern Studies Group. Perhaps appropriately for an organization that sometimes espouses a "postnational" agenda, the group's own frontiers are somewhat undefined, and many people have come in and out of its orbit over the years. Those that have formed the core of the group are: from the founding meeting at George Mason University in 1992: Ileana Rodríguez, Patricia Seed, Javier Sanjinés, José Rabasa, Robert Carr, María Milagros Lopéz, and myself; from our meeting at Ohio State University in 1994: Michael Clark, Marcia Stephenson, and Walter Mignolo; from our 1995 meeting in San Juan, Puerto Rico: Sara Castro Klarén, Abdul Karim Mustapha, Fernando Coronil, Alberto Moreiras, Gareth Williams, María Josefina Saldaña, and John Kraniauskas. Friends and fellow travelers who have contributed to or intersected, sometimes critically, with the work of the group include Tom Moylan, Marc Zimmerman, Kenneth Andrien (who helped organize the Ohio State meeting), Julio Ramos, Juan Zevallos, James Sanders, George Yúdice, Alba María Paz Soldán, Ricardo Kaliman, José Mazzotti, Richard Conn, Doris Sommer, Roger Lancaster, Ricardo Salvatore, Beatriz González, Rosaura Sánchez, José David Saldívar, Agustín Lao, Ramón Grossfogel, and Jon Beaseley-Murray. Ileana Rodríguez deserves a special mention. She both inspired the formation of the group and has provided the moral force that has kept it going.

Perhaps the most charismatic member of the group was María Milagros Lopéz. Mili, as her friends called her, was a social psychologist at the

University of Puerto Rico with a background as a militant in the Puerto Rican Socialist Party and an activist in the Puerto Rican women's movement. After battling severe depression for several years, Mili took her own life at the beginning of the holiday season in December 1997. At the time, she had been working closely with drug addicts in San Juan. This book is dedicated to her memory.

There are three other persons I would like to remember here. I met Pedro Duno through his son Luis, one of the graduate students mentioned above. Pedro, whose academic calling was philosophy, was a legendary figure of the revolutionary left in Venezuela in the stormy period of the armed struggle and its aftermath. He was not afraid of risk or danger, but he was also a man of great wisdom, kindness, and generosity. His loss will be felt not only by his immediate family and friends (among whom I count myself), but also by the Venzuelan left, which faces great challenges in the coming period. The late Carl Marzani was the first to translate and introduce Antonio Gramsci's work in the United States. Though we belonged to very different generations of the left, our paths crossed briefly in the early 1980s, when we were both involved in the negotiations surrounding the creation of Democratic Socialists of America. I would have also liked to share this book with Carol Kay, as I shared with her many discussions about movies, politics, and literature before her untimely death last summer. Carol was a feminist and a scholar of eighteenth-century English political philosophy. She made a point of calling herself a liberal; but she was the sort of liberal who believed that there is never a good reason to cross a picket line, especially at a university. Like Mili, Pedro, Carl, and Carol were "friends of the people." I hope there is something of them in this book too.

Earlier versions of sections of the introduction and chapters 1, 2, and 3 appeared in "Negotiating with the Disciplines: A Conversation on Latin American Subaltern Studies," with James Sanders, *Journal of Latin American Cultural Studies* 6, no. 2 (1997); "Writing in Reverse: On the Project of the Latin American Subaltern Studies Group," *Dispositio/n* 46 (1994/1996), a special issue on *Subaltern Studies in the Americas* edited by José Rabasa, Javier Sanjínes, and Robert Carr; "Pedagogy and Subalternity. Mapping the Limits of Academic Knowledge," in *Social Cartography: Mapping Ways of Seeing Social and Educational Change*, ed. Rolland Paulston (New York: Garland, 1997); " 'Máscaras de humanidad': Sobre la supuesta modernidad del *Apologético* de Juan de Espinosa Medrano," *Revista de Crítica Literaria Latinoamericana* (1995); and "Postliteratura: Sujeto subalterno e impasse de las humanidades," *Casa de las Américas* 190 (1993). Significantly different versions of chapter 4 appeared in *Modern Language Quarterly* 57, no. 2 (1996), a special issue on *The Places of History: Regionalism Revisited in Latin America*, edited by Doris Sommer, and in *The Real Thing: Testimonial Discourse in Latin America*, ed. Georg Gugelberger (Durham: Duke Univ. Press, 1996). The critique of Néstor García Canclini's *Hybrid Cultures* that forms the core of chapter 5 was first presented at the Duke Center for Latin American Studies in March 1997. The second half of chapter 6 is based partly on my essay "Does the Project of the Left Have a Future?" *boundary 2* 24, no. 1 (1997). The section on multiculturalism in the same chapter stems from the text of a talk, "America, America: Thoughts on Bilingualism and Biculturalism in the United States," that I was invited to present by the NEH Humanities Seminar at Cleveland State University in 1997. A collage of bits and pieces of various chapters appeared as "Theses on Subalternity, Representation, and Hegemony," in *Postcolonial Studies* 1, no. 3 (1998): 305–19.

The historical phenomenon of insurgency meets the eye for the first time as an image framed in the prose, hence the outlook, of counter-insurgency—an image caught in a distorting mirror. However, the distortion has a logic to it. That is the logic of the opposition between the rebels and their enemies not only as parties engaged in active hostility on a particular occasion but as the mutually antagonistic elements of a semi-feudal society under colonial rule. The antagonism is rooted deeply enough in the material and spiritual conditions of their existence to reduce the difference between elite and subaltern perceptions of a radical peasant movement to a difference between the terms of a binary pair. A rural uprising thus turns into a site for two rival cognitions to meet and to define each other negatively. ¶It is precisely this contradiction which we have used in these pages as a key to our understanding of peasant rebellion as a representation of the will of its subjects. For that will has been known to us only in its mirror image. Inscribed in elite discourse it had to be read as a writing in reverse.
—RANAJIT GUHA, Elementary Aspects of Peasant Insurgency in Colonial India

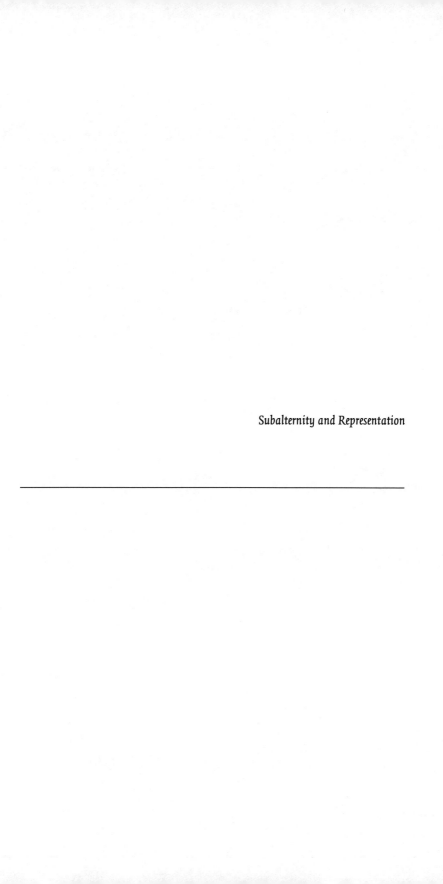

Subalternity and Representation

Introduction

Subaltern studies is about power, who has it and who doesn't, who is gaining it and who is losing it. Power is related to representation: which representations have cognitive authority or can secure hegemony, which do not have authority or are not hegemonic. Gayatri Spivak formulated the problem concisely: If the subaltern could speak—that is, speak in a way that really mattered to us—then it wouldn't be subaltern.[1]

This is a book about the relationship between subalternity and representation. It involves, as one of the readers of the manuscript noted, privileging in the idea of subaltern studies the sign "studies" over the sign (and the reality) "subaltern." It argues that what subaltern studies can or should represent is not so much the subaltern as a concrete social-historical subject, but rather the difficulty of representing the subaltern as such in our disciplinary discourse and practice within the academy.

But, of course, the question of what the subaltern is is itself not something separate from that discourse and practice. Spivak is trying to tell us that, almost by definition, the subaltern is subaltern in part because it cannot be represented adequately by academic knowledge (and "theory"). It cannot be represented adequately by academic knowledge because academic knowledge is a practice that actively *produces* subalternity (it produces subalternity in the act of representing it). How can one claim to represent the subaltern from the standpoint of academic knowledge, then, when that knowledge is itself involved in the "othering" of the subaltern?

The subaltern presents itself to academic knowledge as something like Jacques Lacan's category of the Real: that which resists symbolization, a gap-in-knowledge that subverts or defeats the presumption to "know" it. But the subaltern is not an ontological category. It designates a subordinated *particularity*, and in a world where power relations are spatialized that means it must have a spatial referent, a form of territoriality: South Asian, Latin American, "in the Americas," "in a U.S. frame."[2] Antonio Gramsci's invention of the idea of the subaltern as a cultural-political category was deeply connected with his attempt to conceptualize the "South"—the Catholic, agrarian, region of Italy, where the peasantry remained the largest social class. It goes without saying that the "South" is a part of Europe that closely resembles the postcolonial world (Gramsci himself was from Sardinia, which makes him in a way a "postcolonial" intellectual too).

Subaltern studies is tied to area studies if only because the idea of "area" itself designates in the metropolitan academy a subalternized space and the corresponding epistemological problem of "knowing the other."[3] But, of course, *from* postcolonial Latin America, Asia, or Africa, the other is (among other things) precisely the metropolitan academy and its information retrieval apparatus: the contemporary forms of what Edward Said calls Orientalism. The arguments I deploy in this book concern questions of history, ethnography, cultural theory, and literary interpretation drawn mainly from Latin American studies. That is because the urgencies that underlie these arguments stem directly from my own personal, intellectual, and political involvement with Latin America. Without those urgencies, the question of the subaltern would have remained abstract or virtual for me. Nevertheless, I do not see this book solely or even mainly as a contribution to Latin American studies (although I hope it is at least that). It is not even really a book about subaltern studies. I would like it to be read instead as something like a "regional" contribution to a critique of academic knowledge—one that maps in particular some of the limits of history, literature, ethnography, deconstruction, and cultural studies to the extent these are implicated in the representation of the Latin American subaltern (or—it is not exactly the same thing—of Latin America *as subaltern*). Because

Latin America is to some extent now "inside" its North American other—
"en las entrañas del monstruo," to recall José Martí's metaphor (with a
Hispanic population of close to thirty million, the United States is today the
fifth largest country of the Spanish-speaking world—out of twenty or so—
and early in the next century will become the third)—this critique cannot
itself be contained within the territorial space the idea of Latin America
designates, but rather opens out onto the question of multiculturalism and
the political future of the United States. For, as Spivak also reminds us,
representation is not only a matter of "speaking about" but also of "speaking for."[4] That is, it concerns politics and hegemony (and the limits of
politics and hegemony). If we are indeed in a new stage of capitalism in
which the teleological horizon of modernity is no longer available—either
because it has been achieved, as in the hypothesis of the "end of history,"
or because it will be indefinitely deferred—then what is required is a new
way of posing the project of the left that would be adequate to the characteristics of this period (or a renunciation of that project). What I will argue
here is that subaltern studies entails not only a new form of academic
knowledge production or self-critique, but also a new way of envisioning
the project of the left in the conditions of globalization and postmodernity.
I am privileging the idea of the "new" here, but the question is also an old
one, one that has to do with an understanding of some of the reasons that
led to the impasse of the left.

My friend Ileana Rodríguez believes that "any cultural statement today
must begin by acknowledging the victory of capitalism over socialism which
has discapacitated structural opposition, and tightened up the space in
which the production of culture as systemic criticism was viable."[5] I should
begin myself then by acknowledging that this book has its origin in a
corresponding defeat and failure, one that I share with Ileana. The defeat
was the defeat of the Sandinistas in the 1990 elections in Nicaragua; the
failure was the scholarly and commercial failure of a book I wrote in
the late 1980s with Marc Zimmerman that was partly about the cultural-
ideological dynamics of the Nicaraguan revolution, *Literature and Politics in
the Central American Revolutions.*[6]

Marc and I were both involved in Central American solidarity politics,
and since we were literary critics it made sense to try to combine that
interest with the tasks of solidarity work. Marc worked as a teacher in
Nicaragua in the early years of the revolution, and edited a series of an-
thologies of Sandinista poetry and testimonio. After the Sandinista victory
in 1979, I visited Nicaragua twice. I got to know some of the writers and
intellectuals working for the revolution, and helped organize a Sister City
relationship between the city I live in, Pittsburgh, and San Isidro, a town on

the highway between Managua and Estelí. *Literature and Politics* came out of that experience. It was meant as a theoretical contribution to the ongoing practice of the Nicaraguan revolution and the revolutionary movements in El Salvador and Guatemala, and so in its own "academic" way it was intended as a form of solidarity politics too.

Our hypothesis in *Literature and Politics* was that the dominant forms of modern Central American literature—poetry in particular—had become a material force—an *ideological practice*, in the sense Louis Althusser gives the term—in the construction of the revolutionary movements that were vying for power in the region. However, as Marc and I struggled to finish the book we were struck with a growing sense of the limitations of literature as a form of popular empowerment and agency—limitations revealed dramatically for us in the debates around the poetry workshop experiment in Nicaragua and in the question of testimonio as a narrative form that resisted in some ways being treated simply as a new kind of literature. We ended *Literature and Politics* with these words: "We return, therefore, in closing to the paradox that has been with us from the beginning of this book: literature has been a means of national-popular mobilization in the Central American revolutionary process, but that process also elaborates or points to forms of cultural democratization that will necessarily question or displace the role of literature as a hegemonic cultural institution" (207).

We didn't know it when we began the book, but we were working against time. We were faced with the usual problem of trying to get on top of a complex and often contradictory social process that was still unfolding. By the mid 1980s, the Guatemalan and Salvadoran revolutionary movements that had seemed so strong at the beginning of the decade were stalemated, and the Sandinistas were in deep trouble. In 1989, Cuba—the main regional supporter of the insurgencies—entered its "Special Period" of near economic meltdown, with the collapse of the Soviet Union. The Sandinistas lost the elections in February 1990. Several months later *Literature and Politics* finally came out, and promptly headed for the limbo of academic books that have missed their moment.

The failure of our book was not only conjunctural but also theoretical. The revolutionary movements in Nicaragua, Guatemala, and El Salvador we were concerned with representing through an aspect of their cultural politics had all, in different ways, articulated themselves as national liberation struggles. We tried to trace the ways in which specific literary movements and figures, forms of ideological hegemony and counter-hegemony, and the "national question" as such had become intertwined in their development. But 1990 was not only the year the Sandinistas lost power; it was also the year when, more or less simultaneous with *Literature and Poli-*

tics. Roberto González Echevarría's *Myth and Archive* and Homi Bhabha's anthology *Nation and Narration* appeared.[7] Doris Sommer had a key essay in *Nation and Narration* that anticipated her own influential study of the relation between narrative literature and the formation of the nation-state in nineteenth-century Latin America, *Foundational Fictions*, which came out a year later.[8]

In different, perhaps competing ways, *Myth and Archive*, *Nation and Narration*, and *Foundational Fictions* (along with Benedict Anderson's earlier *Imagined Communities*) rapidly came to occupy the place we hoped *Literature and Politics* would have: that of defining the main agenda for Latin American literary criticism in the North American academy in the 1990s. Moreover, they defined that agenda as one that was postnational or at least deconstructive of the identitarian claims of the nation and national-liberation struggles. Our book and its claim to relevance had been sideswiped by the emergence in Latin American studies of what has now come to be known as postcolonial criticism.

It was out of this crisis in my own work and political commitments—but also as a way of salvaging aspects of that work and those commitments—that I turned to subaltern studies. I was one of a number of people in Latin American studies at the time, loosely connected with one other, who were beginning to get wind of the South Asian Subaltern Studies Group and to imagine that it had more than a casual relation to our own concerns. We came mainly, but not exclusively, from the field of literary criticism (Marc, Ileana, and I had all worked with Fredric Jameson in the Department of Literature at the University of California, San Diego in the late 1960s). What we shared was a collective sense that the project of the Latin American left that had defined our previous work had reached some kind of limit. We weren't sure, or didn't agree what that limit was exactly, but we were sure that things were changing and that we needed a new paradigm. Borrowing the idea of subaltern studies and the organizational form of an academic collective from the South Asian Group, we decided to found a similar organization in Latin American studies. We met for the first time at George Mason University near Washington D.C. in April 1992. Out of that meeting came a founding statement—originally written as a grant proposal to the Rockefeller Foundation—in which we defined the need for a new paradigm as follows:

> The present dismantling of authoritarian regimes in Latin America, the end of communism and the consequent displacement of revolutionary projects, the processes of redemocratization, and the new dynamics created by the effects of the mass media and transnational

economic arrangements: these are all developments that call for new ways of thinking and acting politically. The redefinition of Latin American political and cultural space in recent years has, in turn, impelled scholars of the region to revise established and previously functional epistemologies in the social sciences and humanities. The general trend toward redemocratization prioritizes in particular the reexamination of the concepts of pluralistic societies and the conditions of subalternity within these societies.⁹

Part of the affinity those of us who drafted that statement felt with the South Asian Subaltern Studies Group was that it also came out of a crisis of the left, a crisis that had spilled over into the academy and South Asian studies. The work of the group, particularly the volumes of *Subaltern Studies*, began to appear around 1980. But the impulse behind it dated back to an earlier questioning of the project of Indian nationalism in the 1970s, a sense that the nationalist impulse had exhausted itself, or had run into a series of internal contradictions: the trauma of partition and the communalist violence that continued to haunt independence, industrialization without prosperity, the inability of the Marxist left to displace the political and cultural hegemony of the bourgeoisie and landlords at the national level, the alarming growth of right-wing Hindu fundamentalism. Implicated in the impasse of Indian nationalism was the inadequacy of a historical model of national development in which the Marxist left was supposed to participate alongside the national bourgeoisie—an industrializing, import-substituting bourgeoisie—to construct an alternative path of economic modernization based on state control of key sectors of the economy, ample Soviet aid, and political hegemony by the nationalist party or bloc.

Ranajit Guha, the founder of the South Asian Group, defines the central problematic of his own work as "the study of [the] *historical failure of the nation to come to its own*, a failure due to the inadequacy of the bourgeoisie as well as of the working class to lead it into a decisive victory over colonialism and a bourgeois-democratic revolution of either the classic nineteenth-century type under the hegemony of the bourgeoisie or a more modern type under the hegemony of workers and peasants, that is a 'new democracy.' "¹⁰ Mutatis mutandis, it was a similar "historical failure of the nation to come to its own" that we were confronting in the crisis of the revolutionary left in Latin America. We noted in our founding statement that "the force behind the problem of the subaltern in Latin America could be said to arise directly out of the need to reconceptualize the relation of nation, state and 'people' in the three social movements that have centrally shaped the contours and concerns of Latin American Studies (as of modern Latin

America itself): the Mexican, Cuban, and Nicaraguan Revolutions" (*Postmodernism Debate* 127).

We saw subaltern studies as "a strategy for our times," to borrow Spivak's phrase. In defining the historical range of our project, therefore, we stressed not only the colonial and national periods, but also the effects of neoliberal hegemony and economic and communicational globalization on Latin America in the decade of the 1980s (our approach to subaltern studies was conditioned by the nearly simultaneous emergence of cultural studies). We conceived subaltern studies as an intervention along the dividing line that produces domination and subordination not only in the past but also in the present. This emphasis on the logic of the present distinguished us in some ways from the historiographic agenda of the South Asian Group and of Latin American historians who were taking up subaltern studies.

But we also stipulated in our founding statement that

> the deterritorialization of the nation-state under the impact of the new permeability of frontiers to capital-labor flows merely replicates, in effect, the genetic process of implantation of a colonial economy in Latin America. . . . It is not only that we can *no longer* operate solely within the prototype of nationhood; the concept of the nation, itself tied to the protagonism of Creole elites concerned to dominate and/or manage other social groups and classes in their own societies, has obscured, *from the start*, the presence of subaltern social subjects in Latin American history. (*Postmodernism Debate* 118)

This was our way of bringing into our work the critique of the nation and nationalism that was gaining currency. We began with the awareness, sometimes from a position close to the revolutionary movements themselves, that even in the Cuban or Nicaraguan revolutions, which sought to base themselves on a broad popular, anti-imperialist appeal, there were deep problems in the relation between the revolutionary vanguard and the "people." We shared with the members of the South Asian Group an interest in the critique of representation developed by poststructuralism. In the main, they were historians or social scientists who began to read Roland Barthes, Michel Foucault, et al. to address a problem that they had come across in the historiography of the Indian subcontinent. That historiography, in both its colonial and nationalist (including Marxist) variants, had been structured by a teleological, statist model of political and economic modernization—what in Latin America is called a *desarrollista* paradigm; when that model began to produce perverse effects they had to find a different way of understanding South Asian social history and institutions.

The structuralist and poststructuralist critique of historicism and of the construction of the discourse of history itself lent itself to this purpose.

Our impulse was in some ways the reverse: we had to turn from literary criticism and theory to social history and ethnographic narrative in order to address a crisis that was beginning to take shape in our own field. That crisis was precipitated by the publication of Angel Rama's book *La ciudad letrada* (*The Lettered City*) two years after his untimely death in an airplane accident in 1982.[11] *La ciudad letrada* was more like the sketch for a book than a fully realized study, and it reveals today many silences and ambiguities. Moreover, its theme had been anticipated, in a way that Rama was not always careful to acknowledge, in the work of a generation of sociologically oriented Latin American literary critics that had emerged in the 1970s, which included (to mention only a few representative names) Agustín Cueva, Jean Franco, Roberto Schwarz, Jaime Concha, Roberto Fernández Retamar, Alejandro Losada, Antonio Cornejo Polar, Hugo Achugar, Hernán Vidal, Carlos Rincón, Beatriz Sarlo, Françoise Perus, Beatriz González, Francine Masiello, Rolena Adorno, Iris Zavala, and Mabel Moraña.[12]

Although Rama himself did not put it this way, *La ciudad letrada* was conceived as a Foucauldian genealogy of the institution of literature in Latin American society, a genealogy meant to challenge the prevailing historicism of Latin American literary studies (without, however, succeeding in breaking entirely with that historicism). The question that genealogy raised for us was that if literature—not just colonial texts or the oligarchic "national romances" Doris Sommer studied in *Foundational Fictions*, but even the "boom" novel of the 1980s and the sort of left-modernist literature Marc Zimmerman and I championed in *Literature and Politics*—was functionally implicated in the formation of both colonial and postcolonial elites in Latin America, then our claim that it was a place where popular voices could find greater and greater expression, that it was a vehicle for cultural democratization, was put in question. Rama's argument explained, on the one hand, how literature came to acquire the kind of ideological centrality it had in Latin American history. At the same time, however, it helped explain what Marc and I had come to see in the process of writing our book about the role of literature in the Central American revolutionary process: the limits of literature as representing/a representation of subaltern subjects. Our own project as literary critics "in solidarity" with Sandinism, not just the project of the Sandinistas themselves, came into crisis. To the extent that it designated an alterity that could not be adequately represented in the existing forms of literature without modifying them in some fundamental way, the subaltern was a way of conceptualizing that crisis.

Those of us who formed the Latin American Group were aware that other people had been grappling with the question of the subaltern in other ways and in other areas of Latin American studies. Some of us had been reading Michael Taussig, who was trying to produce an anthropology that could register how subaltern groups in Latin America created in superstitions, rumors, and stories their own forms of history, political economy, and value-theory (as opposed to simply having these brought into their culture by the activity of a political-theoretical vanguard, as in a Leninist or populist conception of the transmission of class consciousness). In his account of the "devil contract" among field workers in the Cauca valley of Colombia in *The Devil and Commodity Fetishism in South America*, Taussig showed, against the assumption that such ideas were what an earlier Marxist historiography called "survivals," that there was an active relationship between what was clearly a premodern superstition and the very high degree of class-consciousness and militancy evident among these workers. Steve Stern's and Florencia Mallon's argument that Andean peasant movements did not lack concepts of the national but that they were different from the creole concept of nation that eventually prevailed in the Wars of Independence—that they obeyed a different territorial, economic, and historical logic—similarly raised issues that epistemologically and politically looked like subalternist issues. We were familiar with C. L. R. James's *The Black Jacobins* on Toussaint and the Haitian revolution. We knew from the work of John Womack and others why the Mexican revolution went wrong—how the popular sectors were co-opted or repressed in the formation of the postrevolutionary Mexican state. We followed the debate, spurred by the work of Gilbert Joseph, about the character of Latin American bandits. We read Karen Spalding on "oppositional consciousness"; James Scott on "the weapons of the weak"; George Marcus and James Clifford on the problem of representing the other in ethnographic writing; and Daniel Nugent's collection *Rural Revolt in Mexico*—one of the first attempts to explicitly project a subaltern studies approach onto the very different historical contours of modern Latin America and its relations with the United States.

At the same time, we were not satisfied with the way in which the question of the subaltern was being posed in this body of work. It seemed to us that the social scientists in Latin American studies were not raising the issue of subalternity to the theoretical-critical level the South Asian Group had done. They seemed mainly concerned with the question of how to access the subaltern from inside their respective disciplines. They were asking in effect: "How do we push our disciplines a little bit further? How do we read the documents of the archive in a new way, or do a new kind of fieldwork so we can get at the people who are not adequately represented in the historical or ethnographic record?" Writing as a historian, Patricia Seed expressed this dissatisfaction in a much-debated article in the *Latin American Research Review*.[13]

Seed was and in many ways still is an exception among the historians and social scientists, however. It may be that those of us who came from literary criticism experienced the crisis of our discipline in a more acute way than the historians and social scientists. Since we were implicated in the "lettered city" ourselves as teachers, critics, and writers, it was not just a question of studying something that was *outside* the academy—studying bandits or peasant rebellions, or doing anthropological fieldwork. It was a question of looking at our own involvement in creating and reproducing relations of power and subordination as we continued to act within the framework of literature, literary criticism, and literary studies. In other words, we had to take into account the complicity of the academy itself— *our* complicity—in producing and reproducing the elite/subaltern relation.

Rama's *La ciudad letrada* was in a sense a book about the state. It was built on the assumption that if you traced the genealogy of the Latin American "lettered city" from the colonial period to the present, you would not just be describing a literary-cultural institution; you would also be explaining something about the character of the Latin American state. You would have a more Gramscian (or Foucauldian) understanding of the relationship between elite culture and hegemony in Latin America, and so also a way of thinking more precisely about the limits of the state and state-related institutions and practices. Latin American nation-states were not rooted in an organic relation of territoriality with cultural-linguistic ethnicity; in that sense, they seemed to exemplify perfectly Benedict Anderson's idea of the nation as an "imagined community" produced by literature and print technology. Latin American literature not only served those nation-states by producing allegorical "foundational fictions," however; literature was also an ideological practice that interpellated the colonial and creole elites that engendered and ran these states, a form of self-definition and self-legitimization that equated the capacity to write and understand literature with the right to exercise state power.

In Latin American literary criticism written under the aegis of dependency theory in the 1960s and 1970s, literature was conceived as vehicle for the cultural syncretism necessary to the formation of an inclusive nation-state. Rama's idea of "narrative transculturation"—*transculturación narrativa*—exemplified for him by the novels of the "boom," was perhaps the most influential expression of this general idea (I will come back to it in chapter 2). Within Rama's own work, therefore, *La ciudad letrada* signaled the beginning of a radical shift in the conception of literature: where Rama had seen literature before as an *instrument* of state modernization and democratization, it was now seen as implicated in the *inability* of the existing forms of the nation-state in Latin America adequately to represent and incorporate the full range of identities and interests subsumed in their territorial limits (themselves often arbitrary and ambiguous).

The way in which the South Asian Subaltern Studies Group took up the question of the nation and nationalism in India dovetailed with this shift in the conception of cultural agency, even though it reflected a very different historical context: it allowed us to think about the relation of the nation, national culture, gender, race, class, power, and literature in Latin America in a fresh way. Many Latin American colleagues have worried about the wisdom of taking a theory developed for the Indian subcontinent under conditions of English colonial domination that persisted up to and in some cases beyond World War II and translating it to Latin American countries which (on the whole) became formally independent in the early nineteenth century. It is worth recalling, therefore, that the idea of subaltern studies itself comes initially not from postcolonial India but from fascist Italy. It is to be found in Gramsci's sketch of the elements of a "history of the subaltern classes" in the "Notes on Italian History" in the *Prison Notebooks*. The problem Gramsci was trying to explain in the "Notes on Italian History" was the constitutive weakness of the modern Italian state that arose from the Risorgimento of the nineteenth century, Italy's equivalent of a bourgeois revolution. His hypothesis—one that Guha echoes in his remark about the "historical failure of the nation to come to its own"—was that this weakness was due to the inability of that state, formed under the political leadership of advanced bourgeois liberalism, to embody a national-popular will. This was the consequence, Gramsci believed, of the fact that this leadership, unlike the Jacobins in the French revolution, did not pose the question of radical agrarian reform, and therefore was unable to draw the peasantry and more generally the "South" as a whole into the process of national formation. The result was that the Risorgimento was a "passive revolution"—a revolution without mass participation. This failure, in turn, provided the opening for fascism.[14]

For Gramsci the idea of the national-popular functioned at once as a cultural concept—associated with the formation of a national language and new forms of literature and the arts, such as the serial novel—and a political one, designating the possibility of a hegemonic or potentially hegemonic bloc of different social agents in a given national society. The failure of Italian nationalism in the Risorgimento had its roots, Gramsci thought, in the separation produced during the Counter-Reformation between what he called traditional intellectuals (that is, "lettered" intellectuals with a cosmopolitan or universalizing worldview—in Latin American Spanish *letrados*) and the Italian popular classes. Whereas in other parts of Europe, Renaissance humanism and the new secular vernacular literature it produced carried the seeds of both liberalism and nationalism, paradoxically in Italy itself—the birthplace of humanism and modern literature—the literary and artistic intelligentsia remained in thrall to the Church and seigneurial interests, and Italian remained the language of an elite: the "people" continued to use regional dialects. Thus, Gramsci concluded, in Italy "neither a popular artistic literature nor a local production of 'popular' literature exists because 'writers' and 'people' do not have the same conception of the world. . . . [T]he 'national' does not coincide with the 'popular' because in Italy the intellectuals are distant from the people, i.e. from the 'nation.' They are tied instead to a caste tradition that has never been broken by a strong popular or national political movement from below."[15] Rama's genealogy of the "lettered city" and the emerging debate over the role of the literary Baroque in the formation of modern Latin American culture suggested that something roughly similar occurred in Spain and Latin America in the seventeenth and early eighteenth centuries.[16]

It is clear that for Gramsci "subaltern" and "popular" were interchangeable concepts (whether they should be in subaltern studies generally is an issue I take up in chapter 4). In that sense, his recourse to the terminology of "subaltern classes" or "subaltern social groups" (Gramsci used both forms) may simply be an aspect of the Aesopian language of the *Notebooks*— Gramsci's use of euphemisms so as not to alarm the prison censors unduly. If so, "subaltern" should be read as peasants and workers, just as "philosophy of praxis" should be read as Marxism, or "integral" as revolutionary. And there, for many persons who consider themselves Marxists, the matter of the subaltern should properly end.

But Gramsci's idea of the subaltern also suggested the primacy in social conflict of determinations of consciousness, contradiction, and political agency that are in a broad sense *cultural* rather than economic or political (political in the narrow sense of party politics). For Gramsci every relationship of hegemony was necessarily an educational relationship, expressing both a position of moral and intellectual leadership and the possibility of a bloc of different social agents around a common program articulated by that leadership. His argument to this effect in the *Prison Notebooks* was motivated by his awareness—no doubt sharpened by the conditions of his own imprisonment—that the economism of both the Second International and the Comintern had been unable to stem the rise of fascism in the decades after World War I: it was that failure after all that had landed him in jail in the first place.

David Forgacs puts it this way: " 'Culture' in Gramsci is the sphere in which ideologies are diffused and organized, in which hegemony is constructed and can be broken and reconstructed."[17] If this is so, then Gramsci's argument anticipates, and to some extent shapes, the shift that has occurred in (to use Bhabha's phrase) the "location of culture"—a shift that is often identified with postmodernity as such. In the Cold War academy, what prevailed was what José Joaquín Brunner calls a " 'cultured' vision of culture": culture was what happened after you went home from work, so to speak, what was in the "arts and culture" section of the Sunday paper. In the language of deconstruction, it was the "supplement" of the social. The humanities responded by retreating behind the wall of aesthetic formalism, insisting on the autonomy of art from the sphere of practical reason and ideology, thus reifying a sense of artistic and cultural production as a compartmentalized, specialized activity. In Anglo-American literary criticism, the most advanced expression of formalism was the distinction between "intrinsic" and "extrinsic" approaches to the text enshrined in René Wellek and Austin Warren's *Theory of Literature*, the handbook of generations of literature graduate students in the 1950s and 1960s.

Much of this " 'cultured' vision of culture"—which at the same time *overvalued* the heritage of humanism and bourgeois high culture and *undervalued* the humanities as "soft" rather than "hard" in a positivist or empiricist sense—persists today (indeed, one of the caricatures of subaltern studies among historians and social scientists is that it is "culturalist"). Brunner sees this persistence as "a symptom of denial produced by a deeper, and typically modern, tendency: the predominance of the interests, including cognitive, of instrumental reason over the values of communicative rationality; the separation of a technical sphere of progress that includes the economy, science, and material conditions of daily life from the sphere of intersubjectively elaborated and communicated meanings, those found indissolubly anchored in a life-world where traditions, desires, beliefs, ideals, and values coexist and are expressed precisely in culture."[18]

What has begun to change, of course, is that culture is now attributed a new power of agency. It has become increasingly common for historians, anthropologists, political scientists, education theorists, planners, sociologists, even economists of the World Bank or the International Monetary Fund to think about the "cultural sustainability" of development or the need for "social adjustment" of the (often catastrophic) effects of neoliberal economic policies. In an essay that has itself—in its global dissemination—become one of the cultural referents of postmodernity, Jameson argues that this shift in the place of culture is one of the consequences of postmodernism, understanding by postmodernism the "cultural logic" or superstructural effect of globalization. In globalization, which Jameson sees as a new stage of capitalism with its own special characteristics, the Weberian model of modernity, in which culture and the arts function as autonomous or semi-autonomous spheres separate from the sphere of instrumental reason and of religious or practical ethics, breaks down. Culture, Jameson argues, now traverses the social in new and untheorized ways.[19] Indeed, the social as such comes to be seen as an "effect of the signifier": the outcome of struggles over cultural representation rather than their ontological precondition. To register the consequences of this breakdown of the frontiers between the different spheres of modernity requires, Jameson believes, new forms of "cognitive mapping." Subaltern studies might be understood in one way as one of those new forms of postmodernist cognitive mapping.

In Latin America itself, the new concern with culture in the social sciences—which was sometimes designated as the "turn to Gramsci"— was in part a consequence of the rise of authoritarian-technocratic military dictatorships in the 1970s. Prior to then, the equation of democratization with economic modernization (in either capitalist or state-capitalist forms) had prevailed, in forms ranging across the political spectrum from left to right, from dependency theory to the Alliance for Progress. But the experience of the Southern Cone countries (and earlier Brazil) showed that democratization was not necessarily connected to economic modernization, and vice versa, that economic modernization—in both capitalist and nominally socialist or state-capitalist forms—was not always able to tolerate democracy. What began to displace both modernization and dependency theory models, therefore, was an interrogation of the different nonsynchronous "spheres" of modernity (cultural, ethical, ideological, political, legal, etc.) and the "structural causality" of their interaction—an interrogation that required a new attention to subjectivity and identity and a new understanding of the religious, linguistic, and ethnic heterogeneity of Latin American populations (Brunner's own work was framed by the defeat of Allende and the Unidad Popular and the subsequent struggle against the Pinochet dictatorship). The political correlative of the "turn to Gramsci" in the Latin American social sciences was the rise of the new social movements and identity politics, themselves also an effect of globalization and the defeat or deferral of the revolutionary projects of the left.[20]

The new centrality of culture and "identity" paradoxically conferred on the field of literary criticism and theory the function of a conceptual vanguard in Latin American studies. But Gramsci's argument about the cultural dimension of hegemony was also a powerful incentive to move away from the " 'cultured' conception of culture." For Gramsci, the dynamics involved in producing subaltern/elite identities in Italian history posed culture as what traditional intellectuals understood it to be—art, classical music, opera, written literature, belles lettres, literary Italian: in a word, "high culture"—against culture in the way it was understood and lived by the popular classes (for example, in the persistence of regional dialects).

So it was not simply a question of "culture" as such, as if the problem could be adequately addressed by simply having historians or social scientists take up literary studies or art history. Posing the problem of culture in a non-"cultured" way required the development of new forms of transdisciplinary or interdisciplinary practice that actively subverted disciplinary boundaries, that were transgressive in some sense. That was the promise of that belated child of the 1960s that came to be known as cultural studies. One of the central preoccupations of this book is the sometimes convergent, sometimes contradictory, relationship between subaltern studies and cultural studies.

Guha defines subaltern studies as "listening to the small voice of history."[21] In the same spirit, I find it useful sometimes to see both subaltern studies and cultural studies as connected to that "incredulity to metanarratives" Jean-François Lyotard offers as a definition of the postmodern: that is, the crisis or erosion of notions of modernity based on a Eurocentric historicism and a positivist epistemology and ends/means rationality supposedly embedded in the operations of the market, the state, and the corresponding forms of academic disciplinarity. The difference is perhaps that where Lyotard gives "incredulity to metanarratives" the form of a project that can and must take place within the space of globalization— indeed, there seems to be for him no meaningful space for agency outside globalization—subaltern studies might be seen instead as an effort to articulate against that which is hegemonic in globalization something like what has been called (although I do not much care for the term) a "postmodernism of resistance."

Like other forms of postmodernist thought and practice, subaltern studies is driven by a tendency toward epistemological rupture that can be deeply threatening to previous disciplinary agendas. Everyone involved in subaltern studies or cultural studies will be familiar with arguments of the following sort: "You claim to be politicizing academic knowledge, but you forget or ignore that we also have large investments, which include both personal and political investments, in doing literature or history or anthropology or hard science according to disciplinary protocols: political investments because the consequences of our work are about what is true and what is not and they affect therefore the structure of public funding for education and research, how high school courses are taught, how museum exhibits are set up, the uses and limits of technology, what the national narrative is and how it gets told, and so, ultimately, hegemony. The academy may have its distortions and limits, but its authority is ultimately the authority of reason and scientific truth, and it is that authority that is necessary to overcome ignorance, inequality, and oppression. Habermas is right: the project of the Enlightenment is still incomplete. Meanwhile, you people come along talking about deconstruction and undecidability in a virtually incomprehensible language. You mistake texts for the real world; you think you can read the real world the same way you read texts. What you do is more harmful than helpful, in fact, because it isolates academic work from the public."

I offer this harangue—which obviously owes something to the Sokal affair—as a way of trying to capture a sense of the resistance to subaltern studies on the part of colleagues suspicious of the new developments in cultural theory, but with a left or liberal political agenda.[22] But this resistance also appears on the terrain of cultural theory itself, as different tendencies jockey for attention, influence, and institutional support. Let me sketch a few major areas of contention that will be explored in the chapters that follow.

Subaltern studies is often seen as a subset of postcolonial studies. But the fit between subaltern studies and postcolonial studies is not always exact (for one thing, subaltern studies is not limited in its scope to the postcolonial world). In his own essay in *Nation and Narration*, Bhabha argues forcefully for "hybridity" as a central concept in postcolonial studies. Bhabha sees hybridity as one of the effects of colonial power; it is the space in which the colonial or subaltern subject can "translate" and "undo" the binaries imposed by the colonial project itself.[23] I will return to this argument (and to related arguments about hybridity and supplementarity in the work of Gayatri Spivak and Néstor García Canclini) in chapters 4 and 5. But a few words to anticipate what I will say there. I recognize, of course, that there is no identity that is not in some way hybrid, beginning with the fact that we are all the genetic product of two quite different people; that identity is decentered, plural, contingent, provisional, performative; that all signification is founded on absence or lack; that binary taxonomies of populations are a feature of what Foucault calls "biopower"; that what subaltern studies makes visible is precisely the fissured character of the national narrative itself, the way it is intersected by other histories, other modes of production, other values and identities. Nevertheless, at the risk of bending the stick too much in one direction, the main theme of this book is that subaltern studies is bound up precisely with what Bhabha calls "a binary structuring of social antagonism," both in the way subaltern studies represents theoretically the subaltern/dominant relationship and in the way it acts itself as a theoretical-political project within the academy.

The appeal of the hybridity argument for the contemporary academy is an obvious one: it joins the concern with the subaltern and postcoloniality with the "spontaneous ideology" (Althusser) of the humanities, which is a kind of Arnoldian belief in the redemptive value of culture. But that brings us back in a way to Brunner's point about the " 'cultured' vision of culture." By contrast, I want to try to suggest here a sense of the subaltern and subaltern cultural practice as something that appears in antithesis to the authority of "culture" in the way culture is usually understood by the academy.

The question of the relation between new forms of theory emanating (in the main) from the U.S. academy and the nationalist left is at the heart of an argument that has been leveled against subaltern studies in particular and the currency of postcolonial cultural theory in general by intellectuals in, or claiming to speak for, Latin America. I will use as an example of this argument the papers by Hugo Achugar and Mabel Moraña originally presented at the 1997 meeting of the Latin American Studies Association in Guadalajara, Mexico.[24]

Moraña and Achugar make three interrelated points: (1) Subaltern and postcolonial studies represent a North American problematic about identity politics and multiculturalism, and/or a Commonwealth problematic about postcoloniality, which has been displaced onto Latin America, at the expense of misrepresenting its diverse histories and social-cultural formations, which are not easily reducible to either multiculturalism or postcoloniality.[25] (2) Both projects ignore the prior engagement by Latin American intellectuals—on native grounds, so to speak—with the problems of historical and cultural representation identified by Guha and the South Asian Subaltern Studies Group. They involve, therefore, a tacit denegation of the status and authority of Latin American intellectuals and intellectual tradition/s, a willful forgetting of what Achugar calls "el pensamiento latinoamericano." The pervasive influence of "theory" itself may be a kind of cultural imperialism connected to globalization, a new form of U.S.-dominated Pan-Americanism concerned with the "brokering" of knowledge in and about Latin America by the North American academy. (3) By foregrounding the critique of the nation and nationalism and diasporic phenomena such as the Hispanization of the United States, postcolonial and subaltern studies may contribute to incapacitating Latin America's ability to implement its own projects of national or regional identity and development. Beyond an appeal to a subaltern other as a kind of abjection that undermines (any possible) hegemonic representation, subaltern studies in particular lacks a sense of the political as grounded in the continuity of the nation, a more or less active and politically informed citizenry, a Habermasian public sphere, local memory, and projects that seek to affirm the interests of both individual Latin American nation-states and Latin America as a whole in a differential, even antagonistic, relation to globalization.[26]

I believe that the issues that divide subaltern studies from its Latin American critics may be less important in the long run than the concerns we share.[27] I am sensitive in particular to their concern with the prestige and power of the North American academy in an era in which Latin American universities and intellectual life are being decimated by neoliberal policies connected in great measure to U.S. hegemony at all levels of the global system, but particularly in Latin America. But the following might be said provisionally in response to their argument: If in fact globalization entails a displacement of the authority of Latin American intellectuals, then the resistance to subaltern studies is itself symptomatic of a kind of subalternity—the unequal position of Latin American culture, states, economies, and intellectual work in the current world system (I am alluding to Paul de Man's remark that the resistance to theory in literary studies is itself a kind of theory). What Moraña and Achugar (and, in a slightly different register, Beatriz Sarlo, whose position I sketch in chapter 4) invoke against the relevance of subaltern studies and postcolonial theory to Latin America amounts to what I would characterize as a kind of neo-Arielism, to recall José Enrique Rodó's turn-of-the-century characterization of Latin America as Ariel the poet, "the creature of the air": a reassertion of the authority of Latin American literature, literary criticism, and literary intellectuals like themselves to serve as the bearers of Latin America's cultural memory against forms of thought and theoretical practice identified with the United States.

But Arielism almost by definition is, like Bhabha's hybridity, an ideologeme of the " 'cultured' vision of culture." For it is not only "in theory" (subalternist, postcolonial, Marxist and post-Marxist, feminist, queer, or the like), or *from* the metropolitan academy that the authority of the Latin American "lettered city" is being challenged. This is also a consequence of the "failure of the [Latin American] nation to come to its own," and of the changes and struggles that accompany the effects of globalization *inside* Latin America itself, including the emergence of the new social movements. Subaltern studies shares with cultural studies—that is the main point of convergence between the two projects—a sense that democratization implies the displacement of hermeneutic authority to popular reception. But that also means a displacement of the authority of the "lettered city." One can understand and even sympathize with Arielism à la Rodó as a mode of resistance to Anglo-American cultural imperialism at the turn of the century. But by rejecting explicitly or implicitly the validity of forms of oppositionality based on subaltern positionalities in Latin America, Moraña and Achugar's argument may also entail a kind of unconscious *blanqueamiento* à la Sarmiento, which misrepresents the history and character of even those countries they claim to speak for.

For subaltern studies is *not only* a way of thinking about a colonial or formerly colonial other. It may be true that southeastern Brazil and Uruguay are more "European" than, say, parts of Spain or Gramsci's South.[28] But even in *that* Latin America (as in Europe itself) there remain: the problem of male chauvinism and the continuing subordination of women; the widening of the subproletariat and the pauperization of sectors of the middle strata; the continuing, and continually deferred, claims of the surviving indigenous peoples (who, it should be recalled, also live "in modernity"); the persistence of racism and sexism at all levels of society; discrimination against and repression of sexual minorities; the arbitrary criminalization of large sections of the population by the state.

By asserting against subaltern studies the authority of a prior Latin American literary-intellectual tradition, and by identifying that tradition with the affirmation of national or regional identity against a foreign other, Moraña and Achugar undercut their own argument in a way. In order to defend the unity and integrity of individual Latin American nation-states and Latin America itself against their re-subordination in the emerging global system, they are forced to occlude some of the relations of exclusion and inclusion, subordination and domination that operate *within* the frame of those nations and what counts as their "national" culture. But the questions posed by those relations—beginning with the fact that the most important social group that the concept of the subaltern designates is women—are crucial in rethinking and reformulating the political project of the Latin American left in conditions of globalization.

Perhaps the most pointed criticism of the Latin American Subaltern Studies Group, however, has come from within the field of subaltern studies itself. I refer to Florencia Mallon's essay, "The Challenge and Dilemma of Latin American Subaltern Studies," in the journal of record of the American historical profession.[29] In that essay, Mallon argues that the work of the group is too dependent on what she characterizes as Derridean textual deconstruction. She proposes instead a model of subaltern studies based on a program of empirical research into the role of subaltern groups in the formation of Latin American society and politics. "In my experience," she writes, "it is the process itself that keeps us honest: getting one's hands dirty in the archival dust, one's shoes encrusted in the mud of field work; confronting the surprises, ambivalences, and unfair choices of daily life, both our own and those of our 'subjects' " (1507).

There is more than a hint of a disciplinary turf war in Mallon's essay. Its not-so-hidden agenda is to ask in effect: Who speaks for subaltern studies? and to suggest that she and her historian colleagues do more than the "literary" Latin American Subaltern Studies Group. The almost simultaneous publication of Mallon's comparative historical study of the role of peasant communities in the formation of the modern Peruvian and Mexican states, *Peasant and Nation*, seemed to come as a confirmation of her claim that she offered a "better" way of doing subaltern studies. I will deal more extensively with the limitations of *Peasant and Nation* as an instantiation of subaltern studies historiography in chapter 1. Here I simply want to repeat the question I began with: Is it really possible to represent the subaltern from the position of either the disciplinary historian or the literary critic—that is, from the institutional position of the dominant culture?

In part, Mallon's concern reflects the general anxiety of historians and social scientists about "taking the linguistic turn." But this is also more particularly a "Marxist" anxiety about "postmodern" theory. Subaltern studies begins with impeccable Marxist credentials via Gramsci, and in the work of the South Asian Group it is deeply connected to the vicissitudes of the Communist left in the Indian subcontinent, particularly the failed experience of the Naxalite rebellion in the early 1970s.[30] Indeed, a rough and ready characterization of subaltern studies might be that it is a kind of hybrid itself—a "Foucauldian" Marxism (in the sense that many of us involved in subaltern studies come out of Marxism, but don't see that there is a necessary contradiction between Marxism and Foucault, as opposed to Marxists who reject Foucault and poststructuralism *tout court*). However, not everyone identified with subaltern studies would consider himself or herself a Marxist, while others would see in subaltern studies a way of carrying on after what they perceive as Marxism's theoretical and/or political collapse. In turn, most Marxists have tended to see subaltern studies as a kind of "post-Marxist" heresy: an adaptation of solid, British-style "history from below" that somehow got struck down, like Saul on the road to Damascus, by poststructuralism.

The most influential critique of subaltern studies from the position of orthodox Marxism I am aware of comes in the introduction to Aijaz Ahmad's *In Theory*, where Ahmad broaches the issue of the "culturalism" of postcolonial theory in general. He mentions in this respect, along with "the Arnoldian sense of 'high' culture" and "Anglo-American sociologies of culture" (i.e., cultural studies), the "equally amorphous category of 'Subaltern consciousness' which arose initially in a certain avant-gardist tendency in Indian historiography but then gained currency in metropolitan theorizations as well."[31] A footnote directs the reader to the following characterization of Guha's work in particular:

> According to Ranajit Guha, described on the blurb of Subaltern Studies VI . . . as 'guru', the colonial nation was characterized by the 'coexistence' of two 'domains', 'elite' and 'subaltern', structurally connected by the category of 'domination'. The former includes all the colonizing personnel as well as both the 'traditional' and the 'modern' 'elites', communist cadres and Marxist historians; the latter, whose 'domain' is said to be 'autonomous' and traceable to pre-colonial society, includes all the rest. See, for an initial statement, 'On Some Aspects of the Historiography of Colonial India', in Subaltern Studies I. . . . Page 8, where Guha tries to define these terms, is remarkable for its contortions as he undertakes to reconcile a language taken partly from Gramsci and partly from American sociology with the Maoism of New Democracy and 'contradictions among the people', at the founding moment of a project which has subsequently come to be assimilated into a very hybrid and largely dependent kind of poststructuralism. (320–21 n. 7)

A subsequent note by Ahmad draws attention to the fact that in contemporary Indian debates the "inversion of the tradition/modernity binary may be found in very diverse kinds of writing: not only in many of the articulations of the Hindu communalist Right, not only in the neo-Ghandhians . . . but also in many 'subalternist' writings. Partha Chatterjee's [writing] . . . is replete with that kind of inverted logic" (321 n. 8).

Traces of this argument—with its tantalizing hint of a tacit convergence between Hindu fundamentalism and the work of subaltern studies—pop up in the way other Marxist historians (for example, Eric Hobsbawm) have characterized subaltern studies, leading one to suspect that Ahmad is their common source. But Ahmad's language ("the Maoism of New Democracy," and so on) should alert one to an unacknowledged sectarian strain in his characterization of subaltern studies: I refer to the hostility of both "official" Trotskyism and Soviet Marxism to Maoism and other forms of third world Marxism. It remains a question, then, whether Ahmad is making a properly "Marxist" critique of subaltern studies, or whether his hatchet job on subaltern studies should be seen instead as part of a debate within the field of Marxism itself.

My own perspective on subaltern studies is that it is a project of Marxism rather than a *Marxist* project, if that distinction makes any sense. I do not think of subaltern studies therefore as a kind of post-Marxism, unless what is meant by post-Marxism is a new kind of Marxism, or a new way in which Marxism acts within the world.[32] Let me acknowledge in this respect my own enormous debt to the unfinished theoretical legacy of Althusser. The entwining of the terrible personal tragedy of Althusser and his wife and the collapse of Communism have contributed to all but eclipse his figure. But, except for some work in postcolonial and feminist theory, I do not see that Althusser has been much improved on by poststructuralism or deconstruction (which could be seen, in any case, as products of Althusser's students) or other forms of postmodernist social thought. There are many roads Althusser opened up that are only beginning to be traveled. Perhaps the most important of these is the analysis of the mechanism of ideology outlined in the famous "Notes on Ideology" and subsequently elaborated by Nikos Poulantzas, Ernesto Laclau and Chantal Mouffe, and Judith Butler, among others. But it is certainly not the only one. Althusser's critique of historicism; the concepts of overdetermination, contradiction, uneven development, and structural causality; Etienne Balibar's crucial insight into the relation between modes of production and forms of historicity (in the latter part of *Reading Capital*)—all these themes invite the problematic of subaltern studies.

In particular, I would inscribe this book and my understanding of subaltern studies within the idea of what Althusser called "theoretical antihumanism." At the same time, I recognize that in its effort to retrieve the presence of the subaltern as a subject of history, subaltern studies is bound to mark its distance from Althusser's well-known claim that "history is a process without a subject." I believe it is the tension between these two urgencies that is productive of subaltern studies as such.

It should already be apparent that the arguments I review in this book are also in many cases arguments *within* subaltern studies. I say this to emphasize that neither the South Asian nor the Latin American Subaltern Studies Groups can be defined by a single "line"—they are rather (to borrow Pat Seed's characterization) "experimental spaces" in which various agendas and projects talk to each other, so to speak, around a common concern that is at the same time epistemological, pedagogic, ethical, and political. The subaltern serves above all as the signifier for that concern. Since the question of the adequacy of representation is at the core of subaltern studies itself, the reader should be aware that while I believe I am representing the nature of that concern adequately here, there are elements of my own take on it, particularly in chapter 6, in which I try to develop the implications of subaltern studies for reconstructing the project of the left. This is not only the usual scholarly demurral; it is also to indicate that subaltern studies is a pluralistic and collective enterprise, an academic form of alliance politics.

That is all to the good, I think, because it makes of subaltern studies a place where people with different convictions and agendas, but committed to the cause of social equality and emancipation, can work together. On the other hand, if subaltern studies is not connected to a politics, then it risks being recaptured by the very forms of academic and cultural elitism it means to question. I agree with the Latin American critics of subaltern studies I mentioned earlier that what is most urgent today is a defense and rehabilitation of the project of the left. But this must start from an analysis of what went wrong; it cannot be simply a matter of "keeping the Red Flag flying here," as if the collapse of the left had not happened in Latin America as everywhere else. Subaltern studies can help in this task by exploring the gap between the claims of the organized left to represent the subordinated classes and social groups and their actual needs, desires, strategies, and possibilities. What brought about the so-called crisis of Marxism was its identification, in both social democratic and Leninist forms, with an ethos of modernization that ultimately could not deliver the goods, to put it crudely. What is represented in this crisis, then, is not so much the crisis of Marxism as such as the crisis of this identification.

Subaltern studies has been understood as involving centrally an investigation and a critique of the nation-state and of the postcolonial nation-state in particular. More than a "postnational" deconstruction of the force of the—always ultimately ungrounded—figure of the nation, however, I believe that subaltern studies allows us to reimagine the nation in a way that makes sense today, after the collapse of "actually-existing socialism" and the defeat or recession of the revolutionary movements like Sandinism that emerged out of the process of decolonization. David Lloyd has spoken in this regard of the possibility of a "nationalism against the state."[33] I would agree with his slogan, adding, however (and this will be the burden of much of what follows), that to argue for a nationalism against the state is also to argue for *a new kind of state.*

That may seem like an overly ambitious claim, given especially the distance that separates academic theory from both popular "common sense" and power. It used to be said of the late Michael Harrington—the main theorist of U.S. social democracy—that, inverting Gramsci's famous slogan, he exhibited "optimism of the intellect and pessimism of the will." A similar charge might be made against this book. The new "visibility" of culture that Jameson sees as the defining characteristic of the postmodern may simply mask the fact that the real forces that move the world today are elsewhere. Ernesto Laclau has diagnosed the "subtle temptation" of substituting the notion of a universal revolutionary subject—the proletariat—with its "symmetrical other" via the reinscription of the multiplicity of subaltern subject-positions into a new kind of subject of history.[34] The subaltern is an "identity," and if we have learned anything at all in the course of "the long twentieth century" it is that identity is bound up inextricably with division, aggression, and evil. This is what Samuel Huntington—seeking a new focus for U.S. power—means to ponder in his idea of the coming "clash of civilizations."

These are useful warnings. Still, one has to recall the crucial difference between "contradictions among the people" and the contradiction between the people and the power bloc. We do not have the right to expect a non-conflictive, harmonious, self-transparent utopia; but we can expect and demand societies in which forms of conflict and inequality driven by capitalist combined and uneven development and the legacy of slavery, colonialism, and imperialism do not have to exist. Does anyone really believe that the tragedies of "ethnic cleansing" in Bosnia or Rwanda, or the resurgence of Islamic fundamentalism, are completely disconnected from that legacy? I continue to think that the possibility of a new form of radical-democratic politics—perhaps it might be called a "postmodernist" form of communism—is lodged within the problematic of the subaltern. If this book has only a propaedeutic value in this regard it will have served its purpose.

Postscript

As I re-read the manuscript of this book, I notice in it a tendency to make stories more and more prominent. Storytelling, Walter Benjamin reminded us, is a form of artisanal cultural production that is subalternized by capitalism and the rise of the modern novel.[35] Would it be possible to have a work of "theory" that would be composed entirely of stories? Perhaps that is what is still worth thinking about in Borges, despite his overtly reactionary politics (or are those politics related to his function as a storyteller as well?).

1 Writing in Reverse: The Subaltern and the Limits of Academic Knowledge

Jacques Lacan told the following story in his Seminar:

> I was in my early twenties or thereabouts—and at the time, of course, being a young intellectual, I wanted desperately to get away, see something different, throw myself into something practical, something physical, in the country say, or at sea. One day, I was on a small boat, with a few people from a family of fishermen in a small port. At the time, Brittany was not as industrialized as it is now. There were no trawlers. The fisherman went out in his frail craft at his own risk. It was this risk, this danger, that I loved to share. But it wasn't all danger and excitement—there were also fine days. One day, then, as we were waiting for the moment to pull in the nets, an individual known as Petit-Jean, that's what we called him—like all his family, he died very young from tuberculosis, which at that time was a constant threat to

the whole of that social class—this Petit-Jean pointed out to me something floating on the surface of the waves. It was a small can, a sardine can. It floated there in the sun, a witness to the canning industry, which we, in fact, were supposed to supply. It glittered in the sun. And Petit-Jean said to me—*You see that can? Do you see it? Well, it doesn't see you!*

He found this incident highly amusing—I less so. I thought about it. Why did I find it less amusing than he? It's an interesting question. . . . The point of this little story, as it had occurred to my partner, the fact that he found it so funny and I less so, derives from the fact that, if I am told a story like that one, it is because I, at that moment—as I appeared to those fellows who were earning their livings with great difficulty, in the struggle with what was for them a pitiless nature—looked like nothing on earth. In short, I was rather out of place in the picture. And it was because I felt this that I was not terribly amused at hearing myself addressed in this humourous, ironical way.[1]

I am using the figure of Lacan here to stand for the dominant subject of knowledge—the "master thinker." Lacan intended this "little story" to illustrate his theory of the relation between the subject and the visual field (it forms part of his lectures on the gaze and scopic pleasure). But it is also a story about subalternity and representation—in this case, about how the subaltern represents the dominant subject to itself, and thus unsettles that subject, in the form of a negation or displacement: "I was rather out of place in the picture."

In Ranajit Guha's succinct definition, the word subaltern is "a name for the general attribute of subordination . . . whether this is expressed in terms of class, caste, age, gender and office or in any other way."[2] "In any other way" might surely be understood to include the distinction between educated and not (or partially) educated that the apprenticeship in academic or professional knowledge confers. That is what Lacan expresses, from the other side of the subaltern/dominant split, when he says that, as a young intellectual, he wanted to "see something different"—in effect, to exchange the position of the master, alienated from the world of labor and matter, for that of the slave.

For Guha, as for Lacan, the category that defines subaltern identity or "will" is Negation. Guha's epigraph for *Elementary Aspects of Peasant Insurgency* is a passage in Sanskrit from Buddhist scripture, which he translates as follows:

(Buddha to Assalayana): "What do you think about this, Assalayana? Have you heard that in Yona and Kamboja and other neighboring *janapadas* there are only two varnas, the master and the slave? And that having been a master one becomes a slave; having been a slave one becomes a master?"³

To access the peasant rebel as a subject of history requires a corresponding epistemological inversion: "the documentation on insurgency must itself be turned upside down in order to reconstitute the insurgent's project at reversing the world" (Aspects 333). The problem is that the empirical fact of these rebellions is captured precisely in the language, and the corresponding cultural assumptions, of the elites—both native and colonial—the rebellions were directed against. Such a dependency, Guha argues, betrays a bias in the very construction of colonial and postcolonial historiography in favor of the written record and ruling classes and their agents, whose status as such is partly constituted by their mastery of literacy and writing. This bias, evident even in forms of historiography sympathetic to the insurgents, "excludes the rebel as the conscious subject of his own history and incorporates the latter as only a contingent element in another history with another subject" (Aspects 77). Thus, "the historical phenomenon of peasant insurgency meets the eye for the first time as an image framed in the prose, hence the outlook, of counter-insurgency. . . . Inscribed in elite discourse, it had to be read as a writing in reverse" (Aspects 333). (Lacan's story is about a kind of seeing in reverse.)

Guha means by "the prose . . . of counter-insurgency" not only the record contained in the nineteenth-century colonial archive, but also the use, including the use in the present, of that archive to construct the bureaucratic and academic discourses (historical, ethnographic, literary, and so on) that purport to represent these peasant insurgencies and place them in a teleological narrative of state formation. He is concerned with the way in which "the sense of history [is] converted into an element of administrative concern" in these narratives. Since the subaltern is conceptualized and experienced in the first place as something that lacks the power of (self) representation, "by making the security of the state into the central problematic of peasant insurgency," these narratives (of perfection of the state, of lawlessness, of transitions between historical stages, of modernization) necessarily deny the peasant rebel "recognition as a subject of history in his own right even for a project that was all his own" (Aspects 3).

Guha's project is to recover or re-present the subaltern as a subject of history—"an entity whose will and reason constituted the praxis called rebellion"—from the welter of documentary and historiographic discourses that deny the subaltern that power of agency. In that sense, as Edward Said observes in his presentation of the work of the South Asian Subaltern Studies Group, it is a continuation of the insurgency it represents historically.[4] But that means that subaltern studies cannot be not simply a discourse "about" the subaltern. What would be the point, after all, of representing the subaltern *as subaltern*? Nor is subaltern studies simply about peasants or the historical past. It appears and develops as an academic practice in a contemporary setting in which globalization is producing new patterns of domination and exploitation and reinforcing older ones. It responds to the pressure on the university and research and policy institutions to produce the knowledges appropriate to the task of understanding and administering increasingly multicultural populations and a heterogenous transnational working class. Subaltern studies is not only a new form *of* academic knowledge production, then; it must also be a way of intervening politically in that production on the side of the subaltern.

There is a passage in Richard Rodriguez's autobiographical essay *Hunger of Memory* that retells Lacan's story from the other side, the side where the dominant emerges into consciousness of itself as such in a movement of differentiation and splitting from the subaltern. It captures eloquently how academic knowledge is implicated in the social construction of subalternity and, vice versa, how the emergence of the subaltern into hegemony necessarily disrupts that knowledge. *Hunger of Memory* tells the story of Rodriguez's apprenticeship as a Chicano "scholarship boy" majoring in English, first at Stanford and then, as a graduate student, at Berkeley, which gave him the chance to transcend his parochial (in his view), working-class, Spanish-speaking family background. Returning from college to his old neighborhood in Sacramento to take a summer job, Rodriguez observes of his fellow workers:

> The wages those Mexicans received for their labor were only a measure of their disadvantaged condition. Their silence is more telling. They lack a public identity. They remain profoundly alien. . . . Their silence stays with me. I have taken these many words to describe its impact. Only: the quiet. Something uncanny about it. Its compliance. Vulnerability. Pathos. As I heard their truck rumbling away, I shuddered, my face mirrored with sweat. I had finally come face to face with *los pobres*.[5]

What Rodriguez means by *los pobres* is, of course, what Guha means by the subaltern. In fact, I know of no more exact description of the production of subaltern identity as the "necessary antithesis" (the phrase is Guha's) of a dominant subject than this brief passage, built on a conceptual binary of verbal fluency–power versus mutism-subalternity, which as writing the passage also enacts performatively. Though it is not without marks of conflict and irremediable loss that its neoconservative admirers often tend to overlook, *Hunger of Memory* is ultimately a celebration of the power of the university, the traditional humanities curriculum in literature, and English writing skills in particular, to give a " 'socially disadvantaged' child," as Rodriguez describes himself, a sense of self and personal agency.[6]

By contrast, readers of *I, Rigoberta Menchú*, which is also an autobiographical text about how one negotiates between subaltern and elite status in the Americas, will recall that it begins with a strategic disavowal of both the culture of the book and the liberal concept of the authority of personal experience that literature can engender: "My name is Rigoberta Menchú. I am twenty-three years old. This is my testimony. I didn't learn it from a book, and I didn't learn it alone."[7] What *Hunger of Memory* and *I, Rigoberta Menchú* share, along with the fact that they are autobiographical narratives of how a subaltern subject "comes to power," so to speak, is a coincidental connection to Stanford. The decision to include *I, Rigoberta Menchú* in one of the tracks of the Western Culture requirement for Stanford undergraduates was a defining issue in the public debate over multiculturalism and political correctness during the Reagan era, with the much publicized interventions of Dinesh D'Souza, in his bestseller *Illiberal Education*, and then—Secretary of Education William Bennett. The debate was not so much over the use of *I, Rigoberta Menchú* as a document from the world of the subaltern: Western culture has always depended on reports of or from subaltern others. It was rather about placing the text at the center of a required set of readings for undergraduates at a university whose primary function was to reproduce local, national, and transnational elites.[8]

When Gayatri Spivak makes the claim that the subaltern cannot speak, she means that the subaltern cannot speak in a way that would carry any sort of authority or meaning for us without altering the relations of power/ knowledge that constitute it as subaltern in the first place. Richard Rodriguez can speak (or write), in other words, but not as a subaltern, not as *Ricardo Rodríguez*, and not, despite the fact that the United States is today the fifth largest nation of the Spanish-speaking world, in Spanish. The "silence" of the subaltern, its acquiescence or "vulnerability" in Rodriguez's image, is only so from the perspective of the elite status he feels he has attained, his narrative authority. It is what *norms* that authority and status, just as, as Spivak puts it, "subaltern practice norms official historiography."[9] *Los pobres* also have lives, selves, narratives, cognitive mappings. Their silence in the face of Rodriguez is strategic: They do not trust him; they sense that, despite his mestizo features, he is not one of them, that he is a *letrado*—a word that in Latin American vernacular Spanish often carries the negative connotation of an agent of the state or the ruling class.[10] If their narratives were somehow to be produced as texts for us, they would resemble I, Rigoberta Menchú. And if, in turn, such texts were admitted into the hegemony—for example, required as part of a core humanities curriculum reading list at an elite university—this would give lie to Rodriguez's claim to difference and authority, a claim based precisely on his mastery of the codes of Western literature he learned as an English major at Stanford and Berkeley.[11]

Moreover, it is not at all clear that Rodriguez himself can, or wants to, erase all marks of subalternity in his own identity. Henry Staten has noted in an incisive re-reading of Hunger of Memory that

> despite his family ideology of distinction from los pobres, despite his transcendental metaphysics, Richard feels an intense connection with the most abjected Mexicans and longs to make contact with them. . . . In part, these feelings constitute the very "middle-class pastoral" against which he warns (Hunger 6): a cross-cultural class romance in which the bourgeois longs for the physicality and immediacy of the laborer. But in Richard's case it is much more than that, for at least two reasons: first, because he shares the phenotype of the laborers and, second, because his father, though "white" and bourgeois-identified, speaks English poorly, has hands worn by labor, and has been humbled by the life of the subaltern (Hunger 119–20)—like the dark-skinned Mexicans that Richard resembles. Richard's identity splits in relation to this father, who on the one hand represents the self that makes Richard different from los pobres and on the other hand represents los pobres from which Richard is different.[12]

Staten's point is that subalternity is a relational rather than an ontological identity—that is, a contingent, and overdetermined, identity (or identities). Rodriguez cannot himself escape that contingency.

In a sense, the very idea of "studying" the subaltern is catachrestic or self-contradictory. Even as they practice a form of elite academic discourse, Guha and the members of the South Asian Subaltern Studies Group maintain an acute sense of the limits imposed by the inescapable fact that that discourse and the institutions that contain it, such as the university, written history, "theory," and literature, are themselves complicit in the social construction of subalternity. Subaltern studies must itself confront and incorporate the resistance to academic knowledge that Menchú expresses in the concluding words of her testimonio: "I'm still keeping secret what I think no-one should know. Not even anthropologists or intellectuals, no matter how many books they have, can find out all our secrets" (247).[13]

What are the implications of subaltern studies for academic knowledge and pedagogy, then? My own answer in this book is ambiguous. I find within the project of subaltern studies a tension between the need to develop new forms of scholarship and pedagogy—in history, literary criticism, anthropology, political science, philosophy, education, and so forth—and the need for a critique of academic knowledge as such. On the one hand, subaltern studies offers a conceptual instrument for retrieving and registering the presence of the subaltern both historically and in contemporary societies. The breakdown of certain forms of thought associated with the idea of modernity—so the argument might go—has to with their inability to represent adequately the subaltern (the failure of U.S. strategy in the Vietnam War—a strategy designed in the academy, at a moment of tremendous expansion of higher education—was one of the first signs of the traumatic problems caused for public policy by the incomprehension or misunderstanding of subaltern classes or social groups by dominant academic methodologies and disciplines). We are disconnected from the subaltern by virtue of being in a doubly elitist position—that of the academy and that of the *metropolitan* academy. But now we have a "lens"— subaltern studies—that allows us to "see" it. We no longer have to depend on the native informant of classical anthropology, who only told us what we wanted to know in the first place. We can "boot up" the subaltern, so to speak.

That is one idea of subaltern studies, then, and to the extent that subaltern actors and cultural forms become visible in and through our work, this will produce new forms of pedagogy and representation in the humanities and social sciences (because "we are all multiculturalists now").[14] But being able to hear in Menchú's remark the force of the resentment against being "known" by us must imply also what Spivak calls "unlearning privilege": working against the grain of our own interests and prejudices by contesting the authority of the academy and knowledge centers at the same time that we continue to participate in them and to deploy that authority as teachers, researchers, administrators, and theorists.

This understanding of the implications of subaltern studies begins with a rather different question than the first. As we have seen, Guha makes Negation the central category of subaltern identity; what would it mean for that Negation to enter into the space of the academy (as opposed to being represented *from* the academy)? Can our own work incorporate that Negation, and thus become part of the agency of the subaltern?

Guha means by Negation not "dialectical" negation—or sublation *Aufhebung*—but something more like simple Negation or "inversion" in the sense used by Ludwig Feuerbach in his critique of Hegel. For Hegel Negation is one moment in a dialectical process of necessary "development"

(Entwicklung) through "stages" that culminates in the Absolute Spirit (or, in more quotidian terms, in modernity). That is the way both history and thought move. Feuerbach's idea of Negation, by contrast, is non-dialectical and non-teleological. Feuerbach takes over from Hegel the problem of religion as the imaginary form of the Absolute Spirit, but "turns it upside down." Religion is the expression of an alienated possibility of human equality, happiness, and fullness always/already present to consciousness. That possibility becomes attainable not at the end of a historical sequence (in which the idea of the holy will itself change through a teleological process of self-alienation and development), but simply by denegating the authority of religion once and for all. This is Negation as "inversion," as opposed to dialectical sublation. Similarly, for Guha the "general form" of peasant insurgency is "a process of inversion turning, as Manu had warned, the lower [adhara] into the higher [uttara]" (Aspects 76).

In invoking Feuerbach, I am aware from Althusser's discussion of Feuerbach in For Marx that I remain firmly within the domain of an ideological conception of identity. This is also Spivak's point, in her introduction to Selected Subaltern Studies, in noting the essentialism of the concept of subaltern consciousness, but at the same time justifying that essentialism on "strategic"—that is, political—grounds. What is at stake here politically is not the truth of the subject, in the way a deconstructive theoretical practice might reveal this, but rather what constitutes truth for the subject (in the sense of Althusser's remark that "ideology has no outside"—that is, that the very category of the subject is ideological). Guha's claim is that simple inversion is one of the ways in which subaltern groups and classes experience history and the possibility of historical change. It is the dominant groups and classes that see history as a teleological (or cyclical) process which produces them as "world historical" subjects. The historical vision of the subaltern is more particularistic, Manichaean, antihistoricist, reactive, even sometimes "reactionary": mock or deride the symbols of cultural authority and prestige, burn the archives, turn the world upside down, bring back the Golden Age, and everything will be okay again. (In both Gramsci's and Guha's construction of the category of the subaltern there is more than a trace of Friedrich Nietzsche's idea of slave morality, now "inverted" into a positive rather than a negative sign.)

Because cultural signs—speech forms and verbal etiquette, writing, food prohibitions, dress, religious literature and iconography, intertextuality, ritual—sustain relations of subordination and deference in a semifeudal society of "high semioticity" (Guha borrows the concept from Yuri Lotman), peasant insurgency is in an important sense a rebellion against the authority of culture itself: "it would be quite in order to say that insurgency was a massive and systematic violation of those words, gestures and symbols which had the relations of power in colonial society as their significata" (*Aspects* 39). Or, again, "It was this fight for prestige which was at the very heart of insurgency. Inversion was its principal modality. It was a political struggle in which the rebel appropriated and/or destroyed the insignia of his enemy's power and hoped thus to abolish the marks of his own subalternity. Inevitably, therefore, by rising in revolt the peasant involved himself in a project that was negatively constituted" (*Aspects* 75).

Guha shows that peasant insurgencies overflow even the forms of "prescriptive reversal" allowed by culturally sanctioned expressions of social inversion:

> In conditions governed by the norm of unquestioning obedience to authority, a revolt of the subaltern shocks by its relative entropy. Hence the suddenness so often attributed to peasant uprisings and the verbal imageries of eruption, explosion and conflagration used to describe it. What is intended . . . is to communicate the sense of an unforeseen break, a sharp discontinuity. For while ritual inversions help to ensure the continuity of village society by allowing its upper and nether elements to change place at regular intervals and for strictly limited periods, the aim of peasant insurgency is to take it by surprise, put the existing power relation on its head and do so for good. (*Aspects* 36)

If, as Said argues, Guha's project is a continuation of the "negative" logic of the peasant insurgencies it seeks to represent as history, then the question it must pose itself is how it locates itself within the necessarily political project of changing the structures, practices, and discourses that create and maintain subaltern/elite relationships in the present. A historian might say "Guha does this by showing a different way of thinking about social history that produces a new concept of historical subjects and agency, of the nation, the national-popular." But the interests and teleology that govern the project of the historian—its "time of writing," its involvement with the idea of a progressive approximation to truth, the institutional accumulation of knowledge that results, the relation between that knowledge and "good citizenship"—are necessarily different from the "negative" interests and teleology that govern the action of the peasant insurgencies themselves. The project of the historian is still basically a representational project in which, as in Ludwig Wittgenstein's analytic, everything is left as is. Nothing is changed in the past because the past is past; but nothing is changed in the present either, in the sense that the history as such does not modify the existing relations of domination and subordination. Just the opposite, in a way: the accumulation of historical knowledge as cultural capital by the university and knowledge centers deepens already existing subalternities. Paradoxically, then, there might be a moment in which the subaltern would have to array itself *against* subaltern studies, just as, in Guha's account, it arrays itself against the symbols of cultural-religious authority in peasant insurrections.

Dipesh Chakrabarty asks in his essay "Postcoloniality and the Artifice of History" how the postcolonial intellectual can take up unproblematically the discourse of history when history, in its colonial, nationalist, and even Marxist forms, is itself deeply implicated in the production of colonial and postcolonial subalternities?[15] Chakrabarty points instead to the possibility/impossibility of *another* history that would embody what he calls the "politics of despair" of the subaltern in the face of modernity: "a history that deliberately makes visible, within the very structure of its narrative forms, its own repressive strategies and practices, the part it plays in collusion with narratives of citizenships in assimilating to the projects of the modern state all other possibilities of human solidarity" (290). But the "impossibility" of that antimodern history is built into subaltern studies itself as an academic project, because "the globality of academia is not independent of the globality that the European modern has created." Chakrabarty concludes: "The antihistorical, antimodern subject, therefore, cannot speak itself as 'theory' within the knowledge procedures of the university even when these knowledge procedures acknowledge and 'document' its existence" (285).

Extending Chakrabarty's argument, we might repeat the question we asked earlier: If higher education—the academy—itself produces and re-produces the subaltern/dominant relation (because if there is higher then there must be lower education), how can it be a place where the subaltern can emerge into hegemony? Asking that question would oblige the disciplinary historian to confront, along with Chakrabarty, the way in which the discourse of history itself is implicated in the construction of ideology, cultural authority, the state, "Western" modernity. But then that would be to admit that the writing of history is not about the past; it is about the present.

I mean these remarks to introduce a consideration of Florencia Mallon's *Peasant and Nation*, to date perhaps the most explicit and sustained attempt to apply the model of subaltern studies to Latin American history.[16] Mallon is concerned with the ways in which the Jacobin imaginary of national-democratic revolution is transferred into the postcolonial space of nineteenth-century Peru and Mexico. In the process of adapting this imaginary to their own cultural goals and values, Mallon wants to show, "subalterns . . . helped define the contours of what was possible in the making of nation-states"—states being understood in Gramscian fashion as "a series of decentralized sites of struggle through which hegemony is both contested and reproduced" (8).

"From the very beginning," Mallon argues, "the historical combination of democracy and nationalism with colonialism created a basic contradiction within national-democratic discourse [in Latin America]. On the one hand, the universal promise of the discourse identified the potential autonomy, dignity, and equality of all peoples, and people, in the world. In practice, on the other hand, entire groups of people were barred from access to citizenship and liberty according to Eurocentric, class-, and gender-exclusionary criteria." How to recover the voices and projects of the excluded, then? Mallon's starting point is a notion of "communal hegemony" (11), based on kinship and generational (and mainly patriarchal) authority, and collective or semicollective property forms. She tracks in considerable detail the complex intersections between this "communal hegemony," the activity of what she calls "local intellectuals," regional interests and coalitions, the constitutional and repressive machinery of the new nation-states, and the resulting contradictions and negotiations of gender, class, and ethnicity within and between each of these spheres. These intersections reveal in their lines of fracture or joining "alternative nationalisms" (89ff., 220 ff.), which "helped to make the kind of nation-states that Mexico and Peru brought into the contemporary period" (329). Conjunctural differences led to a relatively more authoritarian state in Peru, a relatively more popular-democratic state in Mexico.[17]

To do this kind of history requires, Mallon contends, recovering "local voices" against pressures to expunge or ignore these in favor of a more synthetic historical narrative of the emerging unity of the nation. Such a narrative bears too high a cost: "Simplifying local political and discursive practices denies the dignity, agency, and complexity of rural peoples and facilitates the kinds of racial and dualistic 'otherings' to which they are still subject. When we pretend that oral history, ritual, and communal politics are not arenas of argumentation where power gets consolidated and contested, we submerge dissenting voices and help reproduce a false image of a rural Eden (or idiocy) that has been repeatedly invoked, on the right and on the left, to explain why urban politicians and intellectuals know what is best for innocent, ignorant, or naive rural folk" (329–30).

Two methodological implications—which seem to coincide with Guha's concerns in *Elementary Aspects* (although Mallon mentions Guha's work only in passing)—follow from this: (1) the notion of alternative nationalisms "must affect the possible ways in which we rewrite the past today," among other things by restoring to rural communities the status of a subjects-of-history capable of producing their own national imagined community (330); and (2) "history from a subaltern perspective must also take seriously the intellectual history of peasant action [which] means breaking down the artificial division between analyst as intellectual and peasant as subject—understanding analysis as a dialogue among intellectuals" (10).

Mallon writes at one point in *Peasant and Nation* of the need to seek out the "buried treasures of popular imaginings" (329). The metaphor is perhaps simply unfortunate, in the way most metaphors are; but it may also point to a blind spot in her project. Despite her claim that subaltern historiography requires "negotiations" between intellectuals—that is, professional historians like herself and the local intellectuals of the communities she studies—*Peasant and Nation* is *not* visibly the product of such negotiations. Mallon rarely abandons the role of omniscient narrator. To represent historical representation itself as "dialogue" would have required a very different kind of narrative and narrative form, one in which the writing of the historian (Mallon) was "interrupted" by other forms of oral or written narrative and other teleologies of intellectual practice—those of the "local intellectuals."[18]

What Mallon does instead in *Peasant and Nation* is write in effect the *biography* of the nation-state, showing in that narrative the presence of forms of subaltern agency that other accounts—the state's own "official" history—might have ignored. But this is to leave the frame of the nation, and the inevitability of its present (as well as the authority of history and Mallon's own authority as a historian) intact. In a sense, *Peasant and Nation* solves the problem of the disjunction between what Chakrabarty calls the "radical heterogeneity" of the subaltern and the "monism" of the historical narrative of the nation-state and modernity by demonstrating that peasants and rural people actually *did have* a role in the formation of the modern state in Peru and Mexico in the nineteenth century, that they were not just acted on passively or negatively by the state and its agents. But, to use a Lacanian metaphor, this "sutures" a social and conceptual gap that in some ways it might be better to leave open. *Peasant and Nation* thus partially occludes precisely what it wants to make visible: the dynamics of Negation in subaltern agency.

Part of the problem is that Mallon remains committed to a diachronic narrative form—that is, to a sense of history as development, maturation, "unfolding." By contrast, Guha is concerned with the way in which peasant insurgency "interrupts" the narrative of state formation. That is why he breaks with diachronicity in his own representation of these insurgencies, attempting instead to identify their "elementary aspects"—that is, structural modalities. Peasant intransigence and resistance can and do contribute to the complex adjustments, negotiations, mediations that mold the state historically, because the state must modify its strategies and forms to deal with the subaltern.[19] But, by making the synchronic cut—the time of *Elementary Aspects* is similar to what Walter Benjamin called the *Jetzeit*—Guha is also able to preserve in the representation of these insurgencies the possibility they contain of *another state* and another mode of time or way of being that does not depend on a future-directed, teleological narrative of development.

As I noted in the introduction, Mallon criticizes the approach of the Latin American Subaltern Studies Group as being too centered on a literary-critical idea of textual deconstruction. However, she might have benefited herself in some ways from reading—and perhaps recasting—her *own* text deconstructively. The problem with her desire for access to "local voices" is not so much, as Spivak might have it, phonocentrism—the identification of subaltern presence or truth with voice, as in testimonial narrative. It is rather in the simple fact that the voice (and the writing) of the subaltern is simply *not present* as such in her narrative. There is only her voice and her writing (the alternative histories of foundation by local intellectuals she refers to in her text are paraphrased or re-narrated).

Chakrabarty notes that subaltern studies historiography differs from "history from below" in three main areas: "(a) a relative separation of the history of power from any universalist histories of capital, (b) a critique of the nation-form, and (c) an interrogation of the relationship between power and knowledge (hence of the archive itself and of history as a form of knowledge)."[20] One could conclude that Mallon incorporates the first two of these areas, but not the third. The subaltern is always in a sense *out there* for her, in "the mud of field work" or "the dust of the archives." Despite her appeal to a "dialogue" between intellectuals of different types and social locations, she still sees history in the light of an implicitly positivist model of scholarly objectivity that places her at the center of the act of knowing and representing. Instead of studying how Peruvian and Mexican peasants were or were not involved in state formation, Mallon might have interrogated as a historian the relationship between the archive, Angel Rama's "lettered city," written history, and state formation in nineteenth-century Peru and Mexico. For if Foucault and Gramsci—the two figures she appeals to against Derrida and deconstruction—teach us anything, it is that what we do is implicated in some way or another in social relations of domination and subordination. How could it be otherwise? How could such powerful institutions as the university and the discipline of history not be implicated in power?

In whose interests, finally, is the immense labor of "information retrieval" and narrativization *Peasant and Nation* must have involved being performed? Mallon would agree with Chakrabarty that subaltern studies is a project *within* the university. It is not a *narodnik* project, in other words (the *narodniki* were the Russian populists who in the 1880s said, "We have to go to the people, to the *narod*," and then abandoned whatever their backgrounds were—the university, professions, middle-class family life—and went out to peasant communities and tried to organize there). It is not a way of saying, "Give up what you're doing and go work with communal groups in India or refugees in Guatemala or ACT-UP." But don't we have to admit at some point that there is a limit to what we can or should do in relation to the subaltern, a limit that is not only epistemological but also ethical? a limit constituted by the place of the historian like Mallon or a literary critic like myself in a position that is not the position of the subaltern? The subaltern is something that is on the other side of that position.

The assumption that the project of representing the subaltern from the academy and the subaltern's project of representing itself are commensurable is simply that: an assumption. In truth, it would be more accurate to say that these are different, even antagonistic projects. I believe that the university should "serve the people." To that end, I support making it more accessible, democratizing it, making more financial aid available, moving back in the direction of open admissions, socializing the great private universities. But those things in themselves will not close the gap between our position in the academy and the world of the subaltern. They will not even close the gap between the relatively privileged, powerful (and often private) universities that, on the whole, have become the home of subaltern studies in the United States, and low-ranked, poorly funded urban public universities and community colleges.

That is why it is the "negative" or critical side of the subaltern studies project that I prefer to emphasize here: its concern to register where the power of the university and the disciplines to understand and represent the subaltern breaks down. I sometimes think of subaltern studies as a secular version of the "preferential option for the poor" of liberation theology, one which shares with liberation theology the essential methodology of what Gustavo Gutiérrez calls "listening to the poor."[21] Like liberation theology, subaltern studies entails not only a new way of looking at or speaking about the subaltern, but also the possibility of building relationships of solidarity between ourselves and the people and social practices we posit as our objects of study. In a justly famous passage, Richard Rorty distinguishes between what he calls the "desire for solidarity" and the "desire for objectivity":

There are two principal ways in which reflective human beings try, by placing their lives in a larger context, to give sense to those lives. The first is by telling the story of their contribution to a community. This community may be the actual historical one in which they live, or another actual one, distant in time or place, or a quite imaginary one, consisting perhaps of a dozen heroes and heroines selected from history or fiction or both. The second way is to describe themselves as standing in an immediate relation to a non-human reality. This relation is immediate in the sense that it does not derive from a relation between such a reality and their tribe, or their nation, or their imagined band of comrades. I shall say that stories of the former kind exemplify the desire for solidarity, and that stories of the latter kind exemplify the desire for objectivity.[22]

What is best about subaltern studies, I believe, is driven by something like what Rorty calls "the desire for solidarity"; Mallon's project in *Peasant and Nation*, on the other hand, seems to be driven by "the desire for objectivity."

The desire for solidarity must begin, however, with a relation of what Gutiérrez calls "concrete friendship with the poor": it cannot be simply a matter of taking thought or "conversation," or for that matter of romanticizing or idealizing the subaltern. In that sense, Mallon may have a point about the limits of "textuality" and the virtues of fieldwork. Moreover, in making the shift from "objectivity" to "solidarity," we cannot simply disavow representation under the pretext that we are allowing the subaltern to "speak for itself" (that is Spivak's main point in "Can the Subaltern Speak?"). And there is a way in which the (necessarily?) liberal political slant Rorty gives the idea of solidarity may also be, as the 1960s slogan has it, part of the problem rather than part of the solution, because it assumes that "conversation" is possible across power/exploitation divides that radically differentiate the participants.[23]

Solidarity based on an assumption of equality and reciprocity does not mean that contradictions are suppressed in the name of a heuristic notion of merger or identification with the subaltern: Foucault's point about the embarrassment of "speaking for others" is pertinent here. As the "little story" from Lacan with which I began this chapter illustrates, the act of the subaltern "talking back" necessarily disturbs—sometimes unpleasantly so—our own high-minded discourse of ethical benevolence and epistemological privilege, especially at those moments when that discourse claims to speak for the other. Gutiérrez concludes that the consequences of a preferential option for the poor for the intellectual are symbolized by the structure of an asymptotic curve: we can approximate in our work, personal relations, and political practice closer and closer the world of the subaltern, but we can never actually merge with it, even if, in the fashion of the narodniki, we were to "go to the people."

Those of us who are involved in the project of subaltern studies are often asked how we, who are, in the main, middle- or upper-middle-class academics at major research universities in the United States, can claim to represent the subaltern. But we do not claim to represent ("cognitively map," "let speak," "speak for," "excavate") the subaltern. Subaltern studies registers rather how the knowledge we construct and impart as academics is structured by the absence, difficulty, or impossibility of representation of the subaltern. This is to recognize, however, the fundamental inadequacy of that knowledge and of the institutions that contain it, and therefore the need for a radical change in the direction of a more democratic and non-hierarchical social order.

2 Transculturation and Subalternity: The "Lettered City" and the Túpac Amaru Rebellion

Shanta Nag, who came from a generation of middle-class women whose mothers were already educated, tells the story of how she learned to read the alphabet. It was sometime around the turn of the century. Her mother would sit across the table teaching her elder brother and she would stand (beside her) silently watching the proceedings. In a few months, without anybody suspecting it, she had learned to read the first two books of the Bengali primer. The only difficulty was that in order to read, she had to hold the book upside down.—PARTHA CHATTERJEE, The Nation and Its Fragments

In his foreword to *Selected Subaltern Studies*, Edward Said situates Ranajit Guha and his colleagues as "part of the vast post-colonial cultural and critical effort that would also include novelists like Salman Rushdie, Garcia Marquez, George Lamming, Sergio Ramirez, and Ngugi Wa Thiongo, poets like Faiz Ahmad Faiz, Mahmud Darwish, Aimé Cesaire, theoreticians and political philosophers like Fanon, Cabral, Syed Hussein Alatas, C. L. R. James, Ali Shariati, Eqbal Ahmad, Abdullah Laroui, Omar Cabezas . . . ," in the sense that the group's work is, like theirs, a "hybrid, partaking jointly of European and Western streams and of native Asian, Caribbean, Latin American, or African strands," a hybrid which adumbrates the shape of a new, postcolonial humanism.[1]

But where Said envisions a new type of literary intellectual as the protagonist of decolonization, the admittedly paradoxical intention of subaltern studies itself is to displace the centrality of intellectuals, and what intellectuals recognize as culture and the written record, in social history and policy generation. This means being skeptical about seeing the literary intellectual as subaltern, even when it is the case of anticolonial intellectuals, as in Said's list. In much postcolonial criticism, it seems that a subject—someone, say, like Salman Rushdie or Toni Morrison—who is not exactly subaltern, who is distinguished from the subaltern precisely by having the status and prestige of an author, is being made to stand in for the subaltern.[2]

There is a kind of cultural narcissism about the authority of literary culture and our own place within that authority involved in this substitution—an elite cultural narcissism which subaltern negativity is precisely often directed *against*. This will sound too Manichaean to some. Said himself notes that the subalternist project risks becoming a separatist one, in the manner (he says) of radical feminism.[3] The warning is symptomatic of an uneasiness on his part about the relation of the culture of high modernism, which he defends, and what Dipesh Chakrabarty calls the "politics of despair" of the postcolonial subaltern. The specter that haunts Said as a Palestinian intellectual is, of course, that of Islamic religious fundamentalism—the sort of fundamentalism that pronounced the *fatwa* against Rushdie or that animates the suicide bombers of Hamas. But if only because subaltern culture and politics tend themselves to be Manichaean, it might be worth assuming this risk.

I do not mean to overlook in this way the role of cultural and political *leadership* or the question of "intermediate" strata that can be either subaltern or elite depending on the circumstances (I will come back to these issues in chapters 3 and 4). But I do want to mark provisionally the difference between anticolonial or postcolonial non-European literary intellectuals such as the ones Said names, who have their own complex agendas, and organic intellectuals of the subaltern who both appropriate and distance themselves from the identity and functions of the traditional intellectual. Historians like Florencia Mallon are given to preserving and nurturing the written record, whereas peasant rebels, such as those Guha studies in *Elementary Aspects*, or the Zapatistas in Chiapas today, often want to destroy it, for example, by burning down the municipal archives (as the Zapatistas did). They understand that the written record is also the record of their legal conditions of propertylessness and exploitation.[4]

I observed in my introduction that the circumstances that led me and others to reevaluate our work in the direction of subaltern studies included a growing sense of the inadequacy of the paradigms of leftist literary-political practice in which many of us were in fact formed. In the field of Latin American literary criticism, the most influential of these paradigms was undoubtedly Angel Rama's idea of "narrative transculturation" (*transculturación narrativa*), which continues to serve as something like a Latin American form of the kind of postcolonial high modernism Said champions.[5]

The idea of transculturation—and the neologism itself—was introduced by the Cuban ethnographer Fernando Ortiz in his classic 1940 study *Contrapunteo cubano del tabaco y el azucar* (although the idea also harks back to the earlier notion of cultural *mestizaje* or creolization advanced by Pedro Henríquez Ureña, the founder of modern Latin American literary criticism). Ortiz meant the term to serve as an alternative to *acculturation* as a model for the evolution of modern Cuban culture out of its colonial past. Whereas in processes of acculturation a subordinate culture has to adjust to a dominant one, in transculturation elements of both cultures come into a dynamic relationship of contradiction and combination.

For Ortiz, transculturation designated a social process in which previously antagonistic European, Spanish, and African elements—foods, customs, religious practices, manners, dress, music, and so on—were fused in everyday Cuban life and culture. In Rama's refashioning of the concept, which was based on the coincidence between the literary practice of the "boom" writers and the new political energies released by the impact of the Cuban revolution, it became something like an ideologeme for Latin American intellectual and cultural work in general. As such, transculturation posited the providential role of a "lettered" vanguard of social scientists, pedagogues, artists, writers, critics, and a new type of politician to represent subaltern social classes and groups by developing new cultural and political forms in which their formative presence in Latin American history and society could be made manifest. The work of the great Peruvian novelist José María Arguedas, at the boundary between indigenous and European cultural forms, and between Quechua and Spanish, was exemplary of narrative transculturation in this sense for Rama.

In his foreword to the first edition of Ortiz's book, published at a moment when fascism dominated most of Europe, Bronislaw Malinowski recognized the advantage of transculturation as an ethnographic concept over acculturation, which he associated with the negative effects of European colonialism on Africa and the Pacific. Fernando Coronil echoes this valorization of the term in his own introduction to the recent re-edition of the English translation of *Contrapunteo*, arguing in particular that the appeal of transculturation is that it forces one to recognize that "[what Walter Benjamin called] 'cultural treasures' . . . cease to owe their existence exclusively to the work of elites and become, as products of a common history, the achievement of popular collectivities as well."[6] Coronil wants to establish in this way the normative validity of the concept of transculturation for Latin American studies. That claim presumes, however, that the result of transculturation is an equalization of previous power and status differentials; by contrast, acculturation implies—at least in the way that both Malinowski and Ortiz understand it—a movement away from a subaltern or marginal position toward a dominant or hegemonic one.

Ortiz saw transculturation as something that occurred in ordinary quotidian commodities, objects, and practices, indeed, as a process that *required* the quotidian. Rama, by contrast, privileges a *literary* notion of the actual or potential representational adequacy of intellectuals and high culture in relation to the subaltern. Like Ortiz, Coronil is an anthropologist; but it sometimes seems as if for him it is more Ortiz's *book* that is expressive of transculturation than the quotidian popular practices the book describes. In particular, Coronil cites favorably Rama's claim that "literary works do not exist outside of cultures, but crown them [*las coronan*]. To the degree that these cultures are the multitudinous creations of centuries, the writer becomes a producer, dealing with the work of innumerable others: a sort of compiler (Roa Bastos might have said), a brilliant weaver in the vast historical workshop of American society."[7]

In other words, for Rama and for Coronil transculturation is something that takes place *between* high (or academic) culture and subaltern culture, rather than a feature or resource internal to subaltern culture itself. I would argue that this is a significant shift away from Ortiz's original concept (which is itself not unproblematic). For Rama, literature has the power to incorporate the orality of regional or subaltern cultures, but only at the expense of relativizing the authority of oral culture as such. Although oral culture and literary culture nominally have equal status in transculturation, since literature is also modified by its contact with orality and non-Spanish languages, literature actually remains dominant, since it is the pole toward which transculturation tends.[8] (In the passage that Coronil quotes, literature "crowns" culture: Rama's image of the writer as "weaver"—*tejedor*—seems in its equation of manual and intellectual labor more egalitarian, but the writer has to be a "brilliant weaver," as opposed to just the so-so, or subaltern, kind, who might resemble more what Benjamin means by the "storyteller").

For both Rama and Ortiz transculturation functions as a teleology, not without marks of violence and loss, but *necessary* in the last instance for the formation of the modern nation-state and a national (or continental) identity that would be something other than the sum of its parts, since the original identities are sublated in the process of transculturation itself. The essential historicism of this conception (which has an unacknowledged Hegelian basis) may be glimpsed in Ortiz's vivid sense that "[t]he real history of Cuba is the history of its intermeshed transculturations" and that "[a]mong all peoples historical evolution has always meant a vital change from one culture to another at tempos varying from gradual to sudden." But in Cuban history, Ortiz argues, this process has been dramatically compressed: "[T]he cultures that have influenced the formation of its folk have been so many and so diverse in their spatial position and their structural composition that this vast blend of races and cultures overshadows in importance every other historical phenomenon. . . . The whole gamut of culture run by Europe in a span of more than four millenniums took place in Cuba in less than four centuries." The Spanish conquest in particular meant that "in a single day various of the intervening ages were crossed in Cuba."[9]

There is a hidden agenda of class and racial anxiety in Ortiz's idea of transculturation, which, to my mind, Coronil does not sufficiently bring to light in his presentation of *Contrapunteo*. The anxiety is over the possibility that racial and class violence from below will overturn the structure of privilege inhabited by an upper-class, liberal intellectual like Ortiz in a country like Cuba, where a majority of the population is "black" (in U.S. terms) and, at least until the revolution, overwhelmingly poor (peasant, proletarian, or sub-proletarian). Just as Said's work is haunted by the specter of Islamic fundamentalism, *Contrapunteo cubano* is haunted by the most traumatic episode in early twentieth-century Cuban history: the so-called "Little War" of 1912, in which demobilized black soldiers who had fought for independence in the war against Spain, disillusioned by their disenfranchisement in the new republic, rose up against the government and were ruthlessly crushed.[10]

Rama's refashioning of the idea of transculturation in the very different circumstances of the decade of the 1960s and the literary "boom" in Latin America betrays a similar anxiety. For Rama, transculturation is above all an instrument for achieving Latin American cultural and economic modernity in the face of the obstacles to that modernity created by colonial and then neocolonial forms of dependency. It achieves this by modifying without liquidating entirely the force of the subaltern ethnicities, languages, histories, and cultures that have persisted in the course of the continent's experience. Rama argues that cultural conflict in the Americas is not new, but rather

> a continuation of the initial conflict, which was the imposition of Hispanic culture on the indigenous cultures which then led to the Creole and regional extensions of that conflict, particularly as represented by the urban liberal oligarchy that the Republic imposed on tribal communities. It is a conflict that may find some resolution when brazen domination does not take place, when different regions can express and affirm themselves in spite of the unifying forces that confront them. Viewed from this perspective, one can conclude that there is a strengthening of cultures that are understood as interior to the continent, not in the sense that they have rigidly entrenched themselves in their traditions, but in the measure that they continue to experience transculturations without renouncing their soul. (*Transculturación* 71)

It follows that for Rama the only feasible solution for indigenous peoples—as "cultures that are understood as interior to the continent"—is racial-cultural mestizaje, a mestizaje the concept of transculturation both mirrors and models. The alternatives to transculturation are either cultural renunciation or genocide. In an interview shortly before his death in 1983, Rama was asked whether he thought that in Arguedas's last novel, *El zorro de arriba y el zorro de abajo*, published after the author's suicide, there is still a hope for the survival of indigenous culture in Latin America: *hay todavía un lugar para la esperanza de la cultura indígena?* He answered:

> Without a doubt, but not for the survival of indigenous culture, rather for mestizo culture, because indian culture no longer made sense. What Arguedas understood is that for all practical purposes the solution was the muddy solution of mestizaje. That tortuous, and often dirty, road, like life itself, but that was richer in possibilities.[11]

"Richer in possibilities" for whom, though? Neil Larsen observes that, in Rama's concept of transculturation, "[c]ulture in itself becomes the naturalizing and dehistoricizing containment of what is otherwise potentially an emergence of a particular counterrationality directly opposed to that of the absent state mediation."[12] Posing the regional, the archaic, and the subaltern as a problem of integration to the nation-state—that is, in relation to the "incomplete" project of Latin American modernity (to allude to Habermas's well-known concept)—does not permit Rama to think of these as synchronic entities in their own right, with their own historical logic and claims (which may include the claim to a different type of nation-state). From the perspective of transculturation, Rama cannot conceptualize ideologically or theoretically movements for indigenous identity, rights, and/or territorial autonomy that develop their own organic intellectuals and (literary or nonliterary) cultural forms—forms that not only do not depend necessarily on a narrative of transculturation but in many cases feel obliged to resist or contradict such a narrative (by the same token, he was unable to conceptualize the emergence of a grassroots women's movement in Latin America). The idea of transculturation expresses in both Ortiz and Rama a *fantasy* of class, gender, and racial reconciliation (in, respectively, liberal and social-democratic forms).

This fundamental impasse in what was one of the most important paradigms of Latin American cultural theory reminds us of Guha's observation that Indian colonial historiography, "by making the security of the state into the central problematic of peasant insurgency," necessarily denied the peasant rebel "recognition as a subject of history in his own right, even for a project that was all his own" (*Aspects* 3). Guha shares with Rama a sense of the predicament of the postcolonial nation-state. But where Rama is concerned with *integrating* into the state via transculturation subaltern groups that have been previously marginalized or repressed by the state, Guha is concerned with tracking those moments in which, to recall Neil Larsen's phrase above, a "counterrationality" opposed to that of the existing state appears. For Rama, transculturation was ultimately a kind of ideologeme of Latin American modernity. It pointed to the need to forge a new, more complex and inclusive culture and literature—national and continental at the same time—that would break with the colonial heritage in the same way that dependency theory economists were arguing that Latin American economies needed to "delink" from the work market and begin a process of autonomous development.[13] While the theoretical force of dependency theory is certainly long spent in Latin America and the third world generally, some of its underlying assumptions are still with us: for example, the idea, which Rama shared deeply, that it is the responsibility of the left— both the organized political left and the cultural intelligentsia identified with the left—to carry forward the project of elaboration of a national culture left incomplete by the Latin American bourgeoisie, due to its pusillanimous or—to recall André Gunder Frank's apt phrase—"lumpen" character.

Let me offer the following example of this idea. My friend Nelson Osorio is a literary critic who was active in the Chilean Communist Party during the Allende years. After the 1973 coup, he was arrested, tortured, and forced into exile by the Pinochet dictatorship. He eventually settled in Venezuela, where he worked for something close to a decade to compose an encyclopedia of Latin American literature, the *Diccionario Enciclopédico de Literatura Latinoamericana*. The project involved coordinating the participation of hundreds of scholars from all over the world, with the aim of producing a critical totalization of the canon of Latin American literature that also took into account new, noncanonic developments, such as testimonio, oral and written literatures in indigenous languages, literatures in Caribbean languages, and U.S. Latino literature.

I contributed a number of entries to the *Diccionario*. In agreeing to do this, I was acknowledging its "progressive" character as a political-intellectual project. At the same time, however, my own work was pointing to the conclusion that literature had been in Latin America a practice that was constitutive of elite identity. I read Rama's *La ciudad letrada* therefore as a kind *self-criticism* of his own theory of transculturation, a self-criticism framed by the incipient crisis of the project of the Latin American left in the 1980s (Rama himself was expelled from the United States in 1982 by the Reagan administration, under pressure from right-wing Cuban-Americans).

As I noted in the introduction, my own experience with the role of literature in the Central American revolutions made it clear that the metonymic chain (writing/literature/letrados/creole elites/city/nation) Rama sets up in *La ciudad letrada* was not necessarily broken with the attempts to democratize literature such as the literacy campaigns instituted by the Cuban and Nicaraguan revolutions; indeed, it was precisely a sense of the limits of these revolutions in breaking down previous cultural hierarchies that was one of the starting points of the project of the Latin American Subaltern Studies Group.

What has undermined the hegemony of the "lettered city" and the effectiveness of Rama's "narrative transculturation" as a form of cultural modernization is the mutation of the Latin American public sphere caused by tremendous growth in the last thirty or forty years of the audiovisual mass media. The great Brazilian critic Antonio Cándido observed despairingly, in his seminal 1972 essay on literature and underdevelopment, that the rise of the media implied a renewed deferral of the idea of literary culture as a model or formative practice of informed citizenship.[14] Cándido was concerned with the question of why a larger public for written literature had not emerged in the countries of the developing world like Brazil. His answer was that, while the process of capitalist industrialization in the nineteenth century in Western Europe, the United States, Japan, or even peripheral states like Russia or Spain coincided with the expansion of print culture and public education, in countries like Brazil, where industrialization is a relatively recent phenomenon, it coincides asynchronically with the explosion of the media and commercial mass culture. Populations formerly immersed in the primarily oral, iconographic world of rural popular culture can pass, in the process of becoming proletarianized and/or urbanized, directly from that culture to the culture of the media, which Cándido saw as a kind of "urban folklore," without going through print culture. In the countries of the developing world, literature faced an implacable enemy: the mass media.

Cándido saw a crisis of civic identity and competence in the inability of the newly urbanized or urbanizing masses to accede to literature and print culture. He found even the sort of cathechistic theater developed by the Jesuits during the colonial period to teach indigenous peoples Catholic doctrine preferable to the media, because it involved indoctrination in a form of literary high culture. The media, by contrast, function as a sort of "catechism in reverse" (catequismo as avessas).

Like Angel Rama (or Georg Lukács), Cándido was speaking in "Literature and Underdevelopment" as a modern, one of those moderns who believes it is the task of a Marxist-oriented intelligentsia to preserve and defend the institutions of the national culture, formed by the bourgeoisie in their rise to power, from their perversion or degeneration in the hands of that same bourgeoisie, which has abandoned its humanist forms of cultural self-legitimization in favor of the raw power of manipulation of the media and commodity culture. The Diccionario project came out of a similar logic, so it stands to reason that Osorio, who created something like an academic version of Salvador Allende's Popular Unity coalition to sustain it, would want to resist efforts to "decenter" the status of literature as a cultural signifier. He would observe that in order to deconstruct the canon of Latin American literature it must first be constructed as such. I take the point. But the strategic thrust of subaltern studies is that it is necessary to move beyond the parameters of both the nation-state and the literary canon, at least as these are presently constituted. As I will argue in the subsequent chapters, this does necessarily mean moving into either a postnational or a postliterary register; but it does mean rethinking what the nation and literature are and what they can be in a new register.

On this note, I want to introduce four texts related to the Túpac Amaru rebellion (the rebellion was a massive uprising of indian poor peasants and some mestizos that swept through the highlands of Peru between 1780 and 1783, before it was crushed by the colonial authorities). They are, respectively:

1. The Genealogía (Genealogy), written in Spanish by the leader of the rebellion, José Gabriel Condorcanqui Túpac Amaru, which takes the form of a legal document, defending his claim to be descended from the last

Inca, presented to the Real Audiencia de Lima in 1777, three years before the rebellion.

2. The Memorias (Memoirs), also known as Cuarenta años de cautiverio or El cautiverio dilatado, of his brother, Juan Bautista Túpac Amaru, which appeared in Buenos Aires in 1825, also in Spanish.

3. The play Ollantay, written anonymously in Quechua (the author may have been a local priest who had learned to use Quechua) and performed before indigenous audiences—one was said to have included José Gabriel himself—in the years before 1780, but based entirely on the conventions of Spanish Golden Age drama, including the three-act form of the comedia and the figure of the gracioso.

4. Juan de Espinosa Medrano's Apologético en favor de don Luis de Góngora, a treatise on poetry that is generally considered one of the foundational texts of Latin American literary criticism. Written more than a century earlier than the rebellion (the first edition dates from 1662), it also connected to the cultural dynamics of the Andean world in the period leading up to it.

As the brief description above may suggest, Túpac Amaru's Genealogía is immersed in the form and rhetoric of Spanish colonial legalism. It was inspired to a certain extent, although with a more immediately utilitarian purpose, by the narrative genealogy constructed by mestizo writer the Inca Garcilaso a century and a half earlier in his Comentarios reales to justify the right of the remnants of the Inca aristocracy—which he belonged to through his mother—to share in the administration of the viceroyalty with the representatives of the Spanish crown. The rhetorical elaboration of the document, which seems excessive for what is after all a formal legal petition, is intended to establish its author's mastery of the aristocratizing codes of the viceregal "lettered city." It defines a parity between himself and his Spanish and creole interlocutors. In the light of José Gabriel's subsequent role, one can see in the intention of securing his claim to be the direct descendant of the last Inca (and therefore to use the patronymic Túpac Amaru) the seeds of the idea of eventually becoming himself the Inca in a restoration (or, as we will see, a reformulation) of the Inca state, the Tahuansintuyu.

Though the Genealogía has elements of autobiography and family history, it is more like an expanded version of the prueba de limpieza de sangre than an autobiography as such. By contrast, Juan Bautista Túpac Amaru's Memorias, which appears some fifty years later, is an autobiography in the modern sense and reveals an entirely new rhetoric and persona. In the intervening period, the period of the great bourgeois revolutions that the Túpac Amaru rebellion heralds—a sea change has taken place in literary form and sensibility.

The *Memorias* posits Juan Bautista's experience in Spanish prisons as a metonymy of the degradation to which Spanish colonial rule has subjected America. It tells in first person the story of how its narrator is captured after the defeat of the revolt, tried, marched in chains to the coast, and exiled for forty years in the Spanish Bourbon equivalent of the Gulag Archipelago (including a particularly notorious prison in Spanish Africa), from which he eventually makes his way back, not to Peru but to Buenos Aires, after 1820. If the *Genealogía* anticipates the rebellion of 1780 by establishing the legitimacy of José Gabriel's claim to be the descendant of the original Túpac Amaru, the last Inca, the *Memorias* articulates a sense of the continuity between that rebellion and the liberal revolutions of the creoles nearly half a century later. It is a text that revolutionary figures like Simón Bolívar, Bernardino Rivadavia, or José de San Martín must have read with the same sense of instruction and identification that they found in Rousseau's *Confessions*.[15]

If we try to study both the *Genealogía* and the *Memorias* as examples of the appropriation of European literary models by representatives of a regional rebellion against colonial authority—that is, under the aegis of Rama's idea of narrative transculturation—we will rapidly encounter an impasse, however. Neither text figures in the canon of Latin American or, for that matter, Peruvian literature; but it is not simply a question of including them in the canon (although it goes without saying that they should be included in the canon). Rather, the impasse results from a failure of representation Paul de Man identified precisely in Rousseau's *Confessions*. Although in their construction of an allegory of the subject the *Genealogía* and the *Memorias*, like the *Confessions*, evidently "generate history" (the phrase is de Man's)—in the language of speech-act theory, they are *performative*, part of the ideological mise-en-scène of the rebellion and its aftermath—they do not *represent* history.[16] The autobiographical subjects they configure are incommensurate with the actual character of the rebellion, which involves the collective action of large and heterogenous masses of both indigenous and creole populations. The metonymic chain that operates in a testimonial narrative like *I, Rigoberta Menchú* to connect the textual representation of the individual life experience of the narrator to the collective destiny of a class or social group cannot be completed in these texts.

The historian Leon Campbell brings up a related problem. Campbell agrees with scholars of Andean literature like Martin Lienhard or Rolena Adorno that there existed since the Spanish conquest a written literature in both Quechua and Spanish, based on adaptations of European literary, epistolary, and legal models, that nourished the worldview of the leaders of the Andean indigenous communities (we know, for example, that Túpac

Amaru carried on his person an edition of the Inca Garcilaso's *Comentarios reales*). But the documentary archive that has been amassed around the rebellion also reveals in its interstices the existence of a radically different culture, a predominantly non-European, oral (or, more accurately, despite the apparent anachronism, *audiovisual*) culture, developed for and by the rebels—mainly peasants and artisans and the members of their families—who made up the great *tupamarista* and *katarista* armies, and who (on the whole) neither read nor spoke Spanish, nor were particularly concerned to learn. Campbell concludes that there existed what he calls a "dual idiom" of rebellion: on the one hand, literary or legal texts written in Spanish like the *Genealogía* or the proclamations and letters addressed by the rebel leadership to the creoles or colonial authorities; on the other, the non-, or even anti-literary cultural practices deployed by the rebels themselves.[17] The cultural ambivalence displayed by José Gabriel himself (he sometimes wore Inca clothing, other times European-style military uniforms, for example), responded to contradictions in his own ideological formation and position within the colonial system and in his efforts to represent himself as a leader, to both his followers and the colonial authorities.

But the "dual idiom" of the rebellion was not merely conjunctural or tactical, nor does it refer only to divisions in the practices of the leadership. It also coincides with the terms of a well-known historical debate about the nature—reformist or revolutionary?—of the uprising itself. As Campbell puts it:

> When one takes only the Spanish-language literary record into account, the focus of the rebellion appears to be directed exclusively towards the cities and their creole inhabitants and the rebel program focused on material issues, concerned primarily with dismantling the harsh economic reforms of the Bourbons, which impoverished many Peruvians through increased taxes and commercial restrictions.
>
> If, on the other hand, the roles of myth, symbolism and ceremony, of ritual and response, are also examined and their interior meanings better defined, it is clear that not only did these comprise an important part of the literature of the rebellion but that these ideas were often at variance with what the rebels seemed to be asking for in the written proposals. Because the rebel's Spanish language directives were focused on the major commercial centers which had remained loyal to the Crown or creole areas under rebel control . . . they give the rebellion a "tactical rationalism" very characteristic of the times. . . . They also fit nicely with Western definitions of eighteenth-century rebellion as it developed in Europe and America. ("The Influence of Books")

In other words, the historian who chooses literary texts like the *Genealogía* or the *Memorias* as representative of the culture and goals of the rebellion will see essentially a reformist movement, conceived within the language and the legal and cultural codes imposed by the process of European colonization of the Andes, now creolized or transcultured, while the historian who looks beyond these texts to other cultural practices will see something that looks more like a vast revolutionary social movement from below, propelled by the poorest and most exploited sectors of the indian artisans and peasantry, with conjunctural allies among some (very limited) sectors of mestizos, creoles, and *caciques*, and with the ultimate goal of restoring the Inca state or some other form of indigenous hegemony.

I have kept in reserve the question of *Ollantay*, because it is directly connected to this last issue and to José Gabriel Túpac Amaru's claim in the *Genealogía* to be the legitimate descendant of the last Inca. In some ways, *Ollantay* is the most derivative and "European" of the three texts, combining as it does the baroque allegorical model of state theater—as in Calderón's *Life Is a Dream*—with what came to be known as the *comedia tierna* in the Spanish Enlightenment—Jovellanos's *El delincuente honrado* is the best-known example of the genre, which anticipates bourgeois melodrama. At the same time, the play was, as noted, written and performed in Quechua and is based on an Inca story set in the period before the Spanish conquest (this has given rise to a somewhat sterile debate as to whether the play is colonial or precolonial in origin).

Ollantay tells the story of a commoner of the same name who becomes one of the leading generals of the Inca army and who falls in love with Cusi Ccoillor, the daughter of the Inca, Pachacuti. In the course of their affair, Cusi gets pregnant and Ollantay asks the Inca for permission to marry her. Pachacuti reacts violently—the children of the Inca were forbidden to marry commoners—by imprisoning his daughter and her baby and forcing Ollantay to flee to his native province. There he raises an army to challenge the authority of the Inca and Cuzco and to recuperate his Cusi and their child. The war between Ollantay and Pachacuti lasts ten years; in its course Pachacuti dies and is replaced by his son, Túpac Yupanqui, Cusi's brother. Ollantay is eventually defeated, captured, and brought in chains to Cuzco to stand trial for treason with the expectation that he will be put to death. However, through the mediation of his daughter, Yma Sumac, whom he has never seen before, he is forgiven by Túpac Yupanqui, reunited with Cusi, and appointed as a sort of vice-Inca (*inka-rantin*) to rule in Túpac Yupanqui's stead whenever the latter is away from Cuzco.

If we were to interpret *Ollantay* as a "national allegory" (in the sense Jameson gives this term) anticipating the Wars of Independence of the early nineteenth century, Ollantay's frustrated love affair and rebellion against the Inca would appear to symbolize the dissatisfaction of an emergent creole-mestizo class with the still dominant structures of power of the viceregal *ancien régime* in Spain's American colonies. Two points undermine this interpretation, however: (1) as noted, *Ollantay* was composed and performed in Quechua, and therefore for all practical purposes was inaccessible to creole-mestizo audiences; (2) despite its reliance on the formula of the Spanish comedia, the play's models of aesthetic, linguistic, cultural, and political authority are ultimately Andean, rather than European. While the representation of the old Inca against whom Ollantay rebels could certainly be read as a symbol for the Spanish Bourbons, it could also have suggested to the local—mainly indigenous—audiences who saw the play in 1780, as the rebellion was spreading, the not at all "symbolic" possibility of restoring the Inca state as such.

But if that was in fact the message those audiences were reading into *Ollantay*, it came with an interesting twist: the reconciliation suggested by the end of the play, in which the hero is incorporated into the power elite and allowed to marry Cusi, is a "happy ending" at odds with what is known historically about the intransigence of the Incas in these matters. For one thing, the logic of the ending no longer depends on the principle of strict caste authority that prevailed in the traditional Inca system. It suggests, rather, the possibility of a neo-Inca state that allows in some measure for the accession to power of nonaristocratic subjects like Ollantay: that is, a more democratic and egalitarian version of the old Inca state (which depended on conquering and assimilating by force other indigenous city-states, such as the one Ollantay was from).

Should we speak here of the infiltration into or contamination of a "purely" Andean or Inca-centric conception of the state and its territoriality by the concept of enlightened despotism (itself based historically in part on Enlightenment views of the Inca state) or even Jacobin and protodemocratic ideas? *Ollantay* is certainly a product of transculturation. At both aesthetic and ideological levels the play involves an unstable and potentially explosive combination of Andean and European cultural and linguistic elements. Even the relative purity of its Quechua is testimony to its status as a written text (transcribed examples of oral Quechua from the period show a greater degree of regional or class diversity).[18] But it is important to see this as a transculturation *from below*, based not on the ways in which an emerging creole "lettered city" (and then the creole-dominated nation-state) becomes progressively more adequate to the task of representing the interests of the indigenous population, but rather on how that population appropriated aspects of European and creole literary and philosophical culture to serve its interests. Martin Lienhard argues that we should see *Ollantay* as, in fact, a hegemonic articulation—a way of trying to interpellate ideologically non-Inca indigenous groups and sections of the creole and mestizo population—by a "neo-Inca" Andean elite interested in the possibility of reinstituting a new form of the Inca state in the context of the crisis of authority of European absolutism in the late eighteenth century.[19]

It is important to note, however, that what is involved in the case of *Ollantay* and the Túpac Amaru rebellion is not a distinction between a project that has a concept of nation, articulated in literature and print culture—as in Benedict Anderson's well-known thesis—and one that does not, that is simply tribal or community-based precisely because it lacks the representational capacity to project an "imagined community" beyond those territorial limits. It is a question, instead, of *different* conceptions of the nation, territoriality, and intellectuals and intellectual culture. Steve Stern explains that

> In Peru-Bolivia, in the late colonial period, peasants did not live, struggle, or think in terms that isolated them from the emerging "national question." On the contrary, protonational symbols had great importance in the life of peasants and small-holders. *Yet these protonational symbols were tied not to an emerging creole nationalism*, but to notions of an Andean- or Inca-led social order. Andean peasants saw themselves as part of a wider protonational culture, and sought their liberation on terms that, far from isolating them from an overarching state, would link them to a new and just state.[20]

What seems clear, in retrospect, is that the nation-state the Túpac Amaru rebellion would have created had it been able to succeed would not have been based on the authority of Spanish over indigenous languages: it would have been at a minimum bilingual, but probably also (since the authority of Quechua was connected to Inca domination over other peoples, including Aymara and Shuar speakers) plurilinguistic. And it probably would have ventured some form of agrarian communalism based on a revival of the *ayllu* system. It may or may not have retained an identity as an autonomous part of the Spanish empire (in the same way former British colonies remained part of the Commonwealth). It may or may not have been democratic, but if it remained an elite government, that elite would be racially indigenous rather than creole.

To put this in other words: the idea of the nation does not belong exclusively to the creole elite that formed the Peruvian nation-state. It can also be, as Mallon shows in *Peasant and Nation*, a production of subaltern knowledge and desire. To seek to canonize texts like the *Genealogía* or the

Memorias or even *Ollantay* as pertaining to a now wider sense of "Peruvian" or "Latin American" literature not only obscures the fact of the cultural production of a national-popular imaginary by an indigenous peasantry and its organic intellectuals—a production which, while it may have involved elements of European literary, political, and scientific culture, did so in a way subordinate to its own struggle for meaning and hegemony; it also amounts to an act of appropriation that excludes that population as a subject conscious of its own history, incorporating it only as a contingent element of *another* history (of the modern nation-state, of the Enlightenment, of Peruvian literature), whose subject is also an other (creole or mestizo, Spanish-speaking, letrado, male, propertied).

The tension between the "lettered city" in its evolution toward creole nationalism and the mobilizing discourses of Andean peasant rebellion I have sketched in and around the *Genealogía*, the *Memorias*, and *Ollantay* has its roots a century earlier in Juan de Espinosa Medrano's *Apology*. As its full Spanish title—*Apologético en favor de don Luis de Góngora*—suggests, the text is a response to an attack on the style of poetry associated with the Spanish poet Góngora launched by a Portuguese humanist, Manuel de Faría y Sousa, in the mid-seventeenth century. But if it were only that, it would have little interest for us here. What makes it relevant is that Espinosa combines his defense of Góngora with an intimation of an emerging creole consciousness, making the *Apology* one of the earliest instantiations of Rama's idea of narrative transculturation (the baroque style of writing Espinosa defends in the *Apology* was precisely the style employed by José Gabriel Túpac Amaru in the *Genealogía*).

Some minimal background may be necessary to help understand what is at stake here. The essence of Faría's criticism of Góngora, which had in part a nationalist bias (Portugal struggled for most of the first half of the seventeenth century to become independent from the Spanish Hapsburgs), was that Góngora's poetry lacked the "scientific mystery" (*misterio científico*) plainly evident by contrast in the work of Portugal's national poet, Camões. Espinosa replies in the *Apology* that it is not the proper function of poetry—and by extension, of any and all the forms of secular literature or *letras humanas*, as he calls them—to constitute a corpus of natural or theological *doctrine*. The argument depends on a distinction of a nominalist sort between writing that carries the authority of scientific or religious truth—"la revelada y teológica"—and secular literature—"la escritura humana y poesía secular."[21] Inverting the usual Scholastic hierarchy, Espinosa holds that what counts in poetry is the subtle logic of its linguistic-formal *dispositio*, not the didactic *materia* it presents.

This argument anticipates in some important ways Immanuel Kant's distinction between teleological judgment and aesthetic judgment roughly a century later—that is, the philosophical basis of aesthetic formalism as a form of the modern. Inversely, the concept of decorum that underlies Faría's objection to Góngora depends on a fixed notion of the relation between matter of imitation and style and genre of imitation. By rebutting Faría, then, Espinosa is also making a claim for a sort of literary-cultural modernity, a modernity that is represented for him by Góngora's writing, but which is also a feature of his own. Espinosa's defense of Góngora is formalist, but it is a formalism that has been connected to a defense and promotion of the American (or "Austral," as Espinosa himself—lacking the concept of America—puts it) against the authority of the European. Espinosa's aim is not so much to disconnect the aesthetic from the ideological as to in a sense found the ideological—that is, an emergent creole identity which differentiates itself more and more from metropolitan models—on the aesthetic.

Roberto González Echevarría has argued that the very supplementarity of the situation of the colonial letrado comes to be refunctioned in the Apology as a kind of epistemological privilege or advantage over the European, represented by Faría. In Espinosa's metaphor the American is a parrot (papagayo) who can only repeat loquaciously (que tanto parlase) what is told to it. But this lack of essence also embodies for Espinosa the originality of the American world, because it implies the superiority of a practice of signification such as literature over the given world of nature and tradition, of "letras humanas" and literary criticism itself (also a "secondary" or supplementary activity) over Faría's "scientific mystery."[22]

The Apology is a variation of the literary form of the Quarrel between the Ancients and Moderns, in which Espinosa writes himself, and the creole "lettered city" he represents, into the position of the Modern. If modernity implies—according to the Weber thesis—a necessary process of disillusion, a recognition that the world has lost its magical or auratic character, that charismatic forms of authority are on the wane, then secular literature—Espinosa's "letras humanas y poesía secular"—is both a representation of modernity, and something that, as a cultural practice, actively produces modernity. Weber equates, in the specific historical context of the transition between feudalism and capitalism in Western Europe, capitalist modernity with the rise of Protestantism in northern Europe. For a creole letrado like Espinosa, who was himself a Catholic priest, however, the magical-auratic world displaced by the sort of literary modernity he claims for Góngora could not have been Catholicism as such: in Espinosa's colonial and more precisely Andean context, Catholicism represented—or more accurately represented itself as—a form of modernity. But if not Catholicism, what? Precisely the language, culture, and religions of the subject who comes to constitute the other of the (creole) other: the indian, seen as idolatrous, pagan, a follower of "old religion," preliterary.[23]

This paradox allows us to understand an aspect of Espinosa's relation to his own ethnic heritage (one or both of his parents are thought to have been indigenous). Espinosa translated Virgil into Quechua, and introduced Quechua words and Inca themes in his theater pieces, which, like the *Ollantay*, are based on the model of the baroque comedia or *auto sacramental*. But this is not so much a case of the transculturation of metropolitan literary models by an indigenous organic intellectual, as Raquel Chang-Rodríguez has argued, among others.[24] Rather, secular literature was for Espinosa a cultural practice capable of radically displacing the elements of a traditional indigenous worldview and the social and cultural forms structured around it. What Espinosa was attempting to create by translating Virgil into Quechua or by adapting the comedia to Andean themes, in other words, was the possibility of a literary modernity *in Quechua.*

This is certainly something close to what Rama means by narrative transculturation; indeed, Espinosa's *Apology* could be said to mark one of the moments of origin of the Latin American "lettered city" as such. But it also certainly is not the same thing as upholding the authority of pre-colonial culture or of surviving indian cultures within the colonial matrix. The fact that Espinosa defends the creole against the imputation of being barbarous or uncultured does not mean that the *Apology* is without its own version of the civilization/barbarism binary. For Espinosa, the barbarian is precisely that which cannot be adequately inscribed in the literary text— that is, the *preliterary* and therefore unrepresentable.[25]

The idealization of written literature in the *Apology* constructs a precarious creole or creole-mestizo identity not only against the anteriority and authority of Spanish or metropolitan culture—a move that lends itself to the text's refunctioning of a canonic metropolitan figure such as Góngora, whose literary authority was itself initially contested and precarious in the metropolis, as a register of possibilities for positing such an identity. It also situates that identity in a necessarily differential relation with a subject that is even more deeply subalternized than the creole: more deeply subalternized precisely because of its alleged incapacity for or lack of access to "letras humanas," which, on the other hand, never cease to claim that they represent or speak for this subject adequately. The result is that the creole "lettered city" and the emergent national consciousness its dynamic of transculturation is supposed to embody is marked by what Antonio Benítez-Rojo calls (apropos the theme of the nation in nineteenth-century Latin American novels) a "bifurcated desire"—a desire that seeks to found its authority on an appeal to the local and the native and at the same time to transpose in a utilitarian fashion for the purposes of nation-building the forms of European cultural modernity.[26]

It may be worth recalling in this respect that the Afrikaaners were also "creole" and anticolonial (with respect to the British and the authority of the English language and culture). In contrast to what is happening in South Africa today, however, one could say that, mutatis mutandis, apart-heid won historically and continues to win in Latin America with the defeat of the Túpac Amaru rebellion and the blockade of the Haitian revolution after 1793. Indeed, apartheid may be a more accurate model of what happened and continues to happen in many parts of Latin American culture and society than racial-cultural mestizaje or transculturation.

I have avoided so far the question of the "other" side of Campbell's "dual idiom": that is, the cultural forms of the household workers, peasants, artisans, and mitayos (indians assigned to forced labor for the state or private companies) involved in the uprising. That is because my interest has been to show the limits of the "lettered city" even where it tries to position itself in a relation of expressive solidarity with the subaltern. But a word about the means of transmission of the message of peasant rebellion is perhaps in order. Guha argues in Elementary Aspects that in societies of primary orality such as those of rural India (or by extension the Andean highlands), this transmission depends primarily on rumor. Rumor (as opposed to "news") operates according to a fluid dynamic of anonymity, improvisation, and transitivity. Rumor not only is oral, in other words; it depends on orality and communal structures (the village, the bazaar or local marketplace, the network of women) both for its mode of transmission and the particular truth-effect it carries. To claim, as some nineteenth-century historians of the Indian peasant insurrections did, that "the talk of the market-place was an authentic register of a great deal of useful intelligence" is to acknowledge, Guha observes, "the correspondence between the public discourse of rumour and the popular act of insurrection, that is, of the collaterality of word and deed issuing from a common will of the people" (Aspects 259).

This is not to say that writing and the book (or non-native languages) are necessarily absent from peasant culture: the case of Ollantay is evidence enough of the way in which non-European cultures can appropriate the technology of Western literature. But they appear in a curiously inverted or "negative" way that Rama's idea of literary transculturation would be hard put to engage. Guha observes that in the Indian rebellions, "[t]he want of literacy also made the peasants relate occasionally to a written utterance in such a way as to destroy its original motivation by deverbalizing it and exploit the resulting opacity in order to provide that graphic representation with new 'signifieds' (*signifiés*)." He cites in particular the case of a leader of the Santal rebellion of 1855 who, as a sign of his authority and an instrument of mobilization, waved before his followers a sheaf of papers, "which proved on scrutiny to contain among other things 'an old Book on locomotive[s], a few visiting cards of Mr Burn Engineer' and if the testimony of the semi-official *Calcutta Review* (1856) article is to be believed, a translation in some Indian language of the Gospel according to St John."

Guha continues:

> What is even more remarkable is that the rest of the papers said to have dropped from heaven and regarded by the Santal leaders as evidence of divine support for the insurrection had nothing inscribed on them at all either in writing or in print. 'All the blank papers fell from heaven & the book in which all the pages are blank also fell from heaven,' said Kanhu [the leader of the rebellion]. Clearly thus the conditions of a pre-literate culture made it possible for insurgency to propagate itself not only by means of the graphic form of an utterance divorced from its content but indeed by the writing material acting on its own unscored by graphemes. The principle governing such an extension was essentially the same as that of 'drinking the word' known in some of the islamicized parts of Africa. There the ink or the pigment used for inscribing holy or magical formulae on paper, papyrus, slate or skin and believed to be invested by the sanctity of the message itself, would be washed off and swallowed as a cure for certain ailments. However, there was a difference. While the metonymic projection of supernatural faculties from written word to writing material was used in such instances to leave the cure of physical illness to Allah's grace, the Santals used it merely to legitimize their attempt to remedy the ills of the world by their own arms. (*Aspects* 248–49)

This is a complex passage that deserves attention on many levels. Let it serve here simply to indicate a different way of thinking about the relation of transculturation and subalternity and literature and orality. For certainly there are elements of transculturation—not to speak of postmodernist simulacrum—in the action of the Santal leader.[27] But it is a transculturation governed by and preserving the binary that opposes writing (as an instrument of colonial and landlord rule) and orality (as the form of native peasant culture). The operation is possible in the first place only, as Guha points out, "because of the two-dimensional character of written utterances, which . . . distinguishes them clearly from spoken utterances" (249). There is no synthesis of opposites in this transculturation, however. The use of the book does not overcome the class contradiction between peasant and landlord. Transculturation does not overcome subaltern positionality; rather, subaltern positionality operates and reproduces itself in and through transculturation. Thus, there is no teleological movement toward a "national" culture in which literacy and orality, dominant and subaltern languages or codes, are reconciled.

Shahid Amin makes a related claim in his study of the ways in which Gandhi was perceived by peasants and middle-class nationalists on the occasion of a visit he made to a province of Uttar Pradesh in 1921.[28] For both groups, Gandhi is the signifier of resistance to the existing colonial order, but beyond that what is meant by Gandhi differs radically from one to the other. By the peasants, Gandhi is seen as a holy man or mahatma, possessed of supernatural powers, who has come to restore things as they should be (or were): that is, the "moral economy" of peasant economic and spiritual life disrupted by both colonialism and landlord rule. By the nationalists (who are "lettered" and who include sectors of the local landlord class), he is seen as the political leader of an anticolonial struggle to form an independent Indian state. A series of rumors or stories about Gandhi's *pratap* (miraculous power) are reported in the local nationalist newspaper, *Swadesh*, in preparation for and during his visit. Amin is not claiming that there was no connection between these rumors and stories about Gandhi and the newspaper versions of them, since the newspaper accounts of the miracles contrive to give the stories legitimacy (because of the authority conceded to the written word). They feed back into the rumor-mill of peasant oral culture.

But at a certain point the stories and their textualization in the newspaper diverge, such that the peasants' "ideas about Gandhi's 'orders' and 'powers' were often at variance with those of the local Congress-Khilifat [nationalist] leadership and clashed with basic tenets of Gandhism itself" (342). This divergence has two aspects. First, to be effective as propaganda among the peasants, the newspaper accounts had to be retranslated into spoken (and demotic) language, by being read aloud or paraphrased in the villages. Thus, Amin observes, "even for a large part of the technically literate population printed texts can be deciphered only by a detour through the spoken language. In such readings . . . the story acquires its authentication from its motif and the name of its place of origin rather than from the authority of the correspondent. It spreads by word-of-mouth" (336).

The second aspect emphasizes even more the gap that remains between dominant and subaltern positions in what appears at first sight to be a reciprocal and transcultured relationship. Amin writes:

> The editor of *Swadesh*, who had himself sought to inculcate an attitude of devotion in the district towards the Mahatma, had thus no hesitation in printing rumours about the latter's pratap. It was only when these appeared to instigate dangerous beliefs and actions, such as those concerning demands for abolition of zamindari [landlords], reduction of rents or enforcement of just price at the bazaars, that the journal came out with prompt disclaimers. (337)

Amin's sense of the division between nationalist and peasant readings of Gandhi does not mean (to reiterate a point made earlier) that there cannot be a sense of the national from subaltern positions. Moreover (to recall Said's concern about separatism), subaltern nationalism can (and does) take the form of an ethnic or religious fundamentalism. But, as in the case of *Ollantay*, that fundamentalism would itself be eroded by that which it in turn makes subaltern (Hindu fundamentalism subalternizes women, Muslims, non-Hindus, and tribals; Inca fundamentalism, as a project of nostalgic patriarchal restoration, subalternizes women and non-Inca peoples). The "Chinese boxes" logic of subaltern identity points to a multiethnic and multicultural or culturally (and linguistically) *heterogenous* sense of the national, which is not dependent on a logic of transculturation (although it can incorporate it).

This possibility—which is latent in the very texture of all postcolonial societies, including the United States—has yet to find an adequate contemporary expression in cultural theory or politics; as I will argue in chapter 6, that lack has been disabling for the project of the left. Some hint of what this possibility might entail is provided by an essay Antonio Cornejo Polar published just before his untimely death in 1997.[29] Since it concerns the contemporary situation of the descendants of the Andean population involved in the Túpac Amaru rebellion, it serves as a fitting conclusion to this chapter.

Cornejo's essay begins by acknowledging the fact that in the last half century the urban population of Peru has gone from approximately thirty-five to seventy percent, the greater part of this growth being attributable to immigration from the Andean highlands to coastal cities, above all to Lima. The phenomenon is therefore a diasporic one, even though it takes place within the framework of a single nation-state. This is interesting for Cornejo because it undermines irremediably the Andean basis for the utopian nationalism expressed by Arguedas and earlier Peruvian indigenist writers, who opposed city (coastal, creole-mestizo Peru) to countryside (Andean, indian Peru) in the name of a "new city" that would synthesize the best elements of both. It is widely thought that one of the reasons for Arguedas's suicide, in fact, was his despair at the cultural loss implied by the Andean immigration.

Cornejo argues, however, that it is important to avoid making the migrant simply a passive victim—"la perspectiva que hace del migrante un subalterno sin remedio, siempre frustrado, repelido y humillado, immerso en un mundo hostil que no comprende ni lo comprende" (844). The migrant also imposes himself or herself on the city, remaking it in his or her image of a nostalgic past: "triunfo y nostalgia no son términos contradictorios en el discurso del migrante" (844).

Raymond Williams might speak here of the relation between emergent and residual identities. For Cornejo the subject that appears in this register is not, however, transcultured or hybrid. Rather it is schizophrenic or "decentered," constructed along two axes of identity which are dissimilar and contradictory in a *non-dialectical* way:

> [E]l discurso migrante es radicalmente descentrado, en cuanto se construye alrededor de ejes varios y asimétricos, de alguna manera incompatibles y contradictorios de un modo *no* dialéctico. Acoge no menos de dos experiencias de vida que la migración, contra lo que se supone en el uso de la categoría de mestizaje, y en cierto sentido en el del concepto de transculturacion, no intenta sintetizar en un espacio de resolución armónica. (844–45)

Conversely, Cornejo also rejects the option—which he identifies with the work of Néstor García Canclini—of seeing this identity as "deterritorialized." Instead, the dislocation from the Andes to the space of the city "doubles" the territoriality of the subject, obliging it to speak simultaneously from more than one locus of enunciation: "duplica (o más) el territorio del sujeto y le ofrece o lo condena a hablar desde más de un lugar. Es un discurso doble o múltiplemente situado" (841).

He offers as an example of this doubleness the transcription of the performance of a street comic collected in Lima by two ethnographers interested in the new forms of orality emerging in the context of the Andean diaspora.[30] The performer begins with a reference to "nosotros los criollos" (we the creoles) meant to distinguish his audience from the "provincianos" or "la gente de la sierra"—whom he qualifies as "estos mierdas"—and to identify the speaker himself as a *limeño*. A few minutes later, though, he veers suddenly into an encomium to the Incas and Túpac Amaru, and identifies himself as a *serrano*: "[S]i tú eres provinciano nunca niegues a tu tierra. Yo vivo orgulloso como serrano que soy, serrano a mucha honra, serranazo" (843); which I translate, with some liberties, as "if you're country, never deny your roots. I'm proud to be country, country with honor, super-country."

The ethnographers who collected this performance note that oral performance as such tends to depend on metonymic displacement along an axis of contiguity and free association. Cornejo wonders if this discursive feature does not also lend itself to the enactment of "double" territoriality in the performance, which repeats the spatial itinerary of the rural migrant ("repite el azaroso itinerario del migrante"). In the throes of the signifying chain, the street comic finds "unequal locations" from which he knows he can speak, because they are the locations of his own experience: "tal vez en la deriva del curso metonímico el migrante encuentre lugares desiguales desde los que sabe que puede hablar porque son los lugares de sus experiencias." Cornejo concludes: "Serían las voces múltiples de las muchas memorias que se niegan al olvido" (843; "These would be the multiple voices of the many memories that do not allow themselves to be forgotten" [literally: that negate being forgotten]).

This sense of resistance to forgetting, of negation and "doubling" is also, I would argue, a model for a new discourse of the national; but it is no longer a discourse of the national as the many becoming one; rather it is a discourse of the one becoming many.

3   Our Rigoberta? I, Rigoberta Menchú, Cultural Authority, and the Problem of Subaltern Agency

The epistemological and ethical authority of testimonial narratives like *I, Rigoberta Menchú* is said to depend on their appeal to personal experience. Thus, for example (in my own account of the form):

> By *testimonio* I mean . . . a narrative . . . told in the first person by a narrator who is also the real protagonist or witness of the events he or she recounts. . . . The word *testimonio* translates literally as testimony, as in the act of testifying or bearing witness in a legal or religious sense. . . . The situation of narration in testimonio has to involve an urgency to communicate, a problem of repression, poverty, subalternity, imprisonment, struggle for survival, and so on, implicated in the act of narration itself. The position of the reader of testimonio is akin to that of a jury member in a courtroom. Unlike the novel, testimonio promises by definition to be primarily concerned with sincerity rather than literariness.[1]

"What if much of Rigoberta's story is not true?" the anthropologist David Stoll asks in a book about *I, Rigoberta Menchú* and the uses to which it has been put, a book that attracted considerable international media attention when it appeared late in 1998 (coincident with the final stages of the impeachment trial of President Clinton, which also hinged on questions of evidence and credibility).[2] Referring in part to my own remarks on testimonio quoted above, Stoll argues that "[j]udging by such definitions, *I, Rigoberta Menchú* does not belong in the genre of which it is the most famous example, because it is not the eyewitness account it purports to be" (242). In truth, what Stoll is able to show is that *some* rather than *much* of Menchú's story involves what he calls "mythic inflation" (232). But the point remains: if the power of testimonio is ultimately grounded in the presumption of witnessing and speaking truth to power, then any evidence of "invention" should be deeply troubling.

Gayatri Spivak anticipates one possible reply to Stoll's question when she remarks—in the course of an interview published in 1990—that "perhaps the proper question of someone who has not been allowed to be the subject of history is to say: What is man that he was obliged to produce such a text of history?"[3] As I noted in the introduction, Spivak's notorious claim that the subaltern cannot speak as such is meant to underline the fact that if the subaltern could speak in a way that really *mattered* to us, that we would feel compelled to listen to, it would not be subaltern. Spivak is saying, in other words, that one of the things being subaltern means is not mattering, not being worth listening to. Stoll's argument with Rigoberta Menchú, by contrast, is precisely with the way in which her book in fact "matters." It concerns how the canonization of *I, Rigoberta Menchú* was used by academics like myself and solidarity and human rights activists to mobilize international support for the Guatemalan guerrilla movement in the 1980s, long after (in Stoll's view) that movement had lost whatever support it might have initially enjoyed among the Mayan peasants whom Menchú claims to speak for (and about). The inaccuracies and omissions Stoll claims to find in Menchú's account lend themselves, he feels, "to justify violence" (274). That issue—"how outsiders were using Rigoberta's story to justify continuing a war at the expense of peasants who did not support it" (241)—is the main problem for Stoll, rather than the inaccuracies or omissions themselves. By making Menchú's story seem, in her own words, "the story of all poor Guatemalans," *I, Rigoberta Menchú* misrepresented a more complex and ideologically contradictory situation among the indigenous peasants.

In one sense, of course, there is a coincidence between Spivak's concern, in "Can the Subaltern Speak?," with the production in metropolitan academic and theoretical discourse of a "domesticated Other" and Stoll's concern with the conversion of Menchú into an icon of political correctness in order to sustain a vanguardist political strategy he thinks is profoundly flawed. In a way that seems to echo Spivak, Stoll notes that "books like I, Rigoberta Menchú will be exalted because they tell academics what they want to hear. . . . What makes I, Rigoberta Menchú so attractive in universities is what makes it misleading about the struggle for survival in Guatemala. We think we are getting closer to understanding Guatemalan peasants when actually we are being borne away by the mystifications wrapped up in an iconic figure" (227). But his argument is also explicitly with Spivak, as a practitioner of the very "postmodern scholarship" that privileges a text like I, Rigoberta Menchú (247). I will come back to this point. But for the moment it may be enough to note that where Spivak is concerned with the way in which elite representation effaces the effective presence of the subaltern, Stoll's case against Menchú is precisely that: a way of, so to speak, re-subalternizing a narrative that aspired to (and achieved) hegemony. In this sense, Stoll's book could be seen as a contemporary case of what Ranajit Guha means by "the prose of counter-insurgency"—that is, a discourse that captures the fact of insurgency precisely through the cultural assumptions and practices of the elite and the state agencies that the insurgency is directed against.

Stoll foregrounds in his discussion the elevation of Rigoberta Menchú into a kind of secular saint for politically correct academics and solidarity activists. That concern may explain in part his curious insistence in referring to her familiarly by her first name, even though the force of his book is precisely to discredit her personal authority. Why does it seem proper to refer, as we habitually do, to Rigoberta Menchú as Rigoberta? The use of the first name is appropriate to address, on the one hand, a friend or significant other, or, on the other, a servant, child, or domestic animal— that is, a subaltern. But is it that we are addressing Rigoberta Menchú as a friend or familiar in the work we do on her testimonio? We would not say with such ease, for example, Fred for Fredric Jameson, or Gayatri for Gayatri Spivak, unless we wanted to signal that we have or want to claim a personal relationship with them. Jameson himself observes that while testimonio involves the displacement of the "master subject" of modernist narrative, it does so paradoxically via the insistence on the first-person voice and proper name of the narrator (Jameson nevertheless continues to speak of Rigoberta).[4]

The question of name—of the authority of a proper name—is embedded in the title of Menchú's testimonio, which reproduces its opening lines, Me llamo Rigoberta Menchú, y así me nació la conciencia ("My name is Rigoberta

Menchú, and this is how my consciousness was formed"), dramatically mistranslated in the English edition as *I, Rigoberta Menchú: An Indian Woman in Guatemala*. In an interview some years ago, Menchú was asked about her relationship with Elisabeth Burgos, the Venezuelan anthropologist (ex-wife of Regis Debray) who initiated the conversations in Paris that produced the testimonio. In most editions of the book Burgos appears as the author, and she has been the recipient of the royalties (though she claims to have turned over at least part of these to Menchú). Menchú, however, insists on her right to appear as the author or coauthor: "What is in fact an absence in the book is the rights of the author. . . . Because the authorship of the book, in fact, should have been more precise, shared, no?" ("[L]o que si efectivamente es un vacío en el libro es el derecho de autor. . . . Porque la autoría del libro, efectivamente, debío ser más precisa, compartida, ¿verdad?").[5]

In deference to political correctness, not to say politeness or respect for a person I have met only formally, I make it a point to say Rigoberta Menchú or Menchú. But I have to keep reminding myself on this score. My inclination is also to say Rigoberta. What is at stake in the question of how to address Menchú is the status of the testimonial narrator as a subject in her own right, rather than as someone (or some thing) who exists essentially *for us.* What I have to say here is located in the tension between the injunction to grant Menchú the respect and autonomy she deserves in these terms, and the desire to see myself (my own projects and desires) in or through her.

Does Rigoberta Menchú have a psyche, or is the unconscious itself a form of white-skin privilege? The question seems on the face of it ironic or perverse, given the testimonial narrator's own insistence on the public and collective dimension of his or her narrative persona and social function. In "The Storyteller," Walter Benjamin makes storytelling as such impermeable to psychological introspection, which is instead the province of the bildungsroman.[6] Nevertheless, there is a way in which *I, Rigoberta Menchú* could (should?) itself be read as an oedipal bildungsroman, along fairly familiar lines. The sequence of the narration, which corresponds both to the narrator's coming of age and to the emergence of revolutionary armed struggle among the Mayan communities of Guatemala, goes from an initial rejection of the Mother and motherhood in favor of an Athena-like identification with the Father, Vicente, the *campesino* organizer;[7] to an authority struggle with the Father, who does not want his daughter to learn how to read and write, because he believes that will mean her alienation from the community and traditional women's roles; then to the death of the Father (in 1979, along with other demonstrators, he occupied the

Spanish embassy in Guatemala City to protest military violence; the army surrounded the embassy and set fire to it, killing everyone inside), which leads to a recognition that her Mother is also someone who controls the subversive arts of subaltern speech and rumor; then to the killing of the Mother, again at the hands of the army (she is kidnapped and tortured to death in a military camp); then to the emergence of Menchú as a full speaking subject, an organizer and leader in her own right, represented in the act of narrating the testimonio itself.

Perhaps it might be useful to see the testimonio as such as involving a kind of narrative hybridity: a fusion between what Benjamin means by "storytelling" as a premodern form of wisdom and authority, and the bildungsroman or autobiography, which are paradigmatic forms of "modern," transcultured subjectivity. Like Richard Rodriguez's *Hunger of Memory*, *I, Rigoberta Menchú* not only narrates but also embodies in its textual aporias the tensions involved in this almost classic coming-of-age sequence, which also marks the transition (or, perhaps more correctly, the oscillation) between the orders of tradition and modernity, the local and the global, oral and print culture (Menchú telling her story orally and its textualization by Elisabeth Burgos), ethnographic narrative and literature, the subaltern and hegemony, and—in the Lacanian schema of subject formation—the Imaginary and the Symbolic. For Rodriguez, Spanish is the maternal language of the private sphere that has to be rejected in order to gain full access to the authority (governed by the Law of the Father) of the Symbolic order represented by English—so that *Hunger of Memory* is among other things a celebration of English writing programs and a critique of bilingualism. By contrast, it is Menchú's contradictory and shifting relationship to her Mother, who represents the authority of oral culture and Mayan languages, as much as any specifically political experience, that is at the core of her own process of *concientización* as well as her ability to authorize herself as a narrator.[8]

At the (apparent) cost of relativizing the political and ethical claims a text like *I, Rigoberta Menchú* makes on its readers, my improvised psychoanalytic reading foregrounds its complexity, the fact that its analysis is interminable, that it resists simply being the mirror that reflects our narcissistic assumptions about what it should be. Despite all the misunderstandings her essay has provoked, this was surely Spivak's point in answering the question "Can the Subaltern Speak?" in the negative. She was trying to show that behind the good faith of the liberal academic or the committed ethnographer or solidarity activist in allowing or enabling the subaltern to speak lies the trace of the colonial construction of an other—an other who is conveniently available to speak to us (with whom we *can* speak or feel comfortable speaking with). This neutralizes the force of the reality of difference and antagonism our own relatively privileged position in the global system might give rise to.

Elzbieta Sklodowska has in mind something similar when she argues that, despite its appeal to the authority of an actual subaltern voice, testimonio is in fact a staging of the subaltern by someone who is not subaltern, as in Lyotard's notion of the *differend* (where a dispute is carried out according to the terms and language of one of the parties to the dispute). In particular, testimonio is not, in Sklodowska's words, "a genuine and spontaneous reaction of a 'multiform-popular subject' in conditions of postcoloniality, but rather continues to be a discourse of elites committed to the cause of democratization."[9] The appeal to authenticity and victimization in the critical validation of testimonio stops the semiotic play of the text, Sklodowska implies, fixing the subject in a unidirectional gaze that deprives it of its reality. Fixes the testimonial narrator as a subject, that is, but also fixes us as subjects in what Althusser would have called a relation of double specularity created by the idealization or sublimation of subaltern otherness, which in the end also isolates us from our reality.

At the same time, the deconstructive appeal to the "many-leveled, unfixable intricacy and openness of a work of literature"—the phrase is Spivak's,[10] but it captures the position on testimonio assumed by Sklodowska—also has to be suspect, given that this "unfixable intricacy and openness" happens only in a historical matrix in which written literature itself is one of the social practices which generate the difference that is registered as subalternity in the testimonial text. The limit of deconstruction in relation to testimonio is that it reveals (or produces) a textual unfixity or indeterminacy which not only misrepresents but itself produces and reproduces as a reading effect the fixity of actual relations of power and exploitation in the "real" social text.

Is testimonio then simply another chapter in the history of the "lettered city" in Latin America: the assumption, tied directly to the class interests of the creole elites and their own forms of cultural self-authorization, that literature and the literary intellectual and the urban public sphere they define are or could be adequate signifiers of the national? The question is relevant to the claim made by Dinesh D'Souza, in the throes of the controversy over the Stanford Western Culture requirement, that *I, Rigoberta Menchú* is not good or great literature. D'Souza wrote, to be precise: "To celebrate the works of the oppressed, apart from the standard of merit by which other art and history and literature is judged, is to romanticize their suffering, to pretend that it is naturally creative, and to give it an esthetic status that is not shared or appreciated by those who actually endure the oppression."[11]

I happen to think that I, Rigoberta Menchú is one of the most important works of literature produced in Latin America in the last twenty years. But I would rather have it be a provocation in the academy, a radical otherness, as D'Souza feels it to be, than something smoothly integrated into a curriculum for multicultural citizenship at an elite university like Stanford. I would like students at Stanford, or for that matter at the University of Pittsburgh, where I teach (although the stakes in terms of class privilege and intellectual authority are somewhat different), to feel uncomfortable rather than virtuous when they read a text like I, Rigoberta Menchú. I would like them to understand that almost by definition the subaltern, which will in some cases be a component of their own personal identity, is not, and cannot be adequately represented by literature or in the university, that literature and the university are among the practices that create and sustain subalternity.[12] At the same time, of course, it is precisely the academic canonization of I, Rigoberta Menchú that contributes to its ideological force, as Stoll notes.

Menchú herself is of course also an intellectual, whose formation as such includes a period of training as a lay catechist charged with explaining stories from the Bible to her people. But she is an intellectual in a sense clearly different than what Gramsci called the traditional intellectual—that is, someone who meets the standards and carries the authority of high culture, philosophy, and science—and a sometimes explicit hostility to intellectuals, the state education system, and the authority of book-learning is one of the leitmotifs of her testimonio.[13] The concern with the question of subaltern agency in testimonio depends on the suspicion, noted in chapter 2, that intellectuals and writing itself are themselves complicit in relations of domination and subalternity. Testimonio presents itself to us (that is, to the reading public) as a written text, but it also grants a certain authority or epistemic privilege to orality in the context of processes of modernization that privilege literacy and writing in European languages as cultural norms.

Sklodowska and Spivak are concerned with what Gareth Williams calls the "disciplinary fantasies" implied in the academic staging of testimonio.[14] But perhaps the more urgent question is not so much how intellectuals like ourselves appropriate testimonial narrators like Menchú as, in David Stoll's view, a kind of icon that tells us what we want to hear, as how those narrators appropriate us for their purposes. Sklodowska misunderstands the nature of the claim I am making for testimonio by treating it as if it were an appeal to the documentary authenticity of a subaltern voice. She is, of course, correct to point out that the voice in testimonio is a textual construct, put together by an editor who exists in a very different locus of enunciation than the one represented by the testimonial narrative-voice itself. Her implication is that we should beware of a metaphysics of presence perhaps even more in testimonio, where the convention of fictionality has been suspended, than in other texts. But something of the experience of the body in pain or hunger or danger—what René Jara calls "a trace of the Real"—also inheres in testimonio.[15]

That is certainly the sense of the extraordinary passage in which Menchú narrates the torture and execution of her brother by the army in the town plaza of Chajul. She describes how, at the climax of the massacre, the witnesses experience an almost involuntary shudder of revulsion and anger, which the soldiers sense and which puts them on their guard:

> After he'd finished talking the officer ordered the squad to take away those who'd been "punished," naked and swollen as they were. They dragged them along, they could no longer walk. Dragged them to this place, where they lined them up all together within sight of everyone. The officer called to the worst of the criminals—the Kaibiles, who wear different clothes from other soldiers. They're the ones with the most training, the most power. Well, he called the Kaibiles and they poured petrol over each of the tortured. The captain said, "This isn't the last of their punishments, there's another one yet. This is what we've done with all the subversives we catch, because they have to die by violence. And if this doesn't teach you a lesson, this is what'll happen to you too. The problem is that the Indians let themselves be led by the communists. Since no-one's told the Indians anything, they go along with the communists." He was trying to convince the people but at the same time he was insulting them by what he said. Anyway, they [the soldiers] lined up the tortured and poured petrol on them; and then the soldiers set fire to each one of them. Many of them begged for mercy. Some of them screamed, many of them leapt but uttered no sound—of course, that was because their breathing was cut off. But— and to me this was incredible—many of the people had weapons with them, the ones who'd been on their way to work had machetes, others had nothing in their hands, but when they saw the army setting fire to the victims, everyone wanted to strike back, to risk their lives doing it, despite all the soldiers' arms. . . . Faced with its own cowardice, the army itself realized that the whole people were prepared to fight. You could see that even the children were enraged, but they didn't know how to express their rage. (178–79)

Reading this passage, we also experience this rage—and possibility of defiance even in the face of the threat of death—through the mechanism of identification, just as we do at the moment in Schindler's List when the women in the Kraków concentration camp, who have been congratulating each other on surviving the selection process, suddenly realize that their children have been rounded up in the meantime and are being taken to the gas chambers in trucks. These are instances of what Lacan calls tuché: moments where the experience of the Real breaks through the repetitious passivity of witnessing imposed by the repression itself. By contrast, romanticizing victimization would tend to confirm the Christian narrative of suffering and redemption that underlies colonial or imperialist domination in the first place. In practice such a representation would lead more to a posture of benevolent paternalism or liberal guilt rather than effective solidarity, which presumes in principle a relation of equality and reciprocity between the parties involved.[16]

As it happens, however, the narration of the death of Menchú's brother is precisely one of the passages in I, Rigoberta Menchú whose literal veracity Stoll contests, claiming on the basis of his own interviews in the area Menchú comes from (where he spent several years doing fieldwork) that the torture and massacre of her brother by the army happened in a different way, that Menchú herself could not have been an eyewitness to it (63–70), and that therefore her description is, in his words, a "mythic inflation" (232). It is important to distinguish this claim from the claim subsequently made by some right-wing commentators that I, Rigoberta Menchú is fraudulent. Stoll is not saying that Menchú is making it all up. He does not contest the fact of the murder of Menchú's brother by the army. And he stipulates in his preface that "[t]here is no doubt about the most important points [in her story]: that a dictatorship massacred thousands of indigenous peasants, that the victims included half of Rigoberta's immediate family, that she fled to Mexico to save her life, and that she joined a revolutionary movement to liberate her country" (viii). But, as noted, he does argue, that the inaccuracies, omissions, or misrepresentations in her account make her less than a reliable representative of the interests and beliefs of the people she claims to be speaking for.

Menchú has publicly conceded that she grafted elements of other people's experiences and stories onto her own account. In particular, she has admitted that she was not herself present at the massacre of her brother and his companions in Chajul and that the account of the event came instead from her mother, who (she claims) was there. She says that these interpolations were a way of making her story a collective account, rather than an autobiography.[17] Her remarks, posed against Stoll's questioning of the representativity of her testimonio, allow a new way of reading certain passages in the text: for example, the famous opening paragraph, where

Menchú declares that her story "is not only my life, it's also the testimony of my people."

But, in a way, the argument between Menchú and Stoll is not so much about what really happened as about who has the authority to narrate. What seems to bother Stoll above all is that Menchú has an ideological agenda. He wants her to be in effect a "native informant," who will lend herself to his purposes (of information gathering and evaluation), but she is instead an organic intellectual concerned with producing a text of "local history" (to recall Florencia Mallon's term)—that is, with elaborating hegemony. Though Stoll talks about objectivity and facts, it turns out he also has an ideological agenda. He believes that the attempt of the Marxist left to wage an armed struggle against the military dictatorship in Guatemala put the majority of the highland indian population "between two fires," driven to support the guerrillas mainly by the ferocity of the army's counter-insurgency measures rather than by a belief in the justice or strategic necessity of armed struggle.[18] By contrast, the narrative logic of *I, Rigoberta Menchú* suggests that the Guatemalan armed struggle grew necessarily out of the conditions of repression the indigenous communities faced in their attempts to hold the line against land seizures and exploitation by the army, paramilitary death squads, and ladino landowners. For Stoll to sustain his hypothesis, he has to impeach the force of Menchú's testimony, in other words. As he makes clear at the end of his book, Stoll intends not only a retrospective critique of the armed struggle in Guatemala; he also means his book as a caution against enthusiasm for contemporary movements like the Zapatistas in Mexico. Indeed, for Stoll, rural guerrilla strategies as such "are an urban romance, a myth propounded by middle-class radicals who dream of finding true solidarity in the countryside," a myth which has "repeatedly been fatal for the left itself, by dismaying lower-class constituents and guaranteeing a crushing response from the state" (282). The misrepresentation or simplification of indigenous life and rural realities that a text like *I, Rigoberta Menchú* performs colludes with this urban romance.

But is the problem for Stoll the verifiability of Menchú's story or the wisdom of armed struggle as such? If it could be shown that all the details in Menchú's account are in fact verifiable or plausible, would it follow for Stoll that the armed struggle was justified? Obviously not. But, by the same token, the gaps, inaccuracies, "mythic inflations," and so on that he finds in Menchú's account do not necessarily add up to an indictment of the armed struggle. Maybe the armed struggle was a mistake: Stoll observes that Menchú has sought in recent years to place some distance between herself and the umbrella organization of the left, the UNRG. But that judgment does not itself follow from his impeachment of Menchú's narrative authority. In other words, the question of verifiability is subordinate to the question of Stoll's ideological disagreement with the strategy of armed struggle.

My own view is that under conditions of military and paramilitary rule in which even the most cautious trade unionists and social-democratic or Christian-Democratic elected officials were liable to be "disappeared" and in the context of the Sandinista victory in 1979, it is not surprising that armed resistance came to seem to many people in Guatemala as a desperate but plausible strategy. In particular, it is a long way from saying that not all highland peasants supported the armed struggle to claiming that the guerrilla movement lacked, or lost, significant popular roots among them, that it was imposed on them against their will and interests. But Stoll gives us no more convincing "hard" evidence to support this contention than Menchú does to argue the contrary. Other observers have argued that the guerrillas were in fact relatively successful in recruiting highland indigenous peasants, that the integration of the previously predominantly ladino and Marxist guerrilla groups with significant elements of this population constituted a powerful challenge to the military dictatorship, that it was precisely that possibility that the army was seeking to destroy in the genocidal counter-insurgency war that Menchú describes in her narrative. Who are we to believe? As in the impeachment trial of president Clinton, it comes down to a matter of "he said, she said," which in the end will be decided on political rather than epistemological grounds.[19]

Referring to the tasks of the truth commissions established as part of the peace process in Guatemala, Stoll notes that "[i]f identifying crimes and breaking through regimes of denial has become a public imperative in peacemaking, if there is a public demand for establishing 'historical memory,' then I, Rigoberta Menchú cannot be enshrined as true in a way it is not" (273). Fair enough. But if the Guatemalan army had simply destroyed the guerrillas and imposed its will on the population, then there would be no truth commissions in the first place. Yet Stoll faults Menchú's story among other things precisely for helping guerrilla leaders "finally obtain the December 1996 peace agreement" (278).

In the process of constructing her narrative and articulating herself around its circulation, Menchú is becoming not-subaltern, in the sense that she is functioning as a "subject of history" (to recall Spivak's point at the beginning of this chapter). But the conditions of her becoming-not-subaltern—her narrative choices, silences, "mythic inflation," "reinvention," and so on—entail necessarily that there are versions of "what really happened" that she does not or cannot represent without relativizing the authority of her own account. It goes without saying that in any social situation, indeed even within a given class or group identity, it is always possible to find a variety of narratives, points of view that reflect contradictory agendas and interests. "A frank account of Chimel [the region Menchú's family is from] would have presented an uninspiring picture of peasants feuding with each other," Stoll notes. "[T]ellers of life stories tend to downplay the incoherence, accident, discontinuity, and doubt that characterize actual lived experience. . . . In Rigoberta's case, she achieved coherence by omitting features of the situation that contradicted the ideology of her new organization, then substituting appropriate revolutionary themes" (192–93).

The existence of "other" voices in Stoll's account makes Guatemalan indigenous communities—indeed even Menchú's own immediate family— seem irremediably riven by internal rivalries, contradictions, different ways of telling. "Obviously," Stoll writes, "Rigoberta is a legitimate Mayan voice. So are all the young Mayas who want to move to Los Angeles or Houston. So is the man with a large family who owns three worn-out acres and wants me to buy him a chain saw so he can cut down the last forest more quickly. Any of these people can be picked to make misleading generalizations about Mayas" (247). But, in a way, this is to deny the possibility of political struggle as such, since a hegemonic project by definition points to a possibility of collective will and action that depends precisely on transforming the conditions of cultural and political disenfranchisement that underlie these contradictions. The appeal to heterogeneity—"any of these people"— leaves intact the authority of the outside observer—that is, Stoll—who is alone in the position of being able to both hear and sort through the various testimonies (but the "outside" observer also has his own social, political, and cultural agendas, and his actions have effects "inside" the situation he pretends to describe from a position of neutral objectivity). It also leaves intact the *existing* structures of political-military domination and cultural authority. The existence of "contradictions among the people"— for example, the interminable internecine fights over land and natural resources within and between peasant communities that Stoll puts so much emphasis on—does not deny the possibility of contradiction between the "people" as such and an ethnic, class, and state formation felt as deeply alienating and repressive (I will return to this issue in the next chapter).

But Stoll's argument, as we have seen, is not only about Guatemala. It is also with the discourses of multiculturalism and postmodernism in the North American academy, which he feels consciously or unconsciously colluded to perpetuate armed struggle, therefore promoting *I, Rigoberta Menchú* as a text and making Menchú into an international icon. Thus, for example: "It was in the name of multiculturalism that *I, Rigoberta Menchú* entered the university reading lists" (243). Or, "[u]nder the influence of postmodernism (which has undermined confidence in a single set of facts) and identity politics (which demands acceptance of claims to victimhood), scholars are increasingly hesitant to challenge certain kinds of rhetoric" (244). Or, "the identity needs of Rigoberta's academic constituency play into the weakness of rules of evidence in postmodern scholarship" (247). Or, "with postmodern critiques of representation and authority, many scholars are tempted to abandon the task of verification, especially when they construe the narrator as a victim worthy of their support" (274).

What starts off as a critique of the truth claims of Rigoberta Menchú's testimonio and the *foquista* strategy of the Guatemalan guerrilla movement metamorphoses into an attack on what the neoconservative writer Roger Kimball calls "tenured radicals" in European and North American universities, including myself. The connection between postmodernism and multiculturalism that Stoll is bothered about is predicated on the fact that multiculturalism (and Menchú's book is, among other things, an argument for understanding Guatemala itself as a deeply multicultural and multilinguistic nation) implies a demand for epistemological relativism that coincides with the postmodernist critique of science. If there is no one universal standard for truth, then claims about truth are contextual: they have to do with how people construct different understandings of the world and historical memory from the same set of facts in situations of radical social inequality, exploitation, and repression. The truth claims for a testimonial narrative like *I, Rigoberta Menchú* depend on conferring on the form a certain special kind of epistemological authority as embodying subaltern experience. But for Stoll this amounts to a "mythic inflation" of the subaltern to favor the prejudices of a metropolitan academic audience, in the interest of a solidarity politics that (in his view) is doing more harm than good. Against such inflation, Stoll wants to affirm the authority of the fact-gathering procedures of anthropology and journalism, in which testimonial accounts like Menchú's will be treated simply as raw material that must be processed by more objective techniques of assessment. "If we focus on text, narrative, or voice, it is not hard to find someone to say what we want to hear—just what we need to firm up our sense of moral worth or our identity as intellectual rebels," he writes (247). But Stoll's own basis for questioning Menchú's account of the massacre of her brother and other details of her story are interviews with people from the region where the massacre occurred, interviews he conducted many years afterward. That is, the only evidence he can put in the place of what he considers Menchú's unrepresentative testimony are *other* testimonies, in which (it will come as no surprise) he can also find things that *he* might want to hear.

There is a section in Shoshana Felman and Dori Laub's book on testimonial representations of the Holocaust that relates to this quandary. It
has to do with a woman survivor who gave an eyewitness account of the
Auschwitz uprising for the Video Archive for Holocaust Testimonies at
Yale. At one point in her narrative the survivor recalls that in the course of
the uprising, in her own words, "All of a sudden, we saw four chimneys
going up in flames, exploding. The flames shot into the sky, people were
running. It was unbelievable."[20] Months later, at a conference on the
Holocaust that featured a viewing of the videotape of the woman's testimony, this sequence became the focus of a debate. Some historians of the
Holocaust pointed out that only *one* chimney had been destroyed in the
uprising, and that the woman had not mentioned in her account the fact
that the Polish underground had betrayed the uprising. Given that the
narrator was wrong about these crucial details, they argued, it might be
best to set aside her whole testimony, rather than give credence to the
revisionists who want to deny the reality of the Holocaust altogether by
questioning the reliability of the factual record.

Laub and Felman note that, on that occasion,

> [a] psychoanalyst who had been one of the interviewers of the woman
> profoundly disagreed. "The woman was testifying," he insisted, "not
> to the number of the chimneys blown up, but to something else more
> radical, more crucial: the reality of an unimaginable occurrence. One
> chimney blown up at Auschwitz was as incredible as four. The num-
> ber mattered less than the fact of the occurrence. . . . The woman
> testified to an event that broke the all compelling frame of Auschwitz,
> where Jewish armed revolts just did not happen, and had no place. She
> testified to the breakage of a framework. That was historical truth."
> (60)

The psychoanalyst was in fact Laub, who goes on to explain:

> In the process of the testimony to a trauma, as in psychoanalytic
> practice, in effect, you often do not want to know anything except
> what the patient tells you, because what is important in the situation
> is the *discovery* of knowledge—its evolution, and its very *happening.*
> Knowledge in the testimony is, in other words, not simply a factual
> given that is reproduced and replicated by the testifier, but a genuine
> advent, an event in its own right. . . . [The woman] was testifying not
> simply to empirical historical facts, but to the very secret of survival
> and of resistance to extermination. The historians could not hear, I
> thought, the way in which her silence was itself part of the testimony,

an essential part of the historical truth she was precisely bearing witness to. . . . This was her way of being, of surviving, of resisting. It is not merely her speech, but the very boundaries of silence which surround it, which attest, today as well as in the past, to this assertion of resistance. (62)

We know something about the nature of this problem. There is not, outside of human discourse itself, a level of social facticity that can guarantee the truth of this or that representation, given that the facts of memory are not essences prior to representation, but rather themselves the consequence of struggles to represent and over representation. That is the meaning of Benjamin's aphorism "Even the dead are not safe": even the memory of the past is conjunctural, relative, perishable. Testimonio is both an art and a strategy of subaltern memory.

It would be yet another version of the "native informant" to grant testimonial narrators like Rigoberta Menchú only the possibility of being witnesses, but not the power to create their own narrative authority and negotiate its conditions of truth and representativity. This amounts to saying that the subaltern can of course speak, but only through us, through our institutionally sanctioned authority and pretended objectivity as intellectuals, which gives us the power to decide what counts in the narrator's raw material. But it is precisely that institutionally sanctioned authority and objectivity that, in a less benevolent form, but still claiming to speak from the place of Truth, the subaltern must confront every day in the form of war, economic exploitation, development schemes, obligatory acculturation, police and military repression, destruction of habitat, forced sterilization, and the like.[21]

Since (in a way that recalls Florencia Mallon's point about the "dust of the archives") Stoll raises directly the question of the authority of anthropology—which, in his view, has the disciplinary franchise of representing the other to us—against what is, for him, its corruption by "postmodernist scholarship," let me say a few words about the relation of Menchú to Mayan tradition. Though it is founded on a notion of the recuperation of tradition, which her interlocutor, Elisabeth Burgos (also an anthropologist), underlines by inserting passages from the *Popol Vuh* at the beginning of some chapters, there is nothing particularly "traditional" about Menchú's narrative: this is not what makes it the representation of "toda la realidad de un pueblo" ("the whole reality of a people"), because there is nothing particularly traditional about the community and way of life that the narrative describes either. Nothing more "postmodern," nothing more traversed by the economic and cultural forces of transnational capitalism—nothing that we can claim anyway—than the social, economic, and cultural contingencies Menchú and her family and friends live and die in. Even the communal mountain *aldea* or village that her narrative evokes so compellingly, with its collective rituals and economic life, turns out on closer inspection as not so much an ancestral Mayan gemeinschaft as a quite recent settlement, founded by Menchú's father, Vicente, on unoccupied lands in the mountains in the wake of its inhabitants' displacement from their previous places of residence, much as squatters from the countryside have created the great slums around Latin American cities, or returned refugees in Central America have tried to reconstruct their former communities.[22]

I do not mean by this to diminish the force of Menchú's insistent appeal to the authority of her ancestors and tradition, but want simply to indicate that it is an appeal that is being activated and, at the same time, continuously revised *in the present*, that it is a response to the conditions of proletarianization and semi-proletarianization that subjects like Menchú and her family are experiencing in the context of the same processes of globalization that affect our own lives. In some ways, a Latino postmodernist performance artist like Gloria Anzaldúa or Guillermo Gómez Peña might be a more reliable guide to Menchú's world than anthropologists like David Stoll or Elisabeth Burgos, who assume they are authorized or authorize themselves to represent that truth for us.

Readers of *I, Rigoberta Menchú* will remember in particular Burgos's perhaps unintentionally condescending remarks in her introduction about Menchú's cooking and clothing ("she was wearing traditional costume, including a multicoloured *huipil* with rich and varied embroidery," and so on [xiv]), and will probably tend to see these as illustrating the self-interested benevolence of the hegemonic intellectual toward the subaltern. But Menchú's clothes are not so much an index of her authenticity as a subaltern, which would confirm the ethical and epistemological virtue of the *bien pensant* intellectual in the first world: both as a field worker in the coffee plantations and as a maid in Guatemala City she had to learn how to dress very differently, as she tells us herself in her narrative. They speak rather to a kind of performative transvestism on her part, a conscious use of traditional Mayan women's dress as a cultural signifier to define her own identity and her allegiance to the community and values she is fighting for.[23]

There is a question of subaltern agency here, just as there is in the construction of the testimonial text itself. Asked, in the same interview where she claims her right to appear as the coauthor of *I, Rigoberta Menchú*, if she thinks that her struggles will have an end, Menchú answers: "I believe that the struggle does not have an end. . . . I believe that democracy does not depend on the implantation of something, but rather that it is a process in development, that it will unfold in the course of History" ("Yo sí creo que la lucha no tiene fin. . . . yo creo que la democracia no depende de una implantación de algo, sino que va a ser un proceso en desarrollo, se va a desenvolver a lo largo de la Historia") (Britten and Dworkin 213; my translation). She sees her own testimonio in similar terms as a conjunctural intervention that responded to a certain strategic urgency, now relativized by what was not or could not be included in it—an imperfect metonym of a different, potentially more complete or representative text, open to the contingencies of memory and history. Except for wanting to be recognized as coauthor, it is not so much that she objects to the way Elisabeth Burgos edited the transcripts of her narrative. Rather, her concern takes the form of a self-criticism:

> Reading it [I, Rigoberta Menchú] now, I have the impression that it's a part, that there are fragments of history itself, no? So many stories one comes across in life, in our experiences with the family, with the land, with so many things. What the book has are fragments and I hope that one day we could redo it, maybe for our grandchildren, maybe after putting in a series of other stories, testimonies, experiences, beliefs, prayers that we learned as children, because the book has a lot of limitations.
>
> Ahora, al leerlo, me da la impresión que es una parte, que son fragmentos de la historia misma, ¿verdad? Tantas anécdotas que uno tiene en la vida, especialmente la convivencia con los abuelos, con la familia, con la tierra, con muchas cosas. Son fragmentos los que tiene el libro y ójala que algun día pudieramos redocumentarlo para publicarlo, tal vez para nuestros nietos, posiblemente después de poner una serie de otras leyendas, testimonios, vivencias, creencias, oraciones, que aprendimos de chiquitos, porque el libro tiene una serie de limitaciones. (Britten and Dworkin 217; my translation)

Note that Menchú distinguishes in this passage between a testimonio— the book I, Rigoberta Menchú ("son fragmentos los que tiene el libro")—and testimonios in the plural as heterogenous and primarily oral acts or practices of witnessing and recounting in her own community, as in "una serie de otras leyendas, testimonios, vivencias, creencias, oraciones." Testimonio in the singular is for her only one, audience-specific (to use the jargon of Communications) form of a much broader testimonial practice in subaltern cultures, a practice which includes the arts of oral memory, storytelling, gossip, and rumor. Where her primary identification in the early part of her narrative is with her father, Vicente—the organizer or public man—these are precisely the arts Menchú acknowledges learning from her mother, whose own life she calls toward the end of her story a "testimonio vivo," or living testimony.[24]

Testimonio in the singular is, of course, the form of this communal practice that *we* get to experience, since we have no direct access to (and, in general, no interest in) that larger practice. Hence the essentially metonymic character of the testimonial text. However, it is not only the voice/experience of the narrator in testimonio that is a metonym of a larger community or group, as in Menchú's claim that her personal story is the story of "todo un pueblo"; the testimonio itself is also a metonym of the complex and varied cultural practices and institutions of that community or group.

What *I, Rigoberta Menchú* forces us to confront is not the subaltern as a "represented" victim of history, but rather as agent of a transformative historical project that aspires to become hegemonic in its own right. Although we can enter into relations of understanding and solidarity with this project, it is not *ours* in any immediate sense and may in fact imply structurally a contradiction with our own position of relative privilege and authority in the global system. Becoming a writer, making a literary text out of an oral narration, using testimonial material to construct a historical narrative in the way Mallon does in *Peasant and Nation*, reading and discussing the text in a classroom, cannot be the solution the "situation of urgency" that generates the telling of the testimonio in the first place requires, although Burgos, Menchú, and the others involved in creating her testimonio were aware from the start that it would be used as a weapon against the counter-insurgency war being waged by the Guatemalan army. But Menchú's own interest in creating the testimonio is not to have it become part of "Western Culture," which in any case she distrusts deeply, so that it can become an object *for us*, a means of getting the whole truth— "toda la realidad"—of her people. It is rather to act strategically in a way she hopes will advance the interests of the people she "represents"—whom she calls "poor" Guatemalans. That is why her testimonio can never be "great literature" in the sense this has for D'Souza: the response it elicits falls necessarily outside of the fields of both literature and anthropology in their present form.[25]

This seems obvious enough, but it is a hard lesson for us to absorb, because it forces us to recognize that it is not the intention of subaltern cultural practice simply to signify more or less artfully, more or less sincerely, its subalternity to us. If that is what testimonio does, then Sklodowska and Spivak are right in seeing it as a kind of postmodernist *costum-*

brismo. While she speaks in the passage quoted above of the possibility of redoing her text, Menchú also makes it clear that returning to testimonio is now beside the point for her, that there are other stories she needs, or wants, to tell. That is as it should be, because it is not only *our* desires and purposes that should count in relation to testimonio.

But we—the we of "*our* desires and purposes" above—are not exactly in the position of the dominant in the dominant/subaltern binary. While we serve the ruling class, we are not (necessarily) part of it. To leave things simply at a celebration of difference and alterity, therefore, is to leave things in the space of a liberal multiculturalism. It is to replace politics with a deconstructive ethics. Part of the appeal of *I, Rigoberta Menchú* that David Stoll objects to resides in the fact that it both symbolizes and enacts concretely a relation of active solidarity between ourselves—as members of the professional middle class and practitioners of the human sciences—and subaltern social subjects. Testimonio implies more than simply being onlookers and reporters of the struggles of others built around identity politics and new points of contention in globalization. We also have a stake in those struggles. Both the economic and ethical bases of our professional lives depend on the idea of *service* and on a network of publicly supported or subsidized institutions and activities. As a class or class-fraction, with local, national, and transnational parameters, intellectuals and professionals have very little to gain and a lot to lose from privatization and the pressure to erode wages and living standards. That realization argues for a tactical alliance between the middle strata and the global/local "poor."

Similarly, though it is based on an affirmation of Mayan identity and culture against a "great narrative" (which has both Marxist and bourgeois-liberal versions) of acculturation and modernization, *I, Rigoberta Menchú* is not so much an appeal to Mayan exceptionalism as a gesture toward a potentially hegemonic political formation in Guatemala that would also include elements of the ladino working class and middle class (and beyond Guatemala, engage the support of progressive forces in the world at large). What Menchú comes to understand, in other words, is that the very possibility of Mayan identity politics and cultural survival has come to depend on an alliance with (what is for her) an other.[26]

The possibility of building such a political formation, based on a coincidence of interests between subaltern subjects and intellectuals and professionals like ourselves who seek to represent them in some way, is also something that David Stoll's argument against Rigoberta Menchú seeks to preclude. In that way too it functions as a text of counter-insurgency. What we share with Rigoberta Menchú, beyond the contradictions that separate our interests and projects, is the desire and need for a *new kind of state* along with new kinds of transnational political-economic institutionality. How do we activate this possibility in the face of the overwhelming ideological hegemony of neoliberalism? That is the question I would like to address in the second half of this book, which concerns in a general way the relation between subaltern studies and cultural studies.

4 Hybrid or Binary? On the Category of "the People" in Subaltern and Cultural Studies

In the preface to *Selected Subaltern Studies* Ranajit Guha adds to his general definition of the subaltern (as, to recall, "a name for the general attribute of subordination . . . whether this is expressed in terms of class, caste, age, gender and office or in any other way") this qualifying sentence: "We recognize of course that subordination cannot be understood except as one of the constitutive terms in a binary relationship of which the other is dominance."[1] The unstated reference is to Ferdinand de Saussure on the question of linguistic value and the role of negation in constituting identity.[2] The implication is that the logic that constitutes subaltern identity is necessarily binary. Starting from the same "structuralist" account of meaning production, Homi Bhabha argues, by contrast, that the resistance of the colonized subject emerges necessarily at the margin of fixed identity or in its catachrestic moment: "[T]he complex strategies of cultural identification and discursive address that function in the name of 'the people' or 'the nation'" are, he writes, "more hybrid in the articulation of cultural differences and identifications—gender, race or class—than can be represented in any hierarchical or binary structuring of social antagonism."³ That understanding, in turn, is the basis of his claim that the philosophical-critical project of deconstruction and the intentions and strategies of subaltern "unmasking" or "speaking back" to power march hand in hand.

Bhabha's argument has become something like an article of faith in postcolonial criticism, as the following critical statements suggest:⁴

> To study the rhetoric of the British Raj in both its colonial and postcolonial manifestations is therefore to attempt to break down the incipient schizophrenia of a critical discourse that seeks to represent domination and subordination as if they were mutually exclusive terms. Rather than examine a binary rigidity between these terms—which is an inherently Eurocentric strategy—this critical field would be better served if it sought to break down the fixity of the dividing lines between domination and subordination, and if it further questioned psychic disempowerment signified by colonial encounter. . . . [H]ow can the dynamic of imperial intimacy produce an idea of nation that belongs neither to the colonizer nor to the colonized? (Sara Suleri)

> The reification of a colonial moment of binary oppositions may speak more to contemporary political agendas than to ambiguous colonial realities. For it often rests on making the case that the world today is infinitely more complicated, more fragmented and more blurred. We need to think through not only why colonial history appears as manichean but also why so much historiography has invested (and continues to invest) in that myth as well. "Strategic essentialism" may represent the *contre-histoire* in racial discourse, the form in which subjugated knowledges make their space. That may be its political virtue. But as a political strategy for rewriting histories that reflect both the fixity *and* fluidity of racial categories, that attend to how people reworked and contested the boundaries of taxonomic colonial states, it is, if not untenable, at least problematic. (Ann Stoler)

> Those unwilling to countenance [the subalternist] critique of nationalism and national identity—their own and others—instead seem anxious—and for me it registers as a kind of anxiety—to preserve essentialisms, by denying hybridity, diasporas and other contextual remakings of identities precisely because such critiques contribute to a fundamental remaking of the conception of both national and political identity. (Pat Seed)

Is subaltern identity hybrid or binary, then? Are Bhabha's and Guha's senses of the subject formed by colonialism commensurate? Is it a kind of essentialism to posit the subaltern as a stable subject-position in the first place, since real people are neither this nor that? Isn't the whole point, as the passages above suggest, to undo the binary taxonomies that were instituted by previous forms of colonial or class power?

Let me begin my answer with what seems like a waffle on the part of Guha himself (Spivak first drew attention to it in "Can the Subaltern Speak?"). In the "Note" appended to his essay "On Some Aspects of the Historiography of Colonial India," Guha offers a somewhat different definition of subaltern identity, the main feature of which is the identification of the subaltern with the category of "the people": "The terms 'people' and 'subaltern classes' have been used as synonymous throughout this note. The social groups and elements included in this category represent the *demographic difference between the total Indian population and those whom we have described as the élite.*"[5]

Guha goes on to note that the colonial elite in India can be subdivided into three categories, each subordinate to the prior one in turn: (1) the *dominant foreign groups* (British officials, businessmen, landlords, missionaries, and so on); (2) the *dominant indigenous groups* (feudal lords, industrial and mercantile bourgeoisie, upper-level native officials); (3) elites at the regional or local level that were either members of the second category or, "if belonging to social strata hierarchically inferior to those of the dominant all-India groups still *acted in the interests of the latter and not in conformity to interests corresponding truly to their own social being.*"

The somewhat tortured syntax of the Guha's sentence mirrors a conceptual problem in his binary taxonomy. Because it could include social groups or identities that could combine elite and subaltern elements (members of lower-caste groups that had moved up in class or administrative terms, for example), or that had lost elite status, the third category of the elite

> was *heterogenous* in its composition and thanks to the uneven character of regional and economic social developments, *differed from area to area.* The same class or element that was dominant in one area according to the definition given above, could be among the dominated in another. This could and did create many ambiguities and contradictions in attitudes and alliances, especially among the lowest strata of rural gentry, impoverished landlords, rich peasants and upper-middle peasants all of whom belonged, *ideally speaking*, to the category of "people" or "subaltern classes," as defined below.

The sentence quoted above from the "Note," equating "people" and "subaltern classes," follows, together with this definition of the subaltern:

The social groups and elements included in this category [the subaltern] represent *the demographic difference between the total Indian population and all those whom we have described as the 'elite'.* Some of these classes and groups such as the lesser rural gentry, impoverished landlords, rich peasants and upper-middle peasants who 'naturally' ranked among the 'people' and the 'subaltern', could under certain circumstances act for the 'elite', as explained above. (44)

As Spivak notes, Guha's identification of the people and the subaltern is the product of what is in effect a *subtraction*, rather than a positive identity that is *internal* to the people-as-subaltern. It is odd, to say the least, to see the same social actor—that is, the "third category of the elite"—appear in two different places in Guha's text, described in almost identical words, but on opposite sides of the elite/subaltern binary.[6] In the first case, despite their classification as the third category of the elite, "ideally speaking" this group or groups may be persuaded to line up with the subaltern groups. In the second case, they are defined as "naturally" ranking among the people or the subaltern, although they "could under certain circumstances act for the 'elite.' " The third category of the elite is, in other words, in an intermediate or liminal subject-position, somewhat akin to the traditional Marxist characterization of the petty bourgeoisie as a class position "vacillating" between the bourgeoisie and the working class, and thus capable of being mobilized politically by either, depending on the correlation of forces.

This indeterminacy creates, as Guha puts it, "an ambiguity which it is up to the historian to sort out on the basis of a close and judicious reading of his evidence." But the problem is not only historical or methodological; it also has to do with the ways in which such an intermediate subject-position is or could be interpellated or "addressed" ideologically. The identity of the people-as-(the) subaltern is *articulatory*, in the sense that, by definition, it cannot be simply the *sum* of already constituted class or group interests and positions, since it refers to something they all have (or could have) in common. In other words, it also redefines those interests and positions.[7]

The category of "the people" in the way Guha uses it derives in particular from the discourse of the Popular Front. Some brief, but—given the enormous historical and ideological distance that separates us from the heyday of the Popular Front—perhaps necessary background. The policy of the Popular (or People's) Front was inaugurated at the Seventh World Congress of the Comintern in 1935, spurred by a keynote address by the Bulgarian Communist leader Georgi Dimitrov.[8] It sought to rectify what was considered the error of the "class against class" line of the so-called Third Period of the Comintern, which coincided with the Depression, and the rise of Stalin and forced collectivization in the Soviet Union. The political hallmark of Third Period Marxism was the unremitting hostility of the parties affiliated with the Comintern to social-democrats, liberals, and non-Communist trade unions and mass organizations. The argument was that capitalism had entered a stage of terminal crisis. The Great Depression showed that capitalism could collapse economically, and the Bolshevik revolution showed that the objective possibility of revolution was imminent on a world scale. The Communist parties represented the most advanced strata of the working class, Leninism the most advanced theoretical form of Marxism. The social-democratic and labor parties, by confining working-class demands to the sphere of electoral politics, reformism, and trade unionism, were the main obstacle to revolutionary consciousness. It was the task of Communists therefore both to create, in competition with the social-democrats, Catholic parties, and liberals, alternative "revolutionary" mass organizations, as in the famous policy of "dual unionism," and at the same time actively to foment insurrection where it seemed possible (for example, the 1929 Shanghai uprising in China and 1932 rebellion in El Salvador).

What intervened in this strategic calculation was the victory of fascism precisely in the country, Germany, in which the Comintern had placed the greatest hopes. To combat the rise of fascism, Dimitrov argued, the broadest possible unity of democratic forces was needed, which required alliances with a wide variety of social forces, organizations, and political parties. Dimitrov named the following specifically in his speech: youth, women, small peasants and farmers ("fascism triumphed because it was able to win over *large masses of the peasantry, owing to the fact that the Social democrats, in the name of the working class, pursued what was in fact an anti-peasant policy*" [Dimitrov, 76]), "Negros" (in reference to the United States in particular), artisans, organized labor, "Catholic, Anarchist and unorganized workers," "the entire toiling population," social-democrats and independent socialists, the churches, the intelligentsia, sectors of the petty bourgeoisie, "the oppressed peoples of the colonies and semi-colonies" and national liberation movements, and what he called "democratic capitalists."

"The people" designated for Dimitrov the extent of the possible unity of all these components in a common identity. That identity, in turn, had to be posed negatively against something that it was *not*, which Dimitrov named variously as capitalists and landlords, "the rich," fascist dictatorship, reactionaries, "the power of finance capital," "the banks, trusts, and monopolies," imperialism, and the "big bourgeoisie," but which could be understood in a general way as the emerging hegemony of fascism. In a similar way, Mao imagined the bloc of the people in China as formed by all social classes and groups with a stake in resisting the Japanese invasion: that is, the national bourgeoisie, poor and middle peasants, the urban proletariat, the intelligentsia and professionals.

There is an evident (and thus often noted) aporia here, in the sense that "the people" names the social or the national as such as bonded by a "fraternal" relation—as in the idea of the "American people"—but at the same time necessarily excludes, by making into an antagonistic other or "enemy" (in the sense this has in fascist political theory itself—e.g., in Carl Schmitt), other class or group components of the nation. However, for Dimitrov—and this is a crucial point—the category of the people is *heterogenous* rather than unitary (as in the fascist idea of Volk), involving social agents with differing identities, goals, and interests. The unity of the people rests therefore precisely on a recognition and tolerance of difference and incommensurability. This is what Mao meant in his famous concept of "contradictions among the people" (*within* the bloc of the people, that is). But this implies in turn that what is not-the-people—i.e., fascism—does *not* allow (or does not allow in the same way) difference and incommensurability. It represents instead a logic of subjection and/or ethnic homogenization. In other words, heterogeneity is *internal* to the people, rather than expressing a general value or characteristic that extends across the whole space of the national community (I will come back to this point in the last chapter).

The political goal of the Popular Front, as Dimitrov expressed it, was not a Soviet-style dictatorship of the proletariat or even a parliamentary social-democratic or labor government, but rather what he called a "united front" government.[9] The character of united front governments is that they must both defend and extend the provisions for democracy, free elections, free speech, constitutional separation of powers of the state, civil rights, habeas corpus, and so forth inscribed in their respective national traditions. They stand precisely for continuity of democratic rights and privileges (seen themselves as "conquests" of the people), against the idea of the fascist state as an "exceptional" regime. Dimitrov conceived of united front governments as *transitional* forms, necessary to stem the high tide of fascism, but lending themselves afterwards to conversion into the sort of "Peoples' Democracies" that were installed in Eastern Europe or China after World War II. (For that reason, I do not mean to suggest that the heterogeneity implied in principle in the concept of "the people" was in fact inscribed effectively in any regime of what came to be called "actually-existing social-ism." It remains, in this sense, an ideal to be realized.)

Dimitrov, however, did not insist on the "transitional" function of united front government. Indeed, his argument seemed to point in a very different direction: that in the conditions of capitalist crisis created by the Depression and the rise of fascism, it was only under the hegemony of the bloc of the people that the liberal-democratic character of the nation-state and the national culture could be achieved and/or defended.

Dimitrov understood that fascism appealed not only to broad sectors of the middle classes and peasantry frightened both by capitalist crisis and revolutionary agitation, but also to sectors of the organized working class.[10] Part of that appeal lay in fascism's claim to represent the identity and the "interests" of the nation. In response, Dimitrov believed, the discourse of the Popular Front should seek to avoid the "national nihilism" characteristic of Third Period Bolshevism and present itself as rooted in particular national cultures: "[P]roletarian internationalism must, so to speak, 'acclimatize itself' in each country in order to sink deep roots in its native land. National forms of the proletarian class struggle and of the labor movement in the individual countries are in no contradiction to proletarian internationalism; on the contrary, it is precisely in these forms that the international interests of the proletariat can be successfully defended." In particular, Dimitrov argues, socialism "will signify the salvation of the nation" (79–80).[11]

In Dimitrov's conception, "the people" is both an objective and a heuristic category. To pertain to "the people" there has to inhere in one's social being some measure of subordination, expressed in the terms of Guha's first definition ("class, caste, age, gender and office or in any other way"). On the other hand, that measure of subordination, in itself, is not enough to guarantee that one lines up on the subaltern side of the subaltern/dominant binary in a given historical conjuncture.

This indeterminacy of the components of the people—which makes them subject to ideological interpellation—recalls Guha's sense of the third category of the elite as a hinge-like subject-position that can move toward either the elite or the subaltern pole, depending on circumstances. But these circumstances, of course, are not simply a matter of interpellation or "hailing." They are also rooted in the structural features of colonial and postcolonial social formations and the logic of capitalist combined and uneven development. Dependency theory in its classic form more than merits the charge of economism. But dependency theorists themselves were already becoming aware by the late 1960s that in national or regional economies disproportionately subject to external market demand, the relations of production and of exchange (between periphery and metropolis) are themselves secured and reproduced in part by noneconomic practices. The structure of dependency involves (or creates) not only contradictory class relations of production (even where there is extensive formal proletarianization, the very characteristics of a dependent economy assure that proletarianization will be highly uneven, as in the case of peasants who are also employed seasonally as agricultural wage laborers). It also produces a general mechanism of power and accumulation that affects negatively everyone not in the bloc formed by the *comprador* landlords and bourgeoisie, the upper levels of the state bureaucracy, the military, and the participating foreign interests. Lacking an extensive internal commodities market that can discipline the demands and expectations of labor and other non-oligarchic social sectors, regimes in such societies tend to require direct political/military control through the repressive apparatuses of the state, most particularly the army and the police. In terms of a distinction Guha makes, they rule more by domination than by hegemony. They rest politically on a very limited mandate, and tend to enter into crisis when there is a major change in the external market demand for their exports.

A metropolitan capitalist economy "runs by itself," so to speak, in the sense that its conditions of expanded reproduction (prices, value of wages, rates of profit, etc.) are (or at least seem to be) determined by the "normal" operations of the market, which all social actors, including labor, formally accept. In postcolonial or peripheral nations or regions, however, the dominant classes or class fractions govern primarily through their political-bureaucratic relations with other classes and interest groups, which in the final analysis depend on their control of administration, patronage, state revenues, and the police and army, rather than through the mechanism of the market, which they do not control. A political (and sometimes cultural-racial) logic intervenes over a logic of economic "interests" or of social identities defined primarily in term of relations of production and property. Formal or informal state repression acts not only on workers and peasants—that is, on the poor—but also on nonhegemonic business sectors, teachers, service employees, the labor aristocracy, students, some categories of professionals, maids and sex workers, and so on. Shifting alliances, or misalliances, can develop between the—mainly rural—poor peasantry, different ethnic, tribal, or religious groups, the formal proletariat, the unemployed, women, the intermediate strata suggested by Guha's "third category of the elite," even sections of the new urban professional classes who have not been allowed, or have been thrown back from, what they consider a sufficient share of political, cultural, and economic power. It is this "overdetermined" logic of uneven development that creates an objective (as opposed to a purely rhetorical or interpellative) basis for the constitution of "the people" as the social subject of national liberation struggle. Something like this is what Ernesto Laclau and Chantal Mouffe have in mind, when they argue in a famous passage in *Hegemony and Socialist Strategy* that in the advanced capitalist democracies there is a proliferation of identity or rights-oriented democratic struggles; but, given their necessarily diverse character, these struggles do not tend to the constitution of the people, that is, toward a binary division of the political space (of the nation) into two antagonistic camps, the camp of the people and the camp of the power bloc. Here is the passage in full:

> It would appear that an important differential characteristic may be established between advanced industrial societies and the periphery of the capitalist world; in the former, the proliferation of points of antagonism permits the multiplication of democratic struggles, but these struggles, given their diversity, do not tend to constitute a 'people', that is, to enter into equivalence with one another and to divide the political space into two antagonistic fields. On the contrary, in the countries of the Third World, imperialist exploitation and the predominance of brutal and centralized forms of domination tend from the beginning to endow the popular struggle with a centre, with a single and clearly defined enemy. Here the division of the political space into two fields is more reduced. We shall use the term *popular subject position* to refer to the position that is constituted on the basis of dividing the political space into two antagonistic camps; and *democratic subject position* to refer to the locus of a clearly delimited antagonism which does not divide society in that way.[12]

Doris Sommer observes that Mouffe and Laclau's distinction here rests, like Fredric Jameson's claim about "national allegory" in third world literature, on an essentialized distinction between first world and third world.[13] The point is well-taken; however, it might be more useful for our purposes here to note that the distinction could also work the other way: that is, a proliferation of rights- or identity-oriented struggles could also be said to be characteristic of so-called third world countries (indigenous peoples' and women's movements have been among the most important political forces in Latin America in the last fifteen years); and, vice versa, the polarization of the political space into two antagonistic camps is also at least a possibility in the advanced capitalist democracies.

If Laclau and Mouffe's idea of a *popular subject-position* suggests the raison d'être of the people as the subject of national liberation struggle, the other side of their distinction—the idea of a proliferation of individualized struggles and a corresponding democratic subject-position—also establishes the deconstructive limit of the people, both in the advanced countries and in the periphery. Hegemonic anticolonial or anti-imperialist nationalist discourse stabilizes the category of the people around a certain narrative (of common interests, community, tasks, sacrifices, historical destiny) that its class or group components may or may not share to the same degree or at all. It rhetorically sutures over the gaps and discontinuities of the subaltern. It is one thing when, as in the case of modern India, the nationalist project is in the hands of a native bourgeoisie and a landlord class that use the appeal to national unity precisely to limit the counter-mobilization from the left and the popular classes. It is another where this occurs in the context of a project identified with and seeking to mobilize the popular classes.

Let me put forward the case of the Sandinistas as an example of this second eventuality, since, as I explained in the introduction, it was my own involvement in solidarity work with the Nicaraguan revolution that oriented me in the direction of subaltern studies in the first place. As is well known, the Sandinistas organized a multi-class front in Nicaragua (the movement's official name was the Sandinista Front for National Liberation) around the figure of Augusto Sandino, the provincial Liberal politician and landowner who led a successful struggle to oust the U.S. Marines from Nicaragua in the late 1920s, only to be assassinated, with the connivance of U.S. interests in Central America, by the founding patriarch of the Somoza dynasty. The front came to power in 1979 with a broad popular mandate to begin a process of radical social change. But as the revolution progressed, under pressure from both internal class conflict and the U.S.-orchestrated Contra war, the front began to unravel. Anti-Somocista sectors of the business community previously allied with the Sandinistas, landless rural workers or peasant small-holders, mothers and urban youth opposed to the draft, and the Miskitus and other indigenous groups became disaffected or demoralized. Particularly after 1985, when the Sandinistas plan for economic stabilization (implemented to control the inflationary effect of the U.S. blockade and currency destabilization) began to cut into the living standards of the urban working class and rural poor peasants, "the people" began to come apart along several different faultlines, with the result that the Sandinistas began to lose hegemony.

Sandino functioned in Sandinista ideology essentially as what Laclau calls an "empty signifier"—a signifier around which the unity of the people or of the "social" as such appears, but which does not in itself have a necessary or bound ideological connotation.[14] But Sandino was not exactly "empty"—that is, capable of being articulated with any and all forms of popular identity. For the Miskitus and the English-speaking Afro-Caribbean population of Nicaragua's Atlantic coast, Sandino—symbolizing in his person the opposition of a Spanish mestizo-Catholic culture to North American imperialism and cultural values—meant something different than for the main population groups of Nicaragua. In response to the CIA-directed campaign to exploit this friction to destabilize the Atlantic coast, the Sandinistas were obliged first to resort to military repression and then to renegotiate the conditions of regional and tribal self-government, somewhat along the lines of the Spanish system of *autonomías*, eventually with some success.[15]

Charles Hale has argued that the Sandinista/Miskitu split was not simply a question of Sandinista cultural insensitivity or incomprehension. Rather,

> the very premises that were integral to the Sandinistas' success in unifying the vast majority of Nicaraguans—encapsulating their demands, forging a broadly endorsed vision of social change, and rallying support for the increasingly urgent efforts to resist the onslaught of counterrevolutionary aggression—directly excluded the Miskitu. Put bluntly, the FSLN forged a counterhegemonic ideology that invalidated central facets of Miskitu Indians' deeply rooted ethnic militancy. . . . [A] radically new version of Nicaraguan nationalism— emphasizing sovereignty, self-sufficiency, and equality with other states—retained a Mestizo standard of cultural homogeneity to which all citizens were expected to conform . . . in which to identify as Miskitu became virtually synonymous with being considered counterrevolutionary.[16]

But the problem of the limits of hegemonic representation crops up even within the "Mestizo standard of cultural homogeneity" Hale refers to. Consider the case of two key constituencies for the Sandinistas: women and poor peasants. In order to mobilize a mainly Catholic or Catholic-identified population, the Sandinistas pushed the idea of liberation theology and the people's church (the poet-priest Ernesto Cardenal was one of the principal ideological architects of the relation between Marxist social thought and Catholic principles, and many prominent Catholic priests and lay intellectuals were identified with the FSLN). But this committed the Front to support *de jure* if not *de facto* the Church's positions against abortion and birth control (it also prevented the Sandinistas from interfacing with the Protestant fundamentalist sects that were gaining ground rapidly among the poorest sectors of the population). The failure to legalize abortion in particular put the Sandinista women's organization, AMNLAE, in a quandary: to the extent that it was a *Sandinista* organization subject to party discipline and supposedly expressive of the unity of "the people" against imperialist aggression, it had to go along with the decision; but to the extent that it sought to represent and incorporate into the revolutionary process women's demands and struggles coming from below in a deeply patriarchal society, it was under pressure to take a different stand (or at least to relativize the Front's official position) on matters like abortion, birth control, divorce, and violence against women. (What made the problem especially difficult was the fact that the question of women's rights and emancipation could not be raised in the first place independent of the revolutionary process itself.)

It is common knowledge today that the Sandinista policy of rural economic development began to encounter resistance not only from the landed elites displaced by the revolution and agrarian reform, but also from the very social group that policy was intended to benefit: the rural poor (many of the recruits to the Contras were poor peasants). María Josefina Saldaña explains this apparent paradox as follows:

> [T]he FSLN identified the itinerant proletariat and *minifundista* formations with preproletariat or precollective consciousness, and interpreted their desires for land as petit bourgeois aspirations toward private property. . . . The FSLN's development model intervened in every aspect of [these groups'] lives without ever granting these sectors of the peasantry the political means for negotiating the terms of the intervention. . . . Consequently, the dispossessed and land-poor peasants had no way of lobbying the Sandinistas from the inside. Of course, this oversight was symptomatic of the party's fundamental disbelief in the consciousness of these two sectors as viable or rational forms of revolutionary consciousness. . . . The Sandinistas were working with idealized revolutionary subjects in agriculture.[17]

Saldaña suggests that one possible solution would have been for the Sandinistas to negotiate "between their own progressive, vanguard nationalist vision [of economic modernization] and the peasants' 'conservative,' but not necessarily antirevolutionary, mass-based nationalist vision of economic development" (166). But this would have implied, as in the case of the Miskitu and the Atlantic coast, an initial openness on the part of the Sandinistas to the worldview of these sectors of the peasantry—their desire for land and personal autonomy, their sense of limited territoriality, their ties to tradition—an openness that would have contradicted the Sandinistas' own self-legitimization as a vanguard party representing the force of historical progress against a reactionary past.

In the course of a debate within the Latin American Subaltern Studies Group about the politics of subaltern studies, Alberto Moreiras argued that "[t]he hegemonic relation is precisely what excludes the subaltern as such." It follows that

> [w]e need a concept of hegemony, but only in order then to go ahead and affirm that our work as transnational subalternists is necessarily posthegemonic. . . . What I am trying to think through is the possibility of grounding a specifically subalternist political practice. If we are populists, we are not subalternists. If we are subalternists, we can still be populists, but that calls for a double register, or a double articulation, at the level of both theory and practice. As academic intellectuals, occupying an important position in what I think we can call without apologies the Ideological State Apparatus, I would say that our function as subalternists is potentially more important than our function as populists. Within populism, we assume the function of representation of the people. . . . Within subalternism, however, our function is counter-representational primarily, perhaps exclusively. Subalternism is on the side of negation, populism is on the side of positivity, strategically essentialist or not.[18]

The problems with ideological mobilization around the category of the people I outlined above would seem to support Moreiras's claim that the subaltern is the remainder or deconstructive supplement left by hegemonic articulation, and that, therefore, subaltern studies should be properly concerned with exploring the limits of hegemony. But this would imply, in turn, that those groups and classes that actually did support the Sandinistas were not subaltern and that the marginalization from the revolutionary process of poor peasants, indigenous groups, some sectors of women, and others was a necessary consequence of Sandinista hegemony as such, rather than the result of ideological and epistemological blind spots within the—mainly male, white or mestizo, middle-class, university-educated—leadership of the movement. Is the problem the idea of hegemony itself? Or would it be possible to imagine a more "multicultural" form of hegemony in which the problems inherent in the Sandinista project—as in other "modernizing" forms of socialism and populist nationalism—do not have to happen in quite the same way? That, in essence, is the question that will occupy us for the rest of this book.

What is at stake in Moreiras's sense of the incommensurability of the hegemonic and the subaltern is the pertinence of deconstruction as a model for new forms of political imagination and practice. To discuss this possibility further, let me return first to the idea of hybridity in Bhabha and postcolonial theory that I sketched at the beginning of this chapter. I will then move on to consider some perhaps unintended but nevertheless troubling consequences of Spivak's concept of the subaltern.

For Bhabha it is precisely the arbitrary or "ungrounded" character of signification revealed by semiotic and structuralist theory that permits subaltern resistance in the first place. The narrative of national-popular identity "forgets" or occludes the actual history that produces that identity. Bhabha draws attention in particular to what he calls the "performative time" of nationalism, quoting Frantz Fanon on "the fluctuating movement the people are just giving shape to": "The present of the people's history is a practice that destroys the constant principles of the national culture that attempt to hark back to a 'true' national past, which is often represented in the reified forms of realism and stereotype." But,

> [t]he people are not simply historical events or parts of a patriotic body politic. They are also a complex rhetorical strategy of social reference where the claim to be representative provokes a crisis within the process of signification and discursive address. We then have a contested cultural territory where the people must be thought in a double-time; the people are the historical "objects" of a nationalist pedagogy, giving the discourse an authority that is based on the pregiven or constituted historical origin or event; the people are also the "subjects" of a process of signification that must erase any prior or originary presence of the nation-people to demonstrate the prodigious, living principle of the people as that continual process by which the national life is redeemed and signified as a repeating and reproductive process. ("DissemiNation" 297).

To read deconstructively against the grain of such narratives implies recognizing the character of both the people and history (the history of the people and world or "universal" history) as hybrid rather than monistic, involving multiple conflicts and crossings of cultures and positions. The articulation of cultural difference and antagonism cannot be a simple binary "us and them," because

> [c]ultural difference does not simply represent the contention between oppositional contents or antagonistic traditions of cultural value. . . . The very possibility of cultural contestation, the ability to shift the grounds of knowledges, or to engage in a 'war of position',

depends not only on the refutation or substitution of concepts. . . . To the extent to which all forms of cultural discourse are subject to the rule of signification, there can be no question of a simple negation or sublation of the contradictory or oppositional instance. . . . The signs of cultural difference cannot then be unitary or individual forms of identity because their continual implication in other symbolic systems always leaves them 'incomplete' or open to cultural translation. . . . Cultural difference is to be found where the 'loss' of meaning enters, as a cutting edge, into the representation of the fullness of the demands of culture. ("DissemiNation" 313)

Attention to the "rule of signification" entails for Bhabha not only an awareness of the semiotic or arbitrary character of any cultural signifier, but also a necessary act of passage into a "Third Space," which represents both the general conditions of language and the specific implication of the utterance in a performative and institutional strategy. This Third Space is also the space of what Bhabha calls, alternatively, hybridity, translation, supplementarity, interdisciplinarity, the borderline, the cutting edge, the loss of meaning.[19]

It is perhaps a cheap shot to conflate Bhabha's Third Space with the "Third Way" of Anthony Giddens and Tony Blair's New Labour. But there is a similar political as well as conceptual problem with his argument. What it seems to confuse is the mechanism of what Althusser called Ideology in General—that is, the way any ideology works to create the subject in an "imaginary relationship" with the Real—from historically concrete ideologies, such that the ground for subaltern resistance becomes the movement of the signifier itself: the ultimate undecidability of any act of meaning production (since signification is founded in the first place on lack and absence). Bhabha recognizes that, according to the dialectic of the master and the slave, the subaltern or (as he prefers) the "marginal" is in a position of epistemological privilege, in the sense that its very condition of subordination both requires and allows it to "see through" the illusion of the authority and presence of the signs of power that it confronts. The moment when the figures of authority are derided, defied, or simply mocked is the moment of subaltern Negation Guha describes (it is the moment in Rigoberta Menchú's testimonio when the villagers react against the violence of the army's spectacle of torture and murder and force the soldiers to retreat). In other words, the subaltern knows, like Segismundo in Calderón's Life Is a Dream, that power is an effect of the signifier. If it did not, it would have no grounds for negation or resistance: it would simply see its subalternity as built into meaning itself, part of the nature of things.

But it does not necessarily follow from this that subaltern ideology is "deconstructive" in exactly this way. The negation of the dominant ideology is accompanied at the same time by the composition of *another ideology*, which posits as authoritative, authentic, and true other forms of identity, custom, value, territoriality, and history. That is because, to recall Althusser's phrase, "ideology has no outside." Social conflict is not between ideology as "false consciousness" and something that is not ideology, say "science" or "hybridity" or deconstruction itself. It is rather conflict between different and antagonistic ideologies, with radically different consequences in terms of human community and possibility. Despite Bhabha's desire to theorize subalternity and social liminality via deconstruction, what his argument suggests is the pervasive hegemony of "culture" itself as an untranscendable horizon. What occurs thereby is a kind of recontainment or reterritorialization of the subaltern within, so to speak, the MLA.[20]

Let me turn to Spivak, whose work represents the other major effort to articulate, through the medium of deconstruction, the consequences of subaltern studies for cultural theory and politics. It is well known that Spivak tries to solve the problem Bhabha's argument (and semiotic anti-essentialism generally) leads to by advancing, apropos in particular subaltern studies historiography, the idea of a "strategic essentialism."[21] Spivak writes: "To investigate, discover, and establish a subaltern or peasant consciousness seems at first to be a positivistic project—a project which assumes that, if properly prosecuted, it will lead to firm ground, to some thing that can be disclosed" (202). But, "since the 'subaltern' cannot appear without the 'thought of the élite,' " in the very movement of its representation, "there is always a counterpointing suggestion in the work of the group that subaltern consciousness is subject to the cathexis of the élite, that it is never fully recoverable, that it is always askew from its received signifiers, indeed that it is effaced even as it is disclosed, that it is irreducibly discursive" (203). Subaltern studies cannot, therefore, produce the subaltern as full, self-transparent presence. What it produces instead is a "subaltern subject-effect": "[T]he texts of counter-insurgency locate . . . a 'will' as the sovereign cause when it is no more than an effect of the subaltern subject-effect, itself produced by the particular conjunctures called forth by the crisis meticulously described in the various *Subaltern Studies*" (204).

It follows that something like Guha's claim that "to acknowledge the peasant as the maker of his own rebellion is to attribute . . . a consciousness to him" (*Aspects* 4) can only be justified on "strategic"—that is, political—rather than ontological grounds: "I would read it [subaltern studies], then, as a *strategic* use of positivist essentialism in a scrupulously visible political interest" (Spivak, *In Other Worlds* 205). What is "strategic" for Spivak about the recovery of the subaltern by Guha and subaltern studies historiography is that it undoes the claim to authority of the dominant culture and forms of knowledge, including the "mode of production narrative" of classical Marxism. Thus, "the [subaltern studies] group places this theory [of subaltern consciousness as emergent collective consciousness] squarely in the context of that tendency within Western Marxism which would refuse class-consciousness to the pre-capitalist subaltern, especially in the theatres of Imperialism" (206). Further, "If in translating bits and pieces of discourse theory and the critique of humanism into an essentialist historiography the historian of subalternity aligns himself to the pattern of conduct of the subaltern himself, it is only a progressivist view, that diagnoses the subaltern as necessarily inferior, that will see such an alignment to be without interventionist value" (207).

At the same time, however, the deconstructive side of Spivak's argument entails that "the arena of the subaltern's persistent emergence into hegemony must always and by definition remain heterogeneous to the efforts of the disciplinary historian. The historian must persist in his efforts in this awareness, that the subaltern is necessarily the absolute limit of the place where history is narrativized into logic" (207). This sense of the subaltern as "absolute limit" to narrativization means that for Spivak the subaltern in the colonial and postcolonial world must be necessarily *other than* "the people," and it must resist in particular the totalization suggested in the Gramscian copula "people-nation." Spivak's critique of Mahasweta Devi's own interpretation of her story "The Breast Giver" as a national allegory is symptomatic in this respect. Such an interpretation, Spivak believes, is the product of Devi's (elite) subject-position as writer and thus colludes unwillingly with "[the] dominant *radical* reader in the Anglo-U.S. [who] reactively homogenizes the Third World and sees it only in the context of nationalism and ethnicity." Devi's interpretation of her own story goes against the very materiality of the character of the wet-nurse she creates in the story, because it implies that "[t]he subaltern must be seen only as the vehicle of a greater meaning." But, "if nationalism is the *only* discourse credited with emancipatory possibilities in the imperialist theatre, then one must ignore the innumerable subaltern examples of resistance throughout the imperialist and pre-imperialist centuries, often suppressed by those very forces of nationalism which would be instrumental in changing the geo-political conjuncture from territorial imperialism to neo-colonialism."[22]

Where, for Guha, the category of the subaltern includes not only both the working class and peasants and agricultural laborers but also sectors of the so-called "middle" strata and identities that are not specifically marked in class terms (and for Gramsci the subaltern is a kind of euphemism for the working class and peasantry), for Spivak the subaltern is that which always slides under or away from representation, like the wet nurse in Devi's story, even the sort of representation that the work of subaltern studies proposes to give it. As such, it is like what Julia Kristeva understands by the abject: something that is beyond the possibility of representation, because simply by emerging into representation—the Symbolic in the Lacanian sense—it loses the character of subalternity.

In other words, the subaltern functions in Spivak's work in a way similar to the "rule of signification" in Bhabha: as a stand-in or trope for supplementarity and for the activity of deconstruction itself. The alterity of the subaltern interrupts the assumption or claim of an elite position to be a, or the, subject of history; but by the same token (since deconstruction has no political allegiance or project specific to it) deconstruction is always bound to interrupt the constitution of the subaltern as a subject of history. Spivak's argument thus rejoins Bhabha's in its insistence that undecidability itself becomes the ground for subaltern resistance, and, vice versa, that subaltern politics are something like the objective correlative of the activity of deconstruction. (What Spivak understands by catachresis—the collapse of the pretension to signify—is for all intents and purposes what Bhabha understands by hybridity.)

The result for Spivak is that subaltern politics can happen only in a process of continuous displacement/deconstruction that subverts the constitutive binaries colonial/native, subaltern/dominant, inside/outside, modern/traditional. In Spivak's own practice the possibility of such a politics is enacted in her personal relationship with Mahasweta Devi, noted above.[23] But the displacement of agency involved here is a double one, for it is not only that Devi functions for Spivak as, in effect, an organic intellectual of the subaltern like Rigoberta Menchú. The place of the subaltern is further displaced from Devi herself to the women represented in her stories: Jashoda, the wet nurse who dies of breast cancer in "Breast Giver"; or the Naxalite guerrilla captured and tortured by the Indian army in "Draupadi." Spivak herself notes, partly in jest, that "the subaltern is the name of the place that is so displaced . . . that to have it speak is like the arrival of Godot on a bus."[24]

These brief remarks obviously cannot do justice to the full range of Spivak's and Bhabha's thinking on the problems of culture, subalternity, and postcoloniality, which they pursue with great rigor and a keen sense of the political and human stakes involved, nor do I mean to suggest that they necessarily arrive at the same place ideologically (Bhabha has sought to open up the possibilities of multiculturalism beyond the limits of "liberal" multiculturalism; Spivak has been an eloquent and tireless voice for the claims of women and feminism in Marxist cultural theory and practice). But it may be that something similar is happening here as happened with the work of Herbert Marcuse, so influential in the configuration of the cultural politics of the New Left in the 1960s. From an elite academic position it is decreed that the only positions from which opposition to the dominant system can be imagined and constructed are those which are the most marginal or liminal. These positions, in turn, are said to be represented in their radical negativity by a form of academic theory—deconstruction in the case of Spivak and Bhabha, Frankfurt School–style critical theory in the case of Marcuse—and by what amounts in both cases to a valorization of modernist aesthetics.

It might be argued that Spivak's articulation of the subaltern as "absolute limit" to symbolization in fact seeks to obey scrupulously Lenin's injunction that revolutionary politics should always seek out the most oppressed strata of the population. But the political problems with this position are not unlike the problems of Third Period Marxism that Dimitrov sought to address. By contrast, Guha's identification of subaltern and the people argues for a more inclusive sense of subaltern identity, without, however, abandoning the idea of binary antagonism as the articulating principle of that identity (without, that is, identifying the people with the heterogeneity of civil society as such—I will come back to this point in the next chapter). I do not mean by this to romanticize the Popular Front, which, as everyone knows, produced its own illusions, limitations, and contradictions; I simply want to suggest that the principle of populardemocratic interpellation that the Popular Front foregrounded is not incompatible with the goals of subaltern studies.

Subaltern studies exists in the tension between a project that is deconstructive of the claims of the nation, nationalism, academic knowledge, and the formal political left to represent the subaltern, and a constructive— "strategic," in Spivak's sense—articulation (or recognition) of new forms of collective political and cultural agency. Two rather different political agendas flow from this double urgency, however. One is support for the new social movements and grassroots resistance, at a sub- or supranational level (this is the option Spivak herself prefers and sees her work connected to). The other is the constitution of a potentially hegemonic political-cultural "popular" bloc, an ideological articulation that in some way or another must invoke the categories of both the "people" and the "nation." In the first case, it is understood that the unity of the nation-state, along with the idea of political hegemony itself, were never representative of the subaltern, and are now, with the advent of globalization, functionally obsolete in any case for the purposes of the left, as is also perhaps the left itself (thus, for Moreiras, subaltern studies should be at the same time "counter-representational," "transnational," and "post-hegemonic"). In the second case, the question is instead whether subaltern studies can contribute to organizing a new form of hegemony from below—what Guha calls a "politics of the people."

It is in relation to this second possibility that I want to take up briefly, in what remains of this chapter and then more extensively in chapter 5, the question of the relation of subaltern studies and cultural studies. When Stuart Hall refers to what he calls "the 'political' aspect of cultural studies," he is alluding to the fact or widespread perception that the emergence of cultural studies as an academic project was connected to the political left, broadly speaking, and to the new social movements in particular.[25] The Birmingham Centre for Contemporary Cultural Studies, which gave the field its name (and where Hall himself served as assistant director in the 1970s), was organized in a working-class city in one of the so-called Red Brick universities created by the Labor government after World War II to democratize higher education in Great Britain. Birmingham sought consciously to develop an organic relation with the English working class in two ways: first, as an academic project connected to the historical formation and protagonism of that class (hence the close affinity of the Centre with British Marxist historians like E. P. Thompson and with Labor sociologists like Raymond Williams or Richard Hoggart, its first director); second, as a place to register and study the social movements that began to appear in the 1970s at the margins of traditional British working-class culture: the punks and youth culture generally, the women's movement, gay rights, the movements of the new Asian and Caribbean immigrants.

The Frankfurt School had introduced the idea of the academic-theoretical study of mass culture in connection with a leftist political agenda. To establish itself both theoretically and generationally, however, Birmingham-style cultural studies felt compelled to move away from the Frankfurt School's blend of Marxist political economy, aesthetic modernism, psychoanalytic theory, and behaviorism, and its problematics of "reification," "false consciousness," "manipulation," "repressive desublimation" (Marcuse), and the like. Where the experience of mass culture by the intellectuals associated with the Frankfurt School coincided with the rise of fascism in the 1930s, so that the two were implicitly linked in their work (for example, in Theodor Adorno's idea of the authoritarian personality in U.S. mass culture), for baby boomers like Hall or myself, capitalist mass culture—especially movies, television, and rock or dance music—was simply *our* culture, or at least an important part of it—a culture, moreover, not at all incompatible with cultural iconoclasm and/or political radicalization. In fact, the reverse seemed to be more the case: mass culture was one of the key terrains on which 1960s radicalism was articulated.[26]

As I noted in the first part of this chapter, the Popular Front conceived of the people in two ways: (1) as heterogenous in composition, but potentially unified in an antagonistic relation with an elite or "power bloc"; and (2) as an active rather than a passive social subject, with its own cultural resources and agendas. Though its own direct connection to the moment of the Popular Front was partially occluded by the anti-Communism of the Cold War, cultural studies was in effect reinventing this argument.[27] By privileging the popular as such and linking it to an ideal of democratic mass culture, Popular Front cultural theory and practice led to the incorporation of significant sectors of leftist intelligentsia, artists, and technicians into the emerging cultural industries of film, commercial music, radio, and in the 1940s television. But within its compass there were also ambiguities, tensions, and struggles over the implications of commercialization. At the same time that the Popular Front encouraged activists to enter the culture industry and sought to organize workers in the burgeoning film and media industries, it tended to equate popular culture essentially with "folk" or traditional culture, privileging in U.S. music, for example, early jazz over bop, rural blues over rhythm and blues and soul, Appalachian folk ballads over country, and just about anything over rock. It was politically correct to listen to early jazz or folk—so the familiar argument went—because these were forms of "people's music" linked to social formations marked by artisanal or precapitalist modes of production, not commercial products of the emerging capitalist culture industries (many forms of what was seen as "folk" music and early jazz in fact depended on radio and record companies for both their production and circulation). Aligned with this bias was the distinction between mass culture and popular culture, which created many confusions and bitter debates (among them, the scandal caused when Bob Dylan decided to present his songs with a rock band using electric instruments in 1964).

These two seemingly contradictory aspects of the Popular Front cultural policy—its openness to the emerging cultural industries and its privileging of folk or premodern cultural forms as repositories of "people's" consciousness and resistance—were in fact both bound up with the desire to see in the space of the "popular" something like a potentially anticapitalist form of cultural agency. Gramsci's conception of subaltern culture as essentially "folkloric," "spontaneous," anchored in "common sense" rather than a scientific conception of the world, shared this problem, as I will try to show in greater detail in chapter 6. Lukács's alternative strategy for the Popular Front—to celebrate from the left the democratic and scientific heritage of bourgeois high culture, as embodied above all in the realist novel—allowed for a certain commonality between the most advanced representatives of that culture and the project of communism, but at the expense of denying the force of both popular culture and aesthetic modernism.

Even with these crucial limitations, however, Popular Front Marxism was (and in many ways still is) more congenial to the development of cultural studies than Frankfurt School critical theory, even where, because of McCarthyism, it has operated more as the "political unconscious" of cultural studies than as an explicit program or theoretical paradigm. It is more congenial because it presupposes that popular and mass culture are forms of subaltern agency, rather than simply "false consciousness" or anachronism. I noted earlier the affinity of Spivak's and Bhabha's arguments with the principles of aesthetic modernism and its goals of estrangement or defamiliarization. That affinity has its roots in the sometimes tacit, sometimes overt and programmatic, equation both the formalists and the Frankfurt School made between modernism and political radicalism. For the Frankfurt School, in particular, modernist art was the place where the negation of the instrumental reason of capitalist society could continue to happen, given the co-optation or "habitualization" of the working class by Fordism and consumerism. Cultural studies, by contrast, comes out of 1960s "youth culture" and proceeds from a sense that modernism—by then canonized and commodified as bourgeois high art—was itself connected to power structures that coincided with or created preconditions for the economic and social divisions (cultural segregations, distinctions, subordinations).[28]

The " 'political' aspect" of cultural studies in its formative moment was to find—and then try to identify with—forms of culture that were antihegemonic. How to define these? By the binary logic that is constitutive of subaltern identity as such, they would have to be cultural forms that were a negation of the values of bourgeois and middle-class culture, even in its avant-garde and/or politically "progressive" forms represented by modernism. That is, they would have to be literally an/other culture; they could not be simply, as Lukács and the dominant line in the Soviet cultural debates proposed, an extension downwards or a democratization of the values and forms of bourgeois high culture. The writer associated—albeit problematically—with the Frankfurt School who understood the utopian dynamic underlying mass culture and who inserted himself within it was, of course, Walter Benjamin. In his great essay "The Work of Art in the Age of Mechanical Reproduction" or in the draft of his project on the Paris Arcades, Benjamin became a kind of bridge between the legacy of the Frankfurt School and cultural studies as it emerged in the 1970s and 1980s.

For Richard Hoggart, the founder of the Birmingham Centre, mass culture was still essentially a displacement of, on the one hand, high culture and, on the other, an "authentic"—that is, premodern—English popular working-class culture—the sort of "organic" class culture E. P. Thompson chronicled in *The Making of the English Working Class*. But as the work of Birmingham progressed, the distinctions between high and low, mass and popular, "authentic" and "commercial," nativist and colonial culture tended to become more and more precarious, as Hall and others worked— via Althusser's seminal essay on ideology—in the direction of collapsing culture and ideology into each other.[29]

The equation Birmingham arrived at was something like the following: To the extent that mass culture is popular in the consumer sense—that is, "pop"—it is also "popular" in the political sense: that is, representative of the people, embodying the social will of the people, national-popular, "progressive." A key work in this respect was Paul Willis's *Learning to Labour*, an ethnography of British working-class youth that sought to describe the "culture of resistance" they created in music, hairstyle, fashion, speech genres, and so on against the forms of cultural standardization proferred by "approved" culture, the school, the family, and the church as part of their indoctrination into capitalist relations of production.[30]

The premium placed in cultural studies—and here the influence of literary reception theory was decisive—on analyzing the quotidian activity of consumers and the nature of the commodities they buy and use led often to the claim that consumption itself constitutes a particular realm of freedom and low-level popular resistance to the ideological forms or reality principle of capitalism, as if consumption itself were a kind of politics (or alternatively that politics functioned now essentially within the logic of commodification and consumer choice—that is, in the domain of civil society rather than of the state and the ideological state apparatuses [ISAs].)[31] Here a supposedly "left" position—theorizing forms of autonomous popular agency—seemed, oddly, to find common ground with something like Francis Fukuyama's thesis of the end of history. For if the market and mass culture (or more generally, civil society) are what permit cultural resistance on the part of subaltern groups, then they become the very condition of subaltern agency rather than that which subaltern negativity confronts. In the United States, the work of Tom Wolfe and the "new journalism" or Camille Paglia could be said to be an anticipatory right-wing populist form of cultural studies, frankly celebratory of the "democratic" implications of the new forms of globalized commodity culture (in a more apocalyptic key, Jean Baudrillard might also be mentioned in this regard).

This points to a paradox at the heart of the project of cultural studies itself. If cultural studies was successful in the reactionary climate in the United States and Great Britain during the years of its emergence, say between 1985 and 1990, it was in part because it was able to march under two banners at the same time: one "red," the other "white," so to speak. The project of transferring the radical agenda of the 1960s to the university—by critiquing disciplinary paradigms, democratizing structures, modifying requirements, dismantling the canon, introducing new forms of theory, creating new inter- or transdisciplinary spaces for academic work— overlapped with a project to reorganize bourgeois hegemony emanating from both the state and private foundations and think-tanks—a project involving crucially the reform and modernization of higher education in the context of globalization and post-Fordism.

The emergence of cultural studies parallels the rise through the ranks of academia of the generation—the baby boomers—that entered academic work in or just after the 1960s, drawn by the tremendous expansion of colleges and universities during that decade. This generational logic, which makes cultural studies in some ways a continuation of the New Left, coincides with the advent of globalization and the increasingly precarious situation of organized alternatives to capitalism reflected in the collapse of the Soviet Union. There appears a generalized sentiment that the humanities have become dysfunctional, tired out, that they no longer function as they should in relation to bourgeois hegemony. The neoconservatives sought, against cultural studies and "theory," to reassert the authority of the traditional humanities and Western Civilization. Their campaign failed, however, because it did not correspond with the perceptions of the elites directly connected to problems of education (educational administrators, research foundations, boards of trustees). These elites decided that the future of education was moving in the directions suggested by cultural studies, communications, interdisciplinarity, multiculturalism, and the like. The idea of restoring the traditional curriculum in the humanities simply was a non-starter *within* the university, where it was clear that, for better or worse, the disciplines were losing both their coherence and function.

The book that perhaps best expresses the contradictory and paradoxical character of the conjuncture that gives rise to cultural studies is Jean-François Lyotard's *The Postmodern Condition* (which not by chance is also a diagnosis of the state of higher education). If one reads it carefully, one realizes that Lyotard is abandoning the posture of the young Trotskyist of *Socialisme ou barbarie*—the "dream of '68"—and instead wants to think about radicalization *within* the limits of the actually existing university and knowledge centers. He is asking in effect the question: How can we refashion the disciplines in an age when their epistemological bases and frontiers are disintegrating? But this is a question that can be answered only *within* the system itself, which in any case now permits a greater flexibility of thought and action, and is sometimes even capable of radicalizing itself. Cultural studies, like other features of globalized culture and social life, would be for Lyotard a practice "not totally subordinated to the goal of the system," yet tolerated by it.[32]

That is because cultural studies is itself in part the consequence of the deconstructive impact of capitalist mass culture on the human sciences via the same process of commodification that postmodernist aesthetic ideology celebrates (or diagnoses) in its sense of the breakdown of the distinction between high and mass culture. In a more traditional Marxist language, it might be said that cultural studies is a superstructural effect of mass culture and globalization; but, of course, it was a collapsed or collapsing Marxism that cultural studies seemed destined in some ways to supplant.

If, as I have suggested, subaltern and dominant, residual and emergent projects come together in cultural studies, there is also inevitably a moment in which their paths begin to diverge, since they represent in the last instance divergent class interests. We can no longer presuppose in this sense that cultural studies is necessarily progressive or counter-hegemonic in political terms: that is, that it is "popular." This realization has given rise to a critique of the "populism" of cultural studies from the left which takes the form, generally, of a return to the Frankfurt School (with or without Habermas, depending on the individual critic's bent). Meaghan Morris's analysis of the assumption of "consumption without production" in the work of British cultural studies, or Jameson's identification of postmodernism with aesthetic populism and his consequent rehabilitation of Adorno are two familiar and influential examples of this critique.[33] Let me take Beatriz Sarlo's book, *Escenas de la vida posmoderna* (*Scenes of Postmodern Life*)—about the effects of postmodern consumer culture in Argentina—as representative of a similar argument in a Latin American context.[34]

As its title suggests, *Escenas* puts Sarlo in the position of the Benjaminian *flaneur*, as she witnesses a series of contemporary cultural practices in Buenos Aires: video games, television, shopping centers, cosmetic surgery, and the like. But unlike the *flaneur*, who expected to see behind the Hydra face of the degraded urban landscape the possibility of an epiphany, a redemption from history, Sarlo criticizes what she calls "media neopopulism." The mass media and new consumer possibilities like video games or malls or TV "zapping" assume the place previously occupied by the school and the family as ideological practices. As such, they generate new subject-positions and identities. They entail, in particular, a displacement from citizen (in Spanish, *ciudadano*) to a public or audience (*público* can mean both things in Spanish), which is itself a media-fetish. The mildly narcotic effect of the video image has greater force than the discourse of the bourgeois public sphere—the domain of Habermas's "communicative rationality"—eroding thus the bases for political opposition or resistance to the dominant. The media-engendered simulacrum displaces the authority of an original; there is no original, or ground of experience, to appeal to. "Televisive epistemology" (Sarlo's phrase) founds its own autoreflexive intertextuality. The masses feel things to be "closer" with TV and shopping, which erase the distinction between the sacred and the profane, the immediate and the distant, and produce in the form of a "quotidian fantasy" a pseudo-universalization of experience and values that transcends class and group differences. The media, in turn, are the mirror of the state (the new kind of state apparatus demanded and produced by neoliberal economies and globalization).

If the media are in fact the producers of legitimation in contemporary societies, this puts into crisis the function of the traditional intellectual in securing hegemony. Sarlo posits against both the traditional literary intellectual and the "media neopopulists" the figure of the "critical intellectual," who can at the same time represent the new forms of consumption (as she does herself in *Escenas*) and produce their critique.[35] Critical thought and therefore effective citizenship are only possible through the distance or perspective provided by the forms of high culture, which require in turn the expansion of literacy and the strengthening of formal education against the media, Sarlo argues (in much the same terms as Antonio Cándido in the essay on "Literature and Underdevelopment" discussed in chapter 2). For Sarlo, the possibility of making a negative critique of the present is a small window of hope in what she sees as an advancing apocalypse of commodification and "soft" authoritarianism. High art in particular remains for her the place where Being, in the Heideggerian sense, resides in the "fallen" landscape of late capitalist consumer society.

Despite the appeal of Sarlo's argument as a portrait of the effects of neoliberal hegemony on middle-class Latin American society, it also shows the limitations of the Frankfurt School critical theory it derives from. For one thing, Sarlo clearly is nostalgic for the return of a bourgeois public sphere that may never have existed as such, or may have existed only precariously and problematically, in Latin America. In this sense, her argument is Habermasian. But she also shares with North American neo-conservatives such as William Bennett or Allan Bloom a notion of com-modified mass culture as "noxious" culture. Under its spell, in effect, community is displaced by communication. She writes: "[a]gainst the neo-populist ideology that finds on the TV screen the energy to restore the social bonds that modernity has corrupted, it is necessary to determine to what point TV requires a society where these social bonds are weak, in order to present itself to such a society as the true defender of a democratic and electronic society menaced and disdained by those who do not listen to its voice or demands" (*Escenas* 87).

But surely something of the *communitarian* also remains in "communica-tion." The discomfort of the traditional intellectual like Sarlo in the face of mass culture and the media is in part a discomfort about democracy and its effects. One of these effects is a displacement of hermeneutic authority from the place of the literary intellectual to popular reception. Silviano Santiago notes that what is at stake for critics like Sarlo "is the preserva-tion, at all costs, in a democratic or would-be democratic society, of the possibility of public opinion, a possibility they believe can be attained only through a devastating critique of the mass media and the proliferation of images they furnish for mass consumption." But the media and the condi-tions of reception they establish imply instead that

> [m]eaning in symbolic and/or cultural production becomes plural and unattainable in its plurality. The "total" meaning (or the totality of meanings) becomes the product of a purposiveness that is no longer necessarily articulated by the traditional institutions of knowledge and their acolytes. The struggle of subaltern and minority groups for their own identity passes necessarily through the search for, and recovery of, cultural objects that have been judged inferior by the modern tradition on the basis of its own centered ("objective") standards of taste.[36]

If we accept Santiago's argument here—and I do—then the problem with cultural studies is not so much what Jameson or Sarlo would call its populism, as the fact that cultural studies is not *popular* enough. In par-ticular, by transferring the formalist program of dehabitualization of per-ception from the sphere of high culture to the forms of mass culture, now seen as more aesthetically dynamic and effective, more capable of produc-ing *ostranenie*, cultural studies may perpetuate unconsciously the modernist aesthetic ideology it supposedly displaces—an ideology that Sarlo and other critics of cultural studies would presumably defend.

For it will be readily appreciated that this is essentially an *intellectual* appropriation of mass culture, which produces something akin to a "pop" form of the romantic sublime or volksgeist. To the degree that mass culture can be re-aestheticized in this way and at the same time pragmatically incorporated into hegemony as a supplement to economic globalization, it becomes possible for the academic disciplines, including the natural sciences, to regroup against the threat that cultural studies would usurp their territory or blur their frontiers. But the anxiety produced by the shift in hermeneutic authority from the traditional intellectual to popular reception is, as Santiago suggests, also provoked by the *unrepresentability* of the effects of that reception in terms of any known form of academic disciplinarity (how can even the most sophisticated opinion poll measure the psychic-ideological effects of a *telenovela* being watched simultaneously by thirty or forty million viewers in an extremely heterogenous and contradictory range of social positions in a country like Brazil?). For Santiago, the electronic media have become in effect the new condition for cultural citizenship.

I perhaps run the risk here of idealizing mass culture in the same way that earlier in this chapter I seemed to idealize the Popular Front. But it is at least open to question whether the scientific-humanistic culture represented by the academy and the bourgeois public sphere, which has a stake both in producing subalternity and in keeping things that way, does more for subaltern social subjects than the unlegislated and unrepresentable proliferation of mass culture and its reception effects. Like all populist statements, this one is slightly demagogic: I understand that the academy and mass culture are not as radically separate as they appear; that (as Jameson has shown) bourgeois high culture and commodity fetishism are linked by a not always hidden logic; that *we* are also interpellated by mass culture, and, vice versa, that all producers and consumers of mass culture pass through or are affected by the education system at some level; that the classroom is a place to negotiate the political and social consequences of consumerism.

But I also remain attentive to Daniel Bell's thesis on the cultural contradictions of capitalism, a thesis that can be said to define the postmodern as such: Capitalism has produced/is producing forms of cultural and technological experience that no longer coincide with the requirements of the capitalist work ethic. The values of consumerism—desublimation, hedonism, "lite" subjects, narcissism, expenditure—undermine the oedipalized character structure and values necessary for the subject-positions of both the exploiter (as authority figure) and the exploited (as abstract labor) in capitalism.

Bell saw this contradiction as portending a legitimation crisis for contemporary capitalist societies—that was the basis of his affinity with neoconservative cultural politics, even while he remained a political liberal.[37] Cultural studies, on the other hand, is in a position to articulate this contradiction as a modality of Mouffe and Laclau's popular subject-position, by articulating a binary division in which the repressive "performance principle" imposed by the law of value and a "pleasure principle" modeled on consumer desire are posed against each other.[38]

But that possibility raises in turn a series of difficult questions: Is the contradiction, as Bell suggested, between capitalist culture (the values of consumerism) and the requirements of capitalist competition (that is, as Marx might have put it, between forces and relations of production)? Or is this the case of a new "regime" or stage of capitalism, in which the law of value has lost its force? Is it consumption as such that interpellates individuals as subjects—as both Sarlo and the "media neopopulism" she criticizes seem to assume—or is it rather the way individuals or groups are already positioned as subjects by class, gender, racial, and other differences that structures how they act as consumers? What is the relation between identity politics and consumption? Is cultural studies in effect a theory of civil society? As such, does it now function theoretically in place of a political left that has become passé or dysfunctional, by positing cultural production and consumption as in themselves forms of popular-democratic agency, perhaps the only ones possible or viable in the current world system? Or does the linkage between consumption and civil society assumed by cultural studies depend ultimately on the political incidence of popular classes and social movements on the state apparatuses (including the ideological apparatuses) and on social institutions generally (the workplace, cultural institutions and industries outside the state, "common sense," quotidian patterns of behavior and expectations, and so on)? What is the relation between the requirements of what Foucault calls "governmentality" and the dynamics of popular and subaltern subject-positions? What, finally, is the relation of cultural studies and subaltern studies?

In the chapter that follows, I will attempt a response to these questions, focusing on the articulation of Latin American cultural studies suggested by Néstor García Canclini in his important and influential book, Hybrid Cultures. But I want to anticipate my answer to the last question in particular: If cultural studies adequately represented the dynamics of "the people," there would be no need for subaltern studies, or no need for it as an intellectual-political formation distinct from, and in some ways antagonistic to, cultural studies.

5 Civil Society, Hybridity, and the "'Political' Aspect of Cultural Studies" (on Canclini)

To take up the question of cultural studies from the perspective of sub-altern studies is in a sense to return to the discussion of transculturation in chapter 2, because transculturation, divested of its connection with literary high culture, could well serve as an ideologeme for postcolonial cultural studies. Are the limitations of cultural studies the same as the limitations of transculturation?

Let me begin my answer with another *petit recit* or "little story" (which carries with it the risk of the sort of "instant" ethnography that cultural studies practitioners are often accused of performing). In the summer of 1996 I was teaching a graduate seminar on Latin American Cultural Studies at the Universidad Andina in Quito, a seminar centered, as it happens, on Néstor García Canclini's *Hybrid Cultures*. About midway through the semester, a sensational story appeared in the news, side by side with reports of the gold medal an Ecuadoran runner had won at the Olympics—the first in that country's history. Two female mestiza *curanderas*, or healers, were accused by the indian village in the southern highlands of Ecuador where they worked of being impostors and blamed for many deaths in the village—not without reason, because presumably at least some of the illness they were supposed to be curing, for which moreover they had charged a lot of money, could have been treated by other means, either modern or traditional. Under interrogation by the village council, the women confessed that they were indeed impostors.

What it means for a curandera, who performs operations like "lifting footsteps," to be an impostor is a question I am not prepared to answer (a medical anthropologist at the Universidad Andina who studied this incident assured me, though, that there are grounds for distinguishing a fake from a qualified practitioner of traditional medicine, just as in Western medicine one can distinguish between a doctor and a quack). What interests me more in any case is how the crime was adjudicated (as in the O. J. Simpson trial in the United States, the affair was covered live on national television and other media, with the participation of multiple experts of various sorts, ranging from shamans to anthropologists and lawyers).

The villagers wanted to be the ones to punish the women on the grounds that their crimes affected the integrity of the community. Both the national and local state authorities felt pressure to bring the women to trial in the nearest city for the civil crime of fraud. This would have meant, however, a police or military operation against the village in order to rescue the women, since the villagers refused to turn them over. Prudently, the governor of the province elected not to take this course of action, thus allowing the villagers to adjudicate the false curanderas. They did so not by killing the women—as had originally been feared by the authorities—but by disrobing and flagellating them publicly, and then driving them out of the village.[1]

This episode became a topic of discussion and debate within the seminar. Several women in the class saw in the brutal punishment meted out to the curanderas by the villagers a toleration of violence against women—a widespread problem in Ecuadoran society generally that women's organizations had been combating, on civil rights grounds—that is, grounds that involved an appeal to formal legality. Others felt that allowing the village to punish the women both reflected and contributed to the "weak" constitutionality of the Ecuadoran state and civil society (the name of Jürgen Habermas was explicitly invoked here). On the other hand, the two indian participants in the seminar—one of whom was from the region where the incident took place—argued that the civil charge of fraud was inadequate both to the objective degree of the damage the false curanderas had inflicted and to the villagers' perception of that damage (assuming these things can be separated in the first place).

All of us involved in the seminar, however, shared an awareness of a paradox latent in the incident: because of the character of Latin American state formation, the primacy of constitutionality and the rule of law is in some ways bound up with its opposite, that is, with dictatorial or "exceptional" regimes. Historically, Latin American armies stem institutionally and derive whatever legitimacy they may claim at least in part from projects to impose constitutions on populations and communities that resisted them for one reason or other.[2] For example, the campaign against Antonio the Counsellor and the peasant utopia of Canudos in Brazil, the subject of both Euclides da Cunha's nineteenth-century classic *Rebellion in the Backlands* and Mario Vargas Llosa's novel *The War at the End of the World*, was a campaign to impose the authority of the Brazilian federal state on what was clearly in some sense a "lawless" community, or a community beyond the law.

Who was right in the case of the curanderas? Modernity or tradition? The village or the state? The principle of the rule of law (but whose law)? Civil society or the state? The organizations concerned with women's rights, or those concerned with indian identity and autonomy—both of which could be said to operate within the terrain of civil society? Does the assertion of women's rights in this case necessarily contradict the assertion of indigenous peoples' rights, or vice versa? Was the action of the village in fact an instance of civil society, as it is usually understood?

In the conflict between Canudos and the Brazilian state, I would have sided with Antonio the Counsellor and his followers against the state, that is, against "Modernity and Progress." In *The War at the End of the World*, Vargas Llosa, by contrast, wants to portray the "tragic" necessity of the extermination of Canudos in the name of modernity. In the conflict over the curanderas, I side both with the claims of the village and with the feminist concern about violence against women. I recognize, of course, that these stances are contradictory. What unifies them is that in each case I am siding with a subaltern position: the position of indigenous people in a deeply racist society; the position of women in a deeply male-chauvinist society. The problem of "the people" is how to side with each of these positions without negating the claims of the other.

The concept of civil society, understood as free associations or relations among autonomous individuals governed by civil law but not under the direct tutelage of the state, has acquired a programmatic character in recent social theory, spilling over from its European origins (and referents) to the periphery of Europe. Mahmood Mamdani has noted that this transference is based on two unanalyzed assumptions: (1) that civil society exists as a fully formed construct in the postcolonial world in the same way it does in Western Europe; and (2) that the main force behind democratization is the contention between civil society and the state, and that postcolonial societies lack a sufficiently developed or strong civil society.[3]

The current authority of the concept of civil society derives in part from its use as a theoretical explanation for the anti-Soviet movements in Eastern Europe and the Soviet Union itself in the 1980s. The argument goes more or less as follows: Given that no independent political parties in the liberal-democratic sense are allowed (what parties there may be are essentially creatures of the state), the central political contradiction in actually existing communist societies is between civil society as such (family, religious organizations, clubs, extra-official trade unions like Solidarity, informal networks, samizdat, new social movements, and so on) and the party-state, which seeks to absorb into itself all of the functions and forms of civil society.[4] It goes without saying that the privileging of the category of civil society is connected to a "postmodernist" disillusion with the capacity of the state to organize society—that is, to produce modernity in either a capitalist or socialist form. Agency is then transferred from the state to the forces that are said to be operating autonomously in civil society: that is, to "culture"—the private sphere—and/or to the market. In this sense, the right-wing articulation of the state versus civil society binary is neoliberalism, and the left-wing articulation is the new social movements or Foucauldian micropolitics.

Because of the incommensurability of the state and the subaltern, civil society seems on the face of it coterminous with the subaltern: hence, for example, Gramsci's claim that "the history [of the subaltern classes] is intertwined with that of civil society."[5] If a good part of the current authority of the concept of civil society derives from Gramsci's argument about the need to fight a "war of position" in the cultural-ethical sphere as well as in the sphere of formal politics, however, it is also Gramsci who makes one of the most telling criticisms of the state versus civil society distinction. In the notes grouped under the title "The Modern Prince," Gramsci takes up the parent form of neoliberalism, which he calls "laissez-faire liberalism." The core idea of laissez-faire liberalism is, Gramsci writes, that "economic activity belongs to civil society, and that the State must not intervene to regulate it." But the distinction of state and market here is "merely methodological" rather than "organic": "in actual reality civil society and the State are one and the same," since "laissez-faire too is a form of State 'regulation,' introduced and maintained by legislation and coercive means. It is a deliberate policy, conscious of its own ends, and not the spontaneous, automatic expression of economic facts. [It] is a political program" (*Notebooks* 160).

The English editors of the *Notebooks*, Quintin Hoare and Geoffrey Nowell Smith, provide a good overview of the variations of Gramsci's own articulation of the state/civil society relation. They point out that civil society in Gramsci is at times something that must be conquered by a hegemonic project *before* it can take over the state, at other times something that must be conquered or hegemonized *from* the state. Sometimes civil society is "culture" and the private sphere (the family, religion, personal interiority); other times it is a "mode of economic behaviour"—possessive individualism; sometimes it is "outside" and in opposition to the state; other times it is what Gramsci calls "the ethical content of the State." Hoare and Smith conclude that "Gramsci did not succeed in finding a single, wholly satisfactory conception of 'civil society' or the State. . . . The State is the instrument for conforming civil society to the economic structure, but it is necessary for the State to 'be willing' to do this; i.e. for the representatives of the change that has taken place in the economic structure to be in control of the State" (*Notebooks* 207, 208).

These variations obviously have to with the question of how hegemony is secured, and with the reciprocal effects of hegemony on values, social forms, and relations of production. They do not amount, however, to a celebration on Gramsci's part of the autonomous character of civil society. At most, they should be read as anticipatory cautions against the totalitarian pretension of the party-state to bring under its control all or most sectors of the economy and all or most forms of independent civic organization and activity. But they do not deny that control of the state—that is, hegemony—is ultimately what is at stake in the activity of civil society itself; and, vice versa, that it is hegemony that configures civil society.

Coming back to my "little story," it would, in any case, clearly be wrong in at least two ways to see the dispute over the false curanderas as one pitting civil society against an authoritarian or unrepresentative state: (1) the concept of civil society—itself linked to bourgeois legality and the market—is inadequate to encompass both the extent of the harm the village felt had been done to it and the means it proposed to remedy that harm; and, (2) in this case, the state did not do badly by the village. In wanting to adjudicate the case collectively, the village was in a sense stating the claims of community *against* civil society; vice versa, the feelings of astonishment or indignation expressed by some of the students in my seminar at what the peasants were doing posed Ecuadoran civil society (middle- or upper-class, urban, modern, white or mestizo, Spanish-speaking, European-identified, "law-abiding") against community (indian, rural, poor peasant, Quichuaspeaking). At least at one level (and it was admittedly an extremely complex incident), in other words, the conflict over who had the authority to try and punish the false curanderas was between civil society on one side, and subaltern community and class (poor peasant) on the other, with both the national and local states in the position of mediator.

Partha Chatterjee draws attention to what he considers the "suppression in modern European social theory of an independent narrative of community. . . . [C]ommunity, in the narrative of capital, becomes relegated to the latter's prehistory, a natural, prepolitical, primordial stage in social evolution."[6] In the colonial world, the dichotomy between civil society and state is displaced by the impossibility of the colonial state to be able to institute an effective civil society, since it cannot recognize the colonized subject as a full citizen. As a result, "[t]he crucial break in the history of anticolonial nationalism comes when the colonized refuse to accept membership in this civil society of subjects":

> They [the colonized] construct national identities within a different narrative [than that of civil society], that of community. They do not have the option of doing this within the domain of bourgeois civil-society institutions. They create, consequently, a very different domain—a cultural domain—marked by the distinctions of the material and the spiritual, the outer and the inner. This inner domain of culture is declared the sovereign territory of the nation, where the colonial state is not allowed entry, even as the outer domain remains surrendered to the colonial power. The attempt is . . . to find, against the grand narrative of history itself, the cultural resources to negotiate the terms through which people, living in different, contextually defined, communities, can coexist peacefully, productively, and creatively within large political units. (237–38).

Chatterjee concludes that "the invocation of the state/civil society opposition in the struggle against socialist-bureaucratic regimes in Eastern Europe or in the former Soviet republics or, for that matter, in China, will produce anything other than strategies seeking to replicate the history of Western Europe" (238). He is referring to the fact that the concept of civil society is tied up with a normative sense of modernity and civic participation, which by virtue of its own requirements (literacy, nuclear family units, attention to formal politics and business news, property or a stable income source) excludes significant sectors of the population from full citizenship. Writing as a Latin American philosopher, Enrique Dussel uncovers an aspect of the genealogy of this association between civil society and modernity in "something that has passed unnoticed by many commentators and critics of Hegel, including Marx": the "dialectical impulse" that connects the emergence of civil society to the project of colonialism itself.[7] Dussel draws attention in particular to the following two passages from Hegel's *Philosophy of Right*:

> Through a dialectical impulse to transcend itself that is proper to it, such a society [capitalist market society] is, in the first place, driven to seek outside itself new consumers. For this reason it seeks to find ways to move about among other peoples that are inferior to it with respect to the resources it has in abundance, or, in general, its industry.

> This development of relations offers also the means of colonization towards which, in either an accidental or systematic way, a completed civil society is impelled.

Dussel comments: "Hegel does not seem to realize [in these passages] that this means [the colonies] must be seized from other peoples. The periphery of Europe is a 'free space' that allows the poor, produced by the contradictions of capitalist development, to become capitalists or property owners themselves in the colonies" (74). His point is that Hegel's idea of civil society, like Habermas's ideal of communicative rationality, requires an "achieved" modernity that is tied to a belief in the necessity of "development" (pedagogic, economic, hygienic, and so on). But, "[f]or Habermas, as for Hegel, the discovery of America is not a constitutive fact of modernity." By contrast, a "sense of the relation between the conquest of America and the formation of modern Europe permits a new definition, a new global vision of modernity, which shows not only its emancipatory but also its destructive and genocidal side" (74–75).[8]

Guha will sometimes argue that the forms of customary law and tradition in the precolonial Indian subcontinent constitute a kind of civil society *avant la lettre*, and that the colonial state imposed by the British existed above and in some ways against this civil society. These forms could function therefore as a site of resistance to the colonial state, which could neither penetrate nor wholly subsume them. In the colonies, the subaltern exists necessarily at the margin of or outside the boundaries of the state, or in its fissures; the (legal-ethical) category of citizen is not coextensive with the (moral-communal) category of person.[9]

In this, and *only* in this historically specific sense, anticolonial struggle is sometimes conceptualized by Guha as a struggle of civil society against the state. What is meant by civil society in this case, however—the "home" of the binary home and the world, the "spirit" of the people, "native" religion, food, art, dress, customs—is essentially identical to what Chatterjee understands by community. In a similar fashion, when the Zapatistas today call upon "Mexican civil society" to stand with them in their struggle against the regional and national state, they mean by civil society the ensemble of social identities in Mexican society committed to democracy and social justice, and by the state the oligarchy of big capitalists and big political bosses.[10] The presence and force of subaltern negativity is not occluded by the use of the concept of civil society in these cases, in other words, although the concept may be problematic in other ways.

How does this pertain to my story? My point is not to celebrate Latin American "difference," in yet another form of what José Joaquín Brunner calls (referring to Gabriel García Marquéz's *One Hundred Years of Solitude*) *macondismo*. After all, the struggle of the village was *not only* about "premodern" cultural identity and authority. Struggles over cultural identity and rights and economic struggles over the effects of globalization are, as Arturo Escobar puts it, "one and the same. . . . Capitalist regimes undermine the reproduction of socially valued forms of identity; by destroying existing cultural practices, development projects destroy elements necessary for cultural affirmation."[11]

The action of the village clearly obeyed a different temporal-spatial logic than the one that governed formal Ecuadoran civil society. If, as Dussel argues, modernity means the full flowering of civil society, then its necessary condition is, in principle—as in Vargas Llosa's *The War at the End of the World*—the repression of the communal logic (and values, interests, and identities) involved in the village's decision to punish the curanderas itself. But the actual outcome of the struggle also suggests that such a communal logic can "coexist peacefully" with modernity and the modern state (though perhaps not with a *capitalist* modernity). The state simply has to "Let It Be," as the Beatles song has it, instead of seeing its *telos* or purpose as liquidating or transforming such practices and belief systems. But for this to happen requires a change in the discourses and interests that construct the state as a subject of history. It is in producing that change that the critical-theoretical intervention proposed by subaltern studies can play a crucial role.[12]

This observation brings me back, after a long detour, to Stuart Hall's point, noted in the last chapter, about the " 'political' aspect of cultural studies," and to my promised consideration of Canclini's *Hybrid Cultures*.[13] In a way that recalls Gayatri Spivak's characterization of subaltern studies as a "strategy for our times," it may be said of Canclini that he has developed a strategic conception of the role of cultural studies and its relation to the state in the context of the effects of globalization on Latin American societies. Presumably (though she never says this in so many words) Canclini would be for Beatriz Sarlo a "media neopopulist." Unlike Sarlo, Canclini accepts the essential premise that there is an autonomous creativity in the sphere of consumer or popular culture that does not depend on being authorized by high culture (to the contrary, if it is authorized by/as high culture, it becomes denatured and loses its oppositional force); that it is not simply a question of manipulation or commercialization (rather, commercialization is one of the *means* by which this autonomous creativity works); that popular and mass culture are not clearly separate entities; that they are no longer bonded by the territorial referent of the nation-state; that, with this crucial modification, they are coextensive with the category of civil society.

For Canclini, the political left in Latin America is stuck in a "Gutembergian" conception of cultural politics, coincident with the political and demographic limits of Angel Rama's "lettered city" (Rama's own theory of narrative transculturation would be one example of this conception).[14] Canclini belongs to that generation in Latin America which participated in the dream of revolution in the 1960s, but which failed and now returns with a new program, better adjusted to actual conditions, which include centrally the collapse of the alternative to capitalism represented by communism. What Canclini realizes, however, is that *capitalist* societies like contemporary Mexico also confront the problem that the narratives which legitimize and organize the state do not coincide or no longer coincide with the multiple logics of civil society. In fact, it is the crisis or sense of inadequacy of the nation-state provoked by globalization—which is also for Canclini the crisis of Gramsci's "national-popular"—that allows the category of civil society to appear in its full light: that is, as what he calls "interpretive communities of consumers," partially detached from a national referent.[15] Yet the nation-state is not yet in the position to allow civil society to be itself, to recognize the rights of citizens to enter into autonomous relations regulated in the last instance by national and/or international civil law.

Canclini shares with the postmodernist turn in general a sense of the limitations of the state and the narratives of state formation and modernization.[16] Where he differs from subaltern studies in particular, however, is that his concept of agency, defined in part by the operations of popular and mass culture, explicitly seeks to transcend the strong binary implied in the elite/subaltern dichotomy. Canclini is interested precisely in "deconstructing" (he uses the term himself) the categories of subalternity and hegemony, at least as these are generally understood in relation to modernization and modernity. For Canclini, as for Homi Bhabha, the category that expresses the dynamic of popular cultures is hybridity rather than subalternity. Hybridity designates sociocultural forms "in which the traditional and the modern are mixed" (2) and which are located necessarily in civil society rather than in the state or in ideological state apparatuses (ISAS).

Here is the core argument of *Hybrid Cultures*, which occurs in the book's central chapter, "The Staging of the Popular":

> The constitutive processes of modernity are thought of as chains of oppositions juxtaposed in a Manichaean fashion:
>
> $$\begin{array}{ccccc} \text{modern} & = & \text{cultured} & = & \text{hegemonic} \\ \downarrow & & \downarrow & & \downarrow \\ \text{traditional} & = & \text{popular} & = & \text{subaltern} \end{array}$$
>
> The bibliography on culture tends to assume that there is an intrinsic interest on the part of the hegemonic sectors to promote modernity and a fatal destiny on the part of the popular sectors that keeps them rooted in tradition. From this opposition, modernizers draw the moral that their interest in the advances and promises of history justifies their hegemonic position: meanwhile, the backwardness of the popular classes condemns them to subalternity. If popular culture modernizes, as indeed happens, this is a confirmation for the hegemonic groups that there is no way out of its traditionalism; for the defenders of popular causes it is further evidence of the way in which domination prevents them from being themselves.
>
> [But] . . . traditionalism is today a trend in many hegemonic social layers and can be combined with the modern, almost without conflict, when the exaltation of traditions is limited to culture, whereas modernization specializes in the social and economic. It must now be asked in what sense and to what ends the popular sectors adhere to modernity, search for it, and mix it with their traditions. A first analysis will consist in seeing how the oppositions modern/traditional and cultured/popular are restructured in changes occurring in handicrafts and fiestas. Next I will stop to analyze some manifestations of urban popular culture, where the search for the modern appears as part of the productive movement of the popular sphere. Finally, we will have to examine how, together with the traditional, other features that have been fatally identified with the popular are being transformed: their local character, their association with the national and the subaltern. (*Hybrid Cultures* 145–46)

For Canclini, six theses on the relation of popular culture and modernity flow from this argument and differentiate his position radically from Gramsci's: (1) "*modern development does not suppress traditional popular cul-*

tures"; (2) "*peasant and traditional cultures no longer represent the major part of popular culture*"; (3) "*the popular is not concentrated in objects*"; (4) "*the popular is not the monopoly of the popular sectors*"; (5) "*the popular is not lived by popular subjects as a melancholic complacency with traditions*"; and (6) "*the pure preservation of traditions is not always the best popular resource for reproducing itself and reelaborating its situation*" (*Hybrid Cultures* 153–68).

The notion of hybridity in Canclini refers to two somewhat different things. The first has to do with the effects of deterritorialization and globalization in "border" situations, such as the one represented by the city of Tijuana (but not only there, since the border is also seen as internal to the nation or "invaginated," to use Derrida's term), in which cultural elements from different historical times and social formations enter into contact and combination. *Hybrid Cultures* includes an important section—"Deterritorializing"—summarizing the results of an interdisciplinary project Canclini participated in to study cultural conflict in Tijuana—one of the most volatile and fastest growing urban conglomerations in the world. The zero-degree of Canclini's vision of Tijuana comes in the following passage:

> On several corners of Revolution Avenue there are zebras. In reality they are painted burros. They are there so that North American tourists can be photographed with a landscape behind them in which images from various regions of Mexico are crowded together: volcanoes, Aztec figures, cacti, the eagle with the serpent. "Faced with the lack of other types of things, as there are in the south where there are pyramids, there is none of that here . . . as if something had to be invented for the gringos," they said in one of the groups. In another group, they pointed out that "it also refers to the myth that North Americans bring with them, that it has something to do with crossing the border into the past, into wilderness, into the idea of being able to ride horseback." (*Hybrid Cultures* p. 236)

In such a setting, Canclini believes, the nation and a national narrative of unity (territorial, linguistic, symbolic, and so on) no longer serve to represent cultural citizenship or to design effective cultural and educational policies. There is a disconnection or misunderstanding (in the Lacanian sense of *méconnaissance*, as that which creates the imaginary unity of the self) between the *idea* of the nation and the heterogeneity of its actual population and the "mixed times" (*tiempos mixtos*) in which they live. Gramsci would have designated this disconnection as a disjunction of the national and the popular. But, like Bhabha, Canclini explicitly rejects this language, seeing it as still anchored in the tradition/modernity binary. He prefers the postmodernist idea of pastiche.[17]

The concept of hybrid culture also designates for Canclini the breakdown of traditional divisions in the field of cultural study and production: for example, the divisions among high, middle, and popular culture, or among mass culture, popular culture, and folklore, or between artisanal production and manufacture, advertising and art, simulacrum and original, and so forth. Since traditional disciplinary protocols for the study of culture in the humanities and social sciences are anchored in one or other of the three pairs of binaries (art history in the "cultured," for instance; anthropology and folklore studies in the popular-traditional), cultural hybridity demands correspondingly hybrid or interdisciplinary ways of thinking about culture, which, in Deleuzian fashion, Canclini calls "nomad social sciences" (Hybrid Cultures 2). "Nomad social sciences" could be taken as Canclini's definition of cultural studies.[18]

It goes without saying that Canclini's way of looking at these issues has the advantage of registering the complex, "impure" ways in which people actually experience and produce culture, whereas the binarism of subaltern studies seems to create artificially Manichaean identities (hegemonic versus subaltern; traditional versus mass; artesanía versus manufacture; or, in my own case, the subaltern "against literature"). Canclini would concur in particular with Bhabha's claim, noted in chapter 4, that the form of the nation is "more hybrid in the articulation of cultural differences and identifications—gender, race or class—than can be represented in any hierarchical or binary structuring of social antagonism." But it is necessary to distinguish between hybridity as a descriptive taxonomy and its possible articulation as a normative concept for cultural studies—as an ideologeme, in other words, which is what it becomes in both Bhabha and Canclini. It should be evident (to answer the question I posed at the start of this chapter) that Canclini's notion of hybridization has a family relation, so to speak, with transculturation, just as transculturation was itself linked to the older idea of mestizaje or creolization as the essence of Latin American identity or identities.[19] The difference is that whereas writers like Angel Rama or Fernando Ortiz saw transculturation as abetting the nation-state's ability to integrate heterogenous populations and regions in the process of producing itself in a modern form, Canclini sees—in more postmodernist fashion—hybridity as something that happens necessarily not only at the margin of the state but, in a sense, against the state, since it calls the representational adequacy of the state and the ISAs into question. Correspondingly, the locus of transculturation shifts for Canclini from high culture—Rama's transculturación narrativa—back to popular and mass culture—Ortiz's emphasis on everyday culture (food, clothing, sociolinguistics, popular music).

If hybridization comes to be in effect coextensive with the dynamics of civil society in Canclini's argument, then despite his appeal to deconstruction—which functions rhetorically for him as something like the theoretical correlative of hybridization—the binary that is not deconstructed is the one that is constitutive of the concept of hybridity itself: the opposition of the state (and ISAs) versus civil society, in which the first is seen as monolithic and reductionist in its concept of the nation and the national, the second as heterogenous, mobile, autonomously creative, subject (through consumer choice and the market) to popular will. If, as we noted in chapter 2, there is implicit in the concept of mestizaje or transculturation a historical teleology of the nation-state, a similar (unrecognized) postnational teleology operates in Hybrid Cultures, since hybridization entails that the process of combination that gives rise to the hybrid is both necessary and providential, breaking down in the practice of everyday life the binary oppositions Canclini as a theorist of culture pretends to deconstruct. Hybridization functions, in other words, as a process of dialectical sublation or transcendence of prior states of dissonance or contradiction in the configuration of a subject, social group or class, national or regional identity. In this sense, Canclini's argument is essentially modernist, rather than anti- or postmodernist, as it appears at first sight. It simply shifts the locus of modernization from the state to civil society.[20]

Underlying Canclini's articulation of cultural studies is the assumption that, by breaking traditional disciplinary frameworks that impede a knowledge of new realities and by allowing for the creation of disciplinary hybrids, we can articulate new ways of thinking and therefore new ways of generating communicational and educational policies. These will in turn encourage an expanded concept of legal and cultural citizenship. As in Lyotard's The Postmodern Condition, this project presupposes that the present stage of capitalism is, "beyond good or evil," the new condition of life—something inevitable, like having to eat or sleep. For both Lyotard and Canclini there is no "outside" of globalization from which to construct an opposition to it—no "tradition," no "third world," no "nature," no autonomous sphere of popular culture, no modernist hermeneutics of depth. It follows that it no longer makes sense to think of the world system and of inter-state relations within it in terms of a (dominant) center and a (dominated or subaltern) periphery. Everything that was the radical project of the 1960s must now take place within this space. But, providentially, it also can take place there, in the sense that globalization and deterritorialization at the same time require and make possible new disciplinary crossings, new protocols in the sciences, a revision of the structure of academic knowledge. Canclini's articulation of cultural studies thus serves as a compensatory substitute for a political practice of the left that is now seen as impossible or undesirable in a postpolitical era. But it also asks us not to abandon all hope; there are still important and urgent tasks: democratizing the bases of knowledge, producing new types of cultural objects and discourses, developing programs for media literacy—even something as simple as giving graduate students a space to work on subjects like telenovelas or Madonna. Evidently, if one can *know*, in an academic sense, what culture is and how it functions in the context of globalization, then instead of remaining trapped in disciplinary divisions that correspond to earlier stages of capitalist development, one can offer a more accurate "cognitive mapping" of the present and of future trends.

But here within Canclini's project reappears the danger I referred to earlier, apropos the academic institutionalization of cultural studies: its tendency to turn into a kind of postmodernist ethnography or costumbrismo. Instead of studying "primitive" tribes or peasants, now we go to Tijuana, or we analyze telenovelas, but we are still looking with the same eyes as the ones who went into the jungle, saying to ourselves in so many words, "Aha. Let's look at the odd customs of these people, these new others!" It is true, of course, that the new others also include ourselves, since we are at once the participant observers and the observed in the field of contemporary culture—one of the strengths of Canclini's work is his recognition of this feedback loop in the work of cultural studies. Canclini is correct to criticize Gramsci's conception of popular culture as pre- or antimodern, so that subaltern negativity is for Gramsci essentially the resistance of "folk" culture or tradition to (capitalist) modernity. But the subaltern does not operate solely within the frame of tradition or "folk" culture; it operates rather within a logic of binary antagonism that may or may not include the opposition of modernity versus tradition. Gramsci's error was in assuming, first, that the subaltern can become hegemonic only by becoming culturally its other—that is, by incorporating into itself the dominant culture by acculturation or transculturation—and, second, that the dominant culture was necessarily modern. Nevertheless, because Canclini collapses the distinction subaltern/hegemonic into the distinctions popular/cultured and traditional/modern, he cannot discern how the dynamic of subalternity continues to operate *within* modernity and hybridization. In the image of María Milagros López, the contemporary subaltern, at the same time, "has nothing in common with the idyllic past and seems resistant to being incorporated into the normative disciplines of modernity."[21]

For Canclini, specific intellectuals, and cultural studies as a new interdisciplinary field, act as mediators and facilitators between the state (and transnational para-state organisms) and civil society. Interpellating the state from the position of cultural studies implies that cultural studies seeks to function in a sense as the "mirror" of the state, representing not what the state is, but the higher form of what the state should be. Canclini's own work offers at once a theoretical model and a new methodology for this practice. But, as in the new forms of Latin American social democracy suggested in Jorge Castañeda's Utopia Disarmed—a book that is in many ways the companion of Hybrid Cultures—Canclini's project remains essentially within the logic of the dominant system, instead of creating a space of opposition or stimulating the contradictions of that system. Moreover, it displaces agency from a popular-democratic subject to a new kind of specific intellectual, now defined in his or her tasks and goals by cultural studies and "theory."

It is not that class or other forms of social inequality and conflict disappear for Canclini, who still considers himself a person of the left (they are vividly present for him in the question of unequal access to cultural production and resources, for example).[22] What does disappear, however, along with the binary hegemonic versus subaltern and the Gramscian copula national-popular, is the possibility of structural change, even of structural reform. For Canclini, the political as such has been partially displaced by a culturalist notion of social agency located in civil society. But social contradictions and struggles that are also struggles "in culture" and in civil society—for example, class struggles at the point of work, struggles for ethnic or community rights or for a more equitable national or regional situation within globalization (what used to be called anti-imperialist struggle), women's struggles for equality, even the micropolitics of the new social movements that seemed to be the new social subject summoned up by (and for) cultural studies—continue to depend on the logic of domination and subordination, contradiction and negation that characterizes subaltern identity as such, even as the social subjects involved may operate within the terrain of hybridization. They are binary rather than (or as well as) hybrid. Civil society itself is a space in which subaltern/dominant relations are produced and reproduced, rather than one pole of a subaltern/dominant, good/bad dichotomy.

If hybridization is seen as coextensive with the market, consumer choice, and possessive individualism, then despite Canclini's own protestations that his work is intended as a contribution to reformulating the project of the left, there is a sense in which it is also, in principle, compatible with globalization and neoliberal hegemony. Does not in fact cultural hybridization via the mechanism of market society accomplish what the left was unable to do: that is, democratize the very bases of identity and value?

Canclini addresses this question himself in the sequel to *Hybrid Cultures*, *Consumidores y ciudadanos*, whose stated purpose is to "defatalize the neo-liberal paradigm."[23] Canclini explicitly recognizes the limits of the market and thus the need to encourage the ability of existing nation-states to resist or modify the more negative consequences of globalization. The logic of his argument is circular: Consumption is or is becoming a key place in which citizenship is exercised in contemporary societies (the book's ruling idea is that *el consumo sirve para pensar*—consumption serves as a way of thinking). But if that is so, then it must be the responsibility of states and/or regional entities to assure access to consumption and the widest range of consumer possibilities—including "national" cultural products (such as Mexican film and popular music), which, in turn, can also function as cultural export commodities. Globalization, by destroying or marginalizing local producers and products, and/or by reducing the living standards of sectors of the population (and thus their possibility to consume) is therefore a potential threat to this kind of cultural citizenship.[24]

As a response to this threat of homogenization, Canclini advances in *Consumidores* the idea of a Latin American "regional federalism" that would be based in part on the work of a regionalized cultural studies. Such a project would involve a proactive concept of cultural policy, entailing state involvement in areas of cultural production that need protection or special cultivation, in remedying unevenness in access to consumption, and in coordinating activities between the public, private, global, and local spheres.

But, as Alberto Moreiras has observed, Canclini's idea of regional federalism—or what Moreiras himself calls "critical regionalism" (taking the term from Kenneth Frampton via Fredric Jameson)—reinstates the subaltern/dominant binary precisely at the heart of a discourse that had seemed intent on eliminating that binary, in the sense that the force of the regional or local can only derive from the relatively disadvantaged situation of Latin American societies in the global system. To the extent that Latin America can claim an epistemological privilege vis-à-vis the center, it is because of this disadvantage. Moreiras puts it this way: "Latin American cultural studies . . . is to be understood as the systematic effort to incorporate Latin American-area based knowledge . . . as primarily knowledge of the Latin American subaltern difference in the global context. . . . Critical regionalism, as a thinking of cultural consumption from regional perspectives, was understood as the thinking of the singular resistance to consumption from within consumption through which regional and local identity formation happens in global times."[25]

But Moreiras also hedges his bet: alongside the "critical" or "negative" dimension of subaltern regionalism, there exists "a certain understanding of local singularity that serves the reproductive interests of the neoliberal order by fostering consumption of (and thus, not coincidentally, annihilating) difference." Moreover, if "local singularity," "negative fissures," "mixed times," hybridity, transculturation, "heterogeneity," and the like are phenomena that are generalizable to *all* societies, in all times and in all places, they cannot as such express the structural particularity of Latin American societies and nation-states, which is that, alongside the relations of subalternity and domination that continue to prevail *within* them, they also continue to remain (or are in the process of becoming) subaltern as a whole in the world system.[26]

Cultural studies emerges initially and gathers force as an effort to "represent" (in the double sense we have been using this term) from within the academy struggles for social equality and recognition that emerge outside it. Canclini, by contrast, offers in a way a disciplinary *solution* for the problems of exploitation, inequality, and ungovernability that afflict our societies. His project subsumes all other contradictions in the state versus civil society contradiction, and then weakens even that contradiction by making cultural studies a heuristic model for a new type of state/nongovernmental organization practice. It might be more interesting to understand why there cannot be a solution to these problems simply by "taking thought" without a change in the power relations that structure identities as privileged or subaltern in the first place, relations that are both embedded in and configure in their interactions a dominant mode of production. This recognition requires, however, thinking strategically the relation between cultural studies and the project of the left. What is valuable in Canclini's own proposal in this regard is the emphasis on the need for the left to go beyond a "Gutembergian" notion of culture and politics, and most especially to begin to operate on the terrain of the mass media. Equally valuable is the idea of "mixed times" that underlies Canclini's concept of hybridity, which suggests a nonlinear, nonhistoricist sense of political agency and intervention. No longer does the project of the left have to be tied to a homogenous and homegenizing narrative of "modernization" ("mixed times" articulates the problematic, analyzed by Althusser and his school, of the interaction in any given social formation of modes of production and their ideological superstructures that survive under and compete with a dominant mode of production).

I have tried to suggest here, however, that cultural studies can also point in the direction of a postpolitical sense of agency, citizenship, and "participation" in globalization. In this mode, it has become the darling of the foundations. In his review of the Routledge Cultural Studies reader, Jameson speaks of "the desire called Cultural Studies," and describes that desire as "the project to constitute a 'historic bloc,' rather than theoret- ically, as the occasion for a new discipline."[27] If my argument here is correct, the formation of such a historic bloc—that is, of a project capable of displacing the hegemony of neoliberalism—depends on cultural studies but will not happen from the position of cultural studies itself, except to the extent that cultural studies is interpellated critically by subaltern studies. Without this interpellation, it seems to me that cultural studies in general will face an impasse similar to the one faced by Canclini. The ruling class, the state at all levels, transnational organisms of various sorts (nongovern- mental or para-governmental), neoliberal hegemony, the university and the network of foundations and research centers need cultural studies because it responds to urgent shifts in the forms of life and knowledge that accom- pany globalization, but they cannot let it be itself: that is, the equivalent of what used to be called a "liberated zone." They want it to be theirs, but by nature and right it belongs to someone else.

6 Territoriality, Multiculturalism, and Hegemony: The Question of the Nation

---

"The subaltern classes, by definition," according to Antonio Gramsci, "are not unified and cannot unite until they are able to become a 'State.' "[1] True. But if to win hegemony the subaltern classes and groups have to become essentially like that which is *already* hegemonic, then in a sense the old ruling classes and the dominant culture win, even in defeat. How does one move from the negativity of subaltern consciousness to hegemony? That is the question posed by Néstor García Canclini's and Homi Bhabha's critiques of the subaltern/dominant binary, Angel Rama's idea of transculturation, and Florencia Mallon's effort to read back into the historical record the effective presence of peasants and peasant communities in the constitution of the modern state in Peru and Mexico. Yet their own answers to this question are unsatisfactory in the ways we have described.

We might rephrase the question as follows: Does the subalternist critique of the nation-form and nationalism, which is based on an awareness of the incommensurability of the subaltern and the nation-state, necessarily preclude it from contributing to a redefinition of the nation-state and its functions? Or is subaltern studies rather a kind of postnationalism? Ranajit Guha begins *Elementary Aspects of Peasant Insurgency* with a critique of Eric Hobsbawm's idea that peasant banditry is prepolitical, arguing instead that it should be understood in a different register of politics than the one represented by the state and the legal forms of colonial civil society, a register that Guha calls the "politics of the people." But Guha also explains the relation of peasant insurrection to colonial power in terms which imply that, while it was not prepolitical, there are limitations to the kind of politics it embodies:

> [Peasant insurgency] was not yet equipped with a mature and positive conception of power, hence of an alternative state and a set of laws and codes of punishment to go with it. This is not to deny of course that some of the more radical of the rural revolts . . . did in fact anticipate power at least to a degree and expressed it, albeit feebly and crudely, in terms of rough justice and punitive violence laced with vengeance. Beyond that, however, the project in which the rebels had involved themselves was predominantly negative in orientation. Its purpose was not so much to reconstitute the world as to reverse it.[2]

The problem is compounded by the manner in which the peasant revolts related to the political-administrative space of the colonial Raj. Guha argues that the rebellions created territoriality in essentially two ways: by relations of consanguinity—that is, the rebellion spread through ethnic groups or affinity (by blood tie or tribal lineage); or by relations of contiguity or "local bond"—the rebellion could leap between one ethnic group and another where these were located in close proximity. Peasant utopias generally function as subnational forms of territoriality, because the nation as a legal abstraction (and more particularly, the colonial or postcolonial state) is experienced as a hostile and unrepresentative space by peasants, in contrast to a remembered or fantasized other space and time that they seek to restore.[3] Thus, while the immediate "fight for land merged in the general struggle for a homeland" (*Aspects* 290) in a way that would later be mobilized by Indian nationalism, "even the most powerful of peasant uprisings were often unable to exceed local boundaries" (278). This meant that the rebellions could be successful only within this limited territoriality, and that they would eventually be thrown back by the overarching power of the colonial state (as is well known, a similar problem affected slave rebellions in the Americas, which, with the exception of Haiti, succeeded in creating only the liminal territoriality of the maroon communities).

Guha concludes: "[T]he domain of rebellion still fell far short of the domain of the nation, and the two arms of territoriality . . . acted to no small extent in putting the brakes on resistance against the Raj. Narrow localism raised its head and impeded the progress of the insurgents at critical moments" (331).

The double articulation of territoriality in peasant rebellions that Guha describes has important implications for conceptualizing contemporary social struggles and movements that are sub- or supranational in character.[4] Nevertheless, it also means that the historical insurgencies that Guha studies could not move from a position of subalternity to one of hegemony. They remained subaltern in the very act of contesting domination because they could not encompass (or create) the nation. That is because, as Gramsci understood, the nation is (or has been) the form of territoriality that corresponds to hegemony (and, vice versa, the nation is in a sense the *effect* of hegemony).[5]

Connected to the limitations of subaltern territoriality is a political problem built into the nature of subaltern identity itself. Guha's definition of the subaltern as "the general attribute of subordination . . . whether this is expressed in terms of class, caste, age, gender and office or in any other way" stresses cultural as well as economic determinants of social identity. Class in the sense of relation of production is one determinant, but not the only one, of subaltern identity (and class is itself also an identity). But this is to say essentially the same thing as U.S.-style identity politics: one identity can be posited only in a differential relation with another. Though Guha posits the coincidence of the subaltern with the people, that identification is in fact precarious, as we saw in chapter 4, because the people constitutes a potentially unitary and hegemonic social bloc, whereas the subaltern designates a subordinated particularity.

This takes us back to the contradiction in the project of subaltern studies itself between retrieving the presence of a subaltern subject and deconstructing the discourses that constitute the subaltern as such: for example, in Gayatri Spivak's point that the very recovery of the "voice" of the subaltern entails also its erasure, since in the mode of representation we give it (in testimonio, for example) it is no longer located in the space of subalternity, but rather has become something like a ventriloquist's dummy. The problem is complicated by the fact that, as Gyan Prakash puts it, "the subalternist search for a humanist subject-agent frequently ended up with the discovery of the failure of subaltern agency: the moment of rebellion carried with it the moment of failure."[6]

Gramsci takes up the question of the relation of subalternity and hegemony at several points in the *Prison Notebooks*. In the section titled "The

Study of Philosophy," he considers the character of Marxism itself as a historical determinism, expressed most strongly perhaps in the mode of production narrative and the idea of its inevitability and universality. Gramsci's hostility to vulgar Marxism is well known; but he takes an unexpected approach to the question of determinism here. He sees determinism as an *integral* feature of the consciousness of subaltern classes and groups: "It should be noted how the deterministic, fatalistic and mechanistic element has been a direct ideological 'aroma' emanating from the philosophy of praxis [Marxism], rather like religion or drugs (in their stupefying effect)." But this, in turn,

> has been made necessary and justified historically by the "subaltern" character of certain social strata. . . . When you don't have the initiative in the struggle and the struggle itself comes eventually to be identified with a series of defeats, mechanical determinism becomes a tremendous force of moral resistance, of cohesion and of patient and obstinate perseverance. . . . Real will takes on the garments of an act of faith in a certain rationality of history and in a primitive and empirical form of impassioned finalism which appears in the role of a substitute for the Predestination or Providence of confessional religions. (336)

But if (belief in) mechanical determinism is an aspect of subaltern culture and identity—the negation of upper-class idealism, Bertolt Brecht's *plumpen Denken*, a constituent part of the "will" of the peasant rebel that Guha is concerned with retrieving from the historical record—Gramsci believes it is also something that must be overcome in the process of struggle. Why? Because

> when the "subaltern" becomes directive and responsible for the economic activity of the masses, mechanicism at a certain point becomes an imminent danger and a revision must take place in modes of thinking because a change has taken place in the social mode of existence. The boundaries and the dominion of the "force of circumstance" become restricted. . . . [I]f yesterday the subaltern element was a thing, today it is no longer a thing but a historical person, a protagonist; if yesterday it was not responsible, because "resisting" a will external to itself, now it feels itself to be responsible because it is no longer resisting but an agent, necessarily active and taking the initiative. (336–37)

For Gramsci, determinism, while understandable as itself a "determined" effect of class division and conflict, is ultimately a fatalistic, even a quasi-religious concept, which holds back the workers' movement.[7] Tacit in these comments is a critique of Stalinism and the commitment of Soviet Marxism to a narrative of historical "necessity" that stressed a teleological link between the so-called "development of the forces of production" and the achievement of socialism. But there is also an underlying assumption about the conceptual limitations of subaltern culture—an identification of the subaltern with Nietzsche's category of slave morality—that is more problematic.

As we noted in the last chapter, Gramsci tends to equate the subaltern as such with the categories of the "traditional," the "folkloric," or (most often) the "spontaneous" (that is why Canclini thought it was necessary to abandon the categories of subalternity and hegemony at the same time, because, in his view, the subaltern can be conceptualized as a subject-position only in relation to a sense of traditional or popular culture that has been overtaken by modernity). By "spontaneous" Gramsci means ideas that "are not the result of any systematic educational activity on the part of an already conscious leading group, but have been formed through every-day experience illuminated by 'common sense,' i.e. by the traditional popular conception of the world—what is unimaginatively called 'instinct,' although it too is in fact a primitive and elementary historical acquisition" (198–99). Noting the lack of reliable documents about subaltern resistance and insurrection, Gramsci observes: "It may be said that spontaneity is therefore characteristic of the 'history of the subaltern classes,' and indeed of their most marginal and peripheral elements; they have not achieved any consciousness of the class 'for itself,' and consequently it never occurs to them that their history might have some possible importance, that there might be some value in leaving documentary evidence of it" (196). The corollary is that the subaltern is incapable of "imagining" a nation in the sense Benedict Anderson talks about the nation as an "imagined community" (vice versa, for Gramsci the difficulty of the dominant literary-humanistic culture in representing the subaltern classes is the Achilles heel of Italian nationalism).[8]

Gramsci is trying to synthesize in the *Notebooks* "spontaneity"—the element of subaltern negativity, which is the dynamic force of social history—and "conscious leadership," which (in his view) is necessary for hegemony. It is not that subaltern movements lack conscious leadership; but the theory possessed by that leadership is limited to the "folkloric" or "popular science." This is the crux of his polemic against Henri de Man (Paul de Man's uncle), which weaves in and out of the *Notebooks*. De Man, one of the leaders of Belgian social-democracy in the period between the wars, had argued the need for putting the empirical fact of popular super-

stitions, folklore, and the like against the "scientific" authority of Marxist theory. Gramsci thought that this amounted to recovering subaltern
thought in its subalternity.[9] At the same time, however, he argued that the
organized left needed to value and incorporate "spontaneous" movements,
whatever their immediate ideological character (which might be in many
cases religious or millenarian). The cost of not doing this could be reaction, restoration, or coup d'état, since the dominant classes and their
representatives do sense the threat to their interests that is implicit in such
movements: "Neglecting, or worse still, despising the so-called 'spontaneous' movements, i.e. failing to give them a conscious leadership or to raise
them to a higher plane by inserting them into politics, may often have
extremely serious consequences" (199).

Gramsci's model of where subaltern "spontaneity" and "conscious leadership" come together is the Turin strike movement of the early 1920s,
which, in his words, "gave the masses a 'theoretical' consciousness of
being creators of *historical* and *institutional* values, of being founders of a
State." He concludes with a suggestive remark on the relation of subalternity to mass politics: "This unity between 'spontaneity' and 'conscious
leadership' or 'discipline' is precisely the real political action of the subaltern classes, in so far as this is mass politics and not merely an adventure
by groups claiming to represent the masses" (198).

Gramsci's reference to a "higher plane" (and the assumption that the
higher plane is constituted by modern politics rather than local culture) is
symptomatic of a latent historicism in his argument: this is not a question
of economic "stages"—Gramsci rejects economic determinism—but of
"stages" of thought and ideology. In particular, his presumption that the
subaltern has no (recorded or written) history is manifestly Hegelian, and
leads him into a detour into outright Eurocentrism.[10] The (implicit) historicism and (explicit) modernism of Gramsci's argument are conjoined in
his well-known ideas about the importance of formal education. For
Gramsci, the elite/subaltern division is itself in part an educational division: "The fundamental division into classical and vocational (professional) schools was a rational formula: the vocational school for the instrumental classes [*classi strumentali* is used interchangeably by Gramsci with
classi subalterni or *classi subordinate*], the classical school for the dominant
classes and the intellectuals" (*Notebooks* 26; parenthetical note by the editors). The separation between traditional and vocational schools thus reproduces the division between elite and subaltern classes. The proliferation
of different types of vocational schools may appear at first sight democratic, in the sense that it is a gesture toward social heterogeneity and
practical (as opposed to theoretical) knowledge. But democracy "must

mean that every 'citizen' can 'govern' and that society places him, even if only abstractly, in a general condition to achieve this." This the vocational school does not and cannot—so Gramsci claims, anyway—provide. By contrast, even something as evidently anachronistic as the philological curriculum in classics allows the student to acquire "a historicizing under-standing of the world and life, which becomes a second—nearly sponta-neous—nature" (Notebooks 40, 39).

But here precisely a problem appears that Gramsci is obliged to recog-nize: the quotidian force of subaltern resentment of and resistance to the process of formal—that is, state- or church-directed—school education. Gramsci notes that "it will always be an effort to learn physical self-discipline and self-control. . . . This is why many people think that the difficulty of study conceals some 'trick' which handicaps them—that is, when they do not simply believe that they are stupid by nature." He con-cludes somewhat pessimistically that, "[i]f our aim is to produce a new stratum of intellectuals, including those capable of the highest degree of specialisation, from a social group which has not traditionally developed the appropriate attitudes, then we have unprecedented difficulties to over-come" (Notebooks 42–43).

But resistance to learning is precisely a modality of subaltern identity, of subaltern negation—the resistance of the "silence" of the pobres in Richard Rodriguez's Hunger of Memory, or the ambivalence to government schools and "books" which Rigoberta Menchú expresses in her testimonio. If the process of formal education itself produces and reproduces the subaltern/dominant relation, how can it be a place where the subaltern can emerge into hegemony? Gramsci counts on the formation of a new type of intellec-tual capable of translating the "spontaneous" character of subaltern cul-ture into the possibility of hegemony—the famous "organic intellectual," who combines at once the resources of formal education with the point of view and commitment to the interests of subaltern social classes and groups. But, as Hunger of Memory illustrates, the very mechanism of formal education would itself efface or problematize the identification of such an intellectual with his or her initial class or group base, in the sense that the intellectual is no longer "one of them" and is in fact speaking in the place of the subaltern—speaking a necessarily different language (history, aes-thetics, philology and literary criticism, science, political economy, formal philosophy, law and civics, and so on).

Gramsci's ideal of formal education as necessary training for "conscious leadership" is related to his understanding of the Leninist concept of the vanguard party as a "collective intellectual" which acts to represent the subaltern in its emergence toward hegemony. The authority of the party is founded on its claim to know the correct strategy and tactics and its ability to impose, via the mechanism of democratic centralism, a will or discipline on its own members and the sometimes recalcitrant popular subject(s) that it claims to represent, in the name of the ultimate interests of that subject. But why and how is the party or party-state authorized to decide what those interests are? Is it necessary to become "educated" to exercise leadership and possess rights, or is one entitled to those rights simply by virtue of being a person? Gramsci critiques the specific character of Stalinism as an ideology and form of bureaucratic centralism; but he does not develop a critique of Leninism as such. Rather, the vanguard party is the "Modern Prince" required by the subaltern to win and exercise hegemony.

Thus Gramsci's argument arrives at a kind of impasse, an impasse that anticipates the current crisis of Marxism itself. Subaltern "spontaneity" (Guha would say negation) is necessary for social struggle to take place—it is the "content" of struggle, so to speak (therefore, "[e]very trace of independent initiative on the part of subaltern groups should . . . be of incalculable value for the integral historian" [Notebooks 55]). But by nature—that is, as subaltern—it resists becoming that which would make it capable of becoming hegemonic, its "form." For Gramsci, there is not enough "history" or "discipline" or "culture" in subaltern consciousness to constitute a hegemonic project; but the party or the party-state that can and does perform the function of "conscious leadership" ends up reproducing in several crucial ways the structure of the dominant/subaltern antithesis.

The problem is that Gramsci cannot imagine hegemony apart from the cultural forms of that which is already hegemonic: that is, "modern" art, culture, science, mathematics, and the like. The subaltern might reply in something like the following words:

I have been moved by the writing emerging from these movements [on behalf of oppressed or marginalized people] that has pointed to the contradiction between Marxism's liberationist rhetorics and its imaginary of social transformation through mastery, dialectical or otherwise. Anyone who has ever been silenced because he or she is female or gay or black or poor would likely, as I do, want to resist the idea that some speech is intrinsically privileged, epistemically, historically, or otherwise. Anyone who has operated from a position marked as marginal needs, at some level, to resist the reification of historical positioning, and its normalization through the authority of knowledge. If such differences of access to authority exist, and they do, the mythology that elevates these differences to the order of being, to an indication of having been chosen for the grace of privileged access, must be resisted strategically, not as false consciousness, but as bad politics.[11]

I would like to use this discussion of Gramsci's ideas about education as a point of departure to consider the problem of the relation of subaltern studies to the contemporary left. In an essay that originally appeared in the *New Left Review* some years ago, Nancy Fraser sees the left as trapped between what she calls, borrowing the term from Charles Taylor, a politics of recognition and a politics of redistribution.[12] The first, in her view, involves questions of cultural injustice, and tends to promote group differentiation in the interests of identity politics; the second involves questions of economic imbalance or injustice that affect people across lines of identity-group differentiation—that is, as general social collectivities (e.g., the "poor") or classes. The result is that the left is

> stuck in the vicious circles of mutually reinforcing cultural and economic subordination. Our best efforts to redress these injustices via the combination of the liberal welfare state plus mainstream multiculturalism are generating perverse effects. Only by looking to alternative conceptions of redistribution and recognition can we meet the requirements of justice for all. (93)

What Gramsci understands as hegemonic articulation might be a way of transcending, or as Fraser puts it, "finessing," this dilemma, because it changes the rules of the game. In a process of hegemonic articulation, it is not clear in advance what the interests and demands of the individuals, parties, groups, or classes involved will be, because they modify their interests and demands in the process itself, since the possibility of hegemony by definition modifies or inverts the structure of subalternity that defined their positional identity in the first place.[13] But can the left still contest for hegemony at the level of the state apparatus, and if it were in fact able to achieve hegemony, what would this mean, given the subnational and transnational parameters that govern the state as a consequence of economic and communicative globalization?

Gramsci's argument was that a given social project becomes hegemonic only to the extent that it can articulate to itself elements of other class or group projects, such that it appears as the embodiment of the interests of the "nation" as such. When it does this, it is in the position of "intellectual and moral leadership": that is, it is hegemonic. What precisely the nation is in territorial or juridical terms—Quebec or Canada, Chechnya or Russia—is less crucial in this respect than the function of the nation as a necessary signifier for hegemonic articulation.

But it may be that with globalization the symbolic territoriality of the nation-state has become a limited one, in the same way as the territoriality of Guha's peasant rebels, and that consequently the notions of hegemony and the "national-popular" have become obsolete, as Canclini argues. This idea carries the corollary that any attempt to stabilize a positional identity— of nationality, class, gender, race, or ethnicity—feeds into the logic of globalization itself, and that therefore resistance must take the form of a constant deconstruction of power relations. If it does not, the danger is that an identity-based politics, even one founded on subaltern identity, may turn into a genocidal politics of "ethnic cleansing."

At the same time, we need to remember the epistemological and political problem Spivak's "strategic essentialism" was meant to address. Deconstruction does not have a politics specific to it; that is, it is not in itself a politics. Politics necessarily involves ideological representation, and it is in the field of culture broadly speaking, seen as the space of disaggregation and construction of ideologies, that such representations take place. Social struggles are not between science and ideology, or between false consciousness and "truth," but rather between contesting class and group ideologies, which may or may not invoke science or an idea of science in their self-legitimization, but do always invoke what Spivak calls the "metalepsis" of positing a (subaltern) subject as sovereign cause.[14]

Fraser is also sensitive to this problem of subjectivity and agency. Arguing in her essay that, in theory, "the scenario that best finesses the redistribution-recognition dilemma is socialism in the economic plus deconstruction in the culture," she nevertheless cautions that "for this scenario to be psychologically and politically feasible requires that people be weaned from their attachment to current cultural constructions of their interests and identities." "This has always been the problem with socialism," Fraser adds. "Although cognitively compelling, it is experientially remote. The addition of deconstruction seems to exacerbate the problem. It could turn out to be too negative and reactive, i.e. too deconstructive, to inspire struggles on behalf of subordinated collectivities attached to their existing identities" (91 n. 46).

In other words, despite the immediate appeal of Fraser's formula of social welfare plus deconstruction, by her own qualification it cannot itself constitute the basis for a hegemonic political articulation—at best it can serve as the ground for practices out of which the possibility of a hegemonic articulation might result. It is not, therefore, a solution to the dilemma of the left she poses.

Probably the closest approximation in the United States in recent years to a potentially hegemonic formation of the left (though some would contest this characterization) was the Rainbow Coalition. The Rainbow achieved precariously and only for a moment that fusion of "spontaneous" and "conscious" leadership Gramsci found in the Turin strike movement. It is with regard to the Rainbow that I want to recall the distinction Ernesto Laclau and Chantal Mouffe draw between popular subject-position and democratic subject-position, introduced in chapter 4 above. This will serve in turn as a lead-in to a consideration of the question of new social movements and the kinds of politics associated with them.

Essentially, what Laclau and Mouffe mean by democratic subject-position is identity politics: that is, politics based on separate group values, interests, and rights; popular subject-position, by contrast, refers to the kind of politics that seeks to produce a division of the political space into two camps: the bloc of "the people" versus the "power bloc." Mouffe and Laclau see the Rainbow Coalition as being governed by an additive logic of the first, or "democratic" type: that is, women plus African Americans plus Latinos plus gays plus labor plus family farmers plus working poor plus unemployed equal the general constituency and appeal of the Rainbow, but each of these groups or categories retains its specificity and internal heterogeneity. There is no overarching interpellation or instance that constitutes all of these groups into "the people" except the figure of Jesse Jackson as such. That is why the Rainbow—which, as those who were involved with it can testify, brought together very diverse social constituencies (for example, feminists, white radicals, and black community organizations) in a way that had not been seen since the Civil Rights movement— essentially collapsed with the collapse of Jackson's presidential campaign. Part of the problem, of course, was that Jackson mortgaged the Rainbow and his own ambitions to the reconstruction of the Democratic Party as a hegemonic force, which is what has given us in the United States Bill Clinton as the "left-wing of the possible." But is there a way to imagine the possibility of Rainbow in terms of Mouffe and Laclau's second political logic: the logic of the people versus power bloc contradiction?

There is no question that the kind of politics represented by the new social movements—that is, politics based in civil society around forms of public voluntary association that depend on the sorts of positional differentiation of interests and values Mouffe and Laclau theorize—are effective in drawing people into action. By contrast, the blueprints for the reconstruction of the left along neo-Fabian, social-democratic lines suggested by books like Todd Gitlin's *The Twilight of Common Dreams* or Richard Rorty's *Achieving Our Country* seem more often than not a matter of getting the middle and upper classes to agree to higher taxes in return for a modicum of social peace; they depend moreover on a kind of Habermasian belief in the primacy of rational dialogue in politics, which in turn assumes a culturally homogenous public.[15]

On the other hand, whatever their strong points in actually mobilizing people, the new social movements remain essentially in the position of "petitioning" the state and power structures from a position of subordination, as Iris Marion Young, who is one of the sharpest theorists of their form and practice, puts it.[16] That is, like Guha's peasant rebellions, they are not hegemonic, they do not address the possibility of changing structural relations of power and control over resources. They depend on the additive logic of *and . . . and . . . and* that Mouffe and Laclau identify in the Rainbow, where the identity and value claims of the one can only be made in distinction to the many, even where solidarity and membership in a larger group are present in principle. It may be enough to mention in this regard the very ambiguous ideological consequences in the United States of the O. J. Simpson trial.[17]

In his *Critique of Dialectical Reason*, Jean-Paul Sartre called the tendency of a group (say, a group of people waiting for a bus) to decompose into separate subgroups or individuals "serialization." What makes serialization all the more debilitating in terms of constructing a hegemonic position from the left, of course, is that it is the instrumental reason of the state, not to speak of corporate merchandising and advertising strategies, to separate populations into classifiable identity groups. That is why for Fraser, mainstream multiculturalism is the "cultural analogue of the liberal welfare state" (87).

Is there, however, a potential implicit in the new social movements and multiculturalism that is not simply additive? That is, is it possible to unify subaltern identities into a "popular" bloc that can oppose frontally the structure of power and actually rearrange the way in which social inequality is created and maintained? It is not only that race and gender issues are "bivalent," as Fraser puts it (76–82)—that is, they involve at the same time a cultural-recognition aspect, and an economic-redistributive one. There is also a heuristic or probabilistic element that enters into the calculation of their effects. It is impossible to determine, independent of concrete struggle, what the horizons of a particular group or class interest are. I believe (but I can't prove), for example, that the demands for cultural recognition and equality of the indigenous communities in Ecuador I talked about in the last chapter or of African Americans in the United States are ultimately incompatible with the expanded reproduction of capitalism. That is, the realization of these demands will require a new mode of production, which I understand basically as a new hegemonic value structure. But it depends finally on the demands. If the demands are essentially for equality of opportunity—equal rights—then they can be contained within neoliberal hegemony; indeed, in some ways they require the market and legislative "interest group" politics to articulate themselves as democratic subject-positions. But if they are demands for *actual* cultural, economic, epistemological, and politico-civic equality, then they will go beyond the possibility of being contained within that hegemony.

In one way, the logic of a politics of difference—identity politics—points in the direction of assuming that hegemony—whether this is thought as "taking" or "becoming" state power—is no longer a possibility, since there is no common ground to constitute the requisite popular subject-position. In Foucauldian fashion, power is understood instead as a relation diffused through all social spaces and practices rather than being centered in the state and the ISAs. Mouffe and Laclau note in this respect that, "if each struggle transforms the moment of its specificity into an absolute principle of identity, the set of these struggles can only be conceived of as an *absolute system of differences*, and this system can only be thought as a closed totality" (*Hegemony* 182). On the other hand, the assertion of any particular identity claim—to the extent that all such claims are predicated on relations of subordination and marginality that derive from features of the history and structure of capitalism itself—must in fact involve, if only tacitly or in a displaced way, a common ground, which Mouffe and Laclau call an "egalitarian imaginary." Thus,

> Pluralism is *radical* only to the extent that each term of this plurality of identities finds within itself the principle of its own validity, without this having to be sought in a transcendant or underlying positive ground for the hierarchy of meaning of them all and the source and guarantee of their legitimacy. . . . [But] this radical pluralism is *democratic* to the extent that the autoconstitutivity of each of its terms is the result of displacements of the egalitarian imaginary. Hence, the project for a radical and plural democracy, *in a primary sense*, is nothing other than the struggle for a maximum autonomization of spheres on the basis of the generalization of the equivalential-egalitarian logic. (*Hegemony* 167)

In their concept of an "egalitarian imaginary" Mouffe and Laclau mean to allude to Charles Taylor's claim—in the essay that is also Fraser's source for her idea of "recognition"—that multiculturalism involves a "presumption of equal worth."[18] In a recent discussion of this essay, Homi Bhabha has noted that, for Taylor, such a presumption "does not participate in the universal language of cultural value . . . for it focuses exclusively on recognition of the excluded." In other words, the presumption cannot be dictated by an ethical principle that exists prior to the claim of cultural recog-

nition itself. Rather, the presumption depends on what Taylor calls a "pro-
cessual judgement" that involves working through cultural difference to
arrive at a new "fusion of horizon." But, Bhabha counters, such a

> working through cultural difference in order to be transformed by the
> other is not as straightforwardly open to the other as it sounds. For
> the possibility of the "fusion of horizon" of standards—the *new* stan-
> dard of judgement—is not all that new; it is founded on the notion of
> the dialogic subject of culture that we had *precisely at the beginning* of the
> whole argument. . . . that makes the fusing of horizons a largely
> consensual and homogenizing norm of cultural value or worth, based
> on the notion that cultural difference is fundamentally synchronous.[19]

What is clear in Bhabha's point about the nonsynchrony of difference is
that it is not an abstract ethical or epistemological "principle" that drives
the "presumption of equal worth": it is rather the *specific* character of the
various relations of subordination, exploitation, and marginalization produced by the history of capitalist modernity itself, involving as it does at all
moments racism and Eurocentrism, colonialism, the destruction or displacement of native and colonial populations, waves of mass immigration,
combined and uneven development, boom and bust cycles, the inability of
liberalism to produce women's equality, and so on. This equation between
identity demands and the structural features of capitalism itself is why
Mouffe and Laclau see "radical democracy" as the fundamental strategy of
the left: pushing identity demands in both their redistributive and recognition aspects to the point where they begin to become (or seem) incompatible with the structural matrix of capitalist hegemony and the functional relation of the state with capitalist interests. The identification they make between political radicalization and "maximum autonomization of spheres"
implies, among other things, "broaden[ing] the domain of the exercise for
democratic rights beyond the limited traditional field of 'citizenship.' . . .
Against those champions of economic liberalism who affirm that the economy is the domain of the 'private,' the seat of natural rights, and that the
criteria of democracy have no reason to be applied within it, socialist theory
defends the right of the social agent to equality and to participation as a
producer and not only as a citizen" (*Hegemony* 185). By contrast, if Bhabha is
right, the thrust of Taylor's position is to recode multiculturalism within
the possibilities offered by the existing institutional-ideological superstructure of globalized capital, including the academy.

Mouffe and Laclau's point about a "plurality of struggles and democratic
demands" means that it is wrong to want to dissolve the positional identity

of this or that social movement or "recognition" demand into the identity of the people or the "working class," because the social movement depends on that positional identity for its articulation and force: the identity is what Lacan called a "point of capture" for libidinal cathexis (point of capture—*point de capiton*—is like those buttons on a mattress which inflect the undifferentiated plane of its surface). That is why the currently fashionable claim (in, for example, Gitlin's *The Twilight of Common Dreams* or Rorty's *Achieving Our Country*, mentioned earlier), that a left politics must eschew identity politics and rights claims as antithetical to "building bridges," is ultimately a middle-class fantasy that simply puts the left on the other, or redistributive side, of the recognition/redistribution dilemma Fraser outlines.

On the other hand, for the left to construct a hegemonic politics *from* subaltern positionalities, identity politics or rights claims have to be articulated in a way that goes beyond liberal multiculturalism. These demands have to be pushed to a limit where they come to be (or seem) incompatible with the perceived needs of capital and of its ideological superstructure. If this can be done, then it would be possible to produce out of these demands, which are by definition contingent, heterogenous, and differentiated, the "collective will" (Gramsci) of a popular subject-position. The various subaltern positionalities would come to understand that the possibility of realizing *their* specific demands is contingent on entering into an alliance with the others to invert the structure of hegemony or domination that makes them subaltern in the first place. What makes it possible for them to enter into this general relation of equivalence, instead of seeing their affirmation of their own identity claims as necessarily autonomous and differential, is that *qua* subaltern, these identity claims contain necessarily a moment of negation that is subversive of *any* claim to hierarchical authority. Even the trope of simple inversion—the first shall be last and the last first, "we have been naught, we shall be all"—which, as Guha shows, often underlies subaltern agency—has at its core a displaced form of the egalitarian imaginary (for if the relation of master and slave can be reversed, then these are simply "roles" and not ontological destinies). In other words, the "egalitarian imaginary" is an essential ("strategically"?), rather than a contingent, aspect of subaltern identity.

Does the "egalitarian imaginary" imply in turn, however, a kind of tacit universalism and a "universal citizen" who can represent the plurality and serve as the articulating principle of alliances, as Mouffe herself argues?[21] Borrowing Iris Young's proposal that the idea of citizenship itself "has been constructed on a separation between the public and the private that has presented the public as the realm of homogeneity and universality while relegating difference to the private," María Milagros López argues that it does not. Such a separation, she notes, "tends to erase the historical marks of oppression, and to oblige alliances among equals to start from scratch." Instead of basing itself on the idea of a public sphere "in which citizens leave behind their particular group affiliations and needs in order to discuss a presumed general interest or common good," the project of radical democracy should aim at the creation of what Young calls a *heterogenous public* that "provides the mechanisms for the effective representation of all voices." López adds: "While, for Mouffe, this risks essentialism, I find it more of a recognition of the historical, nonerasable nature of affiliations that are not subject to changes in formal theorizing and that recognize the importance of affectivity and desire."[22]

A potentially hegemonic articulation of the left would not seek to transcend the new social movements or identity politics, therefore, even in the way Mouffe or Laclau envision this. Instead, it would seek to organize them into something like a postmodernist version of the Popular Front. Would, however, that identity structure or *combinatoire* still articulate, like the historical Popular Front, the various identities as *national*—that is, in a "common" relation to the idea and "interests" of the nation? Does not their interpellation as such risk erasing their specificity (which may include, as in the case of the Miskitus in Nicaragua, a problematic relation to the "nation")? But here also reappears the question I noted earlier in this chapter of the *adequacy* of the nation-state as a territorial form under conditions of globalization. In the imperialist stage of capitalism, as Lenin thought of it, it made sense to see the nation-state as a subject with its own autonomous power of agency, since it was through the state that any number of functions necessary for Fordist corporations had to pass: tariffs and protectionist policies; immigration policy; control of prices and unlimited monopolies or cartels; access to raw materials and markets; labor and social security legislation; techno-bureaucratic infrastructure; the construction—via museums, monuments, education—of the national narrative itself. Conquest of the state meant conquest at least in principle of the "commanding heights" of both the economy and the juridical and ideological apparatuses. That was the point of Lenin's positing a "national" rather than simply a "class" dimension to the contradictions of monopoly capitalism on a global scale.

By contrast, globalization entails, as Spivak puts it, that

[t]he possibility of social redistribution is being taken away from the (of course, often recalcitrant and corrupt) nation-state; and therefore

the possibility of seeking constitutional redress. "Economic citizenship" (Sasskia Sassert)—authority and legitimacy—is passing into the
hands of finance capital markets and transnational corporations. . . .
Because the limits and openings of a particular civil society are classi-
cally tied to a single state, the transnationalization of global capital
requires a post-state system.[23]

Spivak argues that the consequences for the left of globalization are that
the "non-Eurocentric globe-girdling movements of Ecology, Bio-Diversity,
Women, and Alternative Development" are "the *new* face of socialism"
(21). "Euro-U.S. Socialism should acknowledge [them] as the major arena
of struggle against globalization," she claims. "When the United States of
Europe or America consider the future of the U.S. left or the European left
(somewhat more serious) in a restricted focus, they are engaging in a new
version of 'socialism in one "country," ' in a vanguardism that is the flip
side of exploitation" (20).

Spivak's point finds an echo in the idea that "[i]mmigration . . . is now
more than ever the site of the contradictions between the national state and
the global economy"[24] and in recent calls for a "new cosmopolitanism." I
will return shortly to these issues. For the moment, however, I simply want
to note that Spivak's "postnational" understanding of the political consequences of globalization dovetails with her sense of the subaltern as the
deconstructive supplement of the nation, which we sketched in chapter 4.
But the assumption, which she seems to share, that the nation-state was in
fact an autonomous, self-contained subject form in some earlier stage of
capitalism in a way that it is not any longer, is deeply problematic in some
ways. This can be shown, for example, by considering the complex relation
of the Russian revolution itself to the sphere of international capitalism.
From its inception to its eventual collapse, the problem of Soviet Communism was essentially how to construct and maintain a state-socialist economy in a world economy dominated by increasingly sophisticated and tech-
nologically advanced forms of capitalism. As is well known, this was the
key issue in the "socialism in one country" debate Spivak alludes to that led
to the rise of Stalinism in the 1930s. In a sense, the answer Stalin offered
(which in turn rested on the Bolshevik critique of Rosa Luxemburg's internationalism and Lenin's enthusiasm for Taylorism) was that socialism in
one country was possible, but it required the Soviet Union to become like
capitalism in the organization not only of production but of society as a
whole, via the mechanism of so-called "primitive socialist accumulation"
and forced industrialization. That mechanism, however, depended on the
coercive action of the state and party on the working population, especially,

but not only, the peasantry, which had the consequence of alienating significant sectors of that population from the socialist project, or at least what
they perceived as—and what called itself—socialism.

So, in a way, there is nothing particularly new about the effects of capitalist deterritorialization on the nation-state, except perhaps a new pessimism or realism about the possibility of "delinking" both economically
and ideologically from the global economy. In fact, it may be precisely the
partial disabling of the (illusion of) economic autonomy of the nation-
state by globalization that makes the nation-state even more compelling as
a form of territoriality for political-cultural articulation today. There are
two interrelated aspects to this paradox (which have something to do with
Althusser's point about the relative autonomy of the levels of the economic
and the political): first, the national (or local) state is perceived by populations as being susceptible to political-cultural mobilization, whereas the
overall structures and movement of global capital are not; second, the state
has, or, perhaps more importantly, is seen as possessing, the power to
limit or attenuate the consequences of the transnational demographic,
cultural, and capital flows produced by globalization. It is not a question of
being "for" or "against" globalization, then, but of how to position oneself
within globalization. Especially, but not only, in countries where the state
has had historically a tenuous hold on large sectors of the populations it
supposedly contains—as in parts of Latin America and Africa—globalization introduces this question: Even if the state did not "represent" you in
the past, who is now in the position to mediate between you and transnational power structures? Seen in this light, the role of the state and the
question of national "identity" may be prioritized rather than weakened by
globalization.

The loss of faith in and/or antagonism toward the state that is a real
enough feature of contemporary life (in one way or another we all share it)
needs to be reframed in the context of the relation of the state to the
requirements of capitalist political economy. In the post–World War II
long-cycle of capitalist growth, which lasted into the deep recession of the
early 1970s, the state functioned in classic Keynesian terms both as an
engine of accumulation and a means for distribution of wealth and resources through its own vast expansion. To keep accumulation going in
the post-Fordist context of the last quarter century, by contrast, has required a spectacular reduction of the distributive and regulatory functions
of the state. The consequence is that the state at all levels—never in the first
place exactly coincident with the people—is perceived as inefficient, inef-
fective, unrepresentative, hostile: a "cold monster." But this perception is
itself a determined effect of a central contradiction of capitalist hegemony,

whose "economic" requirements now include trashing the state by defunding and privatization at the same time that neoliberal ideology celebrates the mechanisms of the market and civil society over those of state planning. For neoliberalism, the state exists essentially to exercise a police and punitive function that establishes the rules of the game for "rational choice" in a market society. But the attack on the state is not only ideologically determined—that is, impelled by the hegemony of neoliberal political economy; the hegemony of neoliberalism itself expresses a new reality principle of capitalism in its present stage. The left needs to respond that it is not a question of the state as such, but of the (unmediated) subsumption of legitimate and useful state functions to capital logic. The problem is how to generate first the idea and then the institutional form of a different kind of state, one that would be driven by the democratic, egalitarian, multinational, multiethnic, and multicultural character of the people: that is, a "people-state."

An argument advanced by Michael Lind apropos the immigration debate in the United States seems to me pertinent in this regard.[25] Lind claims that to reconstitute itself as a hegemonic political force, the left (Lind himself prefers the idea of a center-left) needs to in effect reterritorialize the American nation-state. It must do this among other ways by reversing its usual policy of de facto tolerance of illegal immigration and supporting tighter controls on immigration generally. By introducing masses of new workers into the U.S. economy who are willing to work for very low wages or earnings and have difficulty organizing collectively, since many of them are undocumented and therefore juridically disenfranchised, more or less uncontrolled immigration constantly erodes the possibility of creating an antagonistic positionality of labor, women, African Americans, even the existing Latino and Asian populations. The contradiction that Lind identifies in the sort of baffled centrism represented by Clinton, whose political model is something like the pre–World War I Bismarckian state, is that it subsumes its political project under the requirements of globalization, which entail free flow of capital, information, technology, and labor. This "free flow" undermines, however, the interests of the very social groups— particularly organized labor and African Americans—who are expected to support Clinton politically.

It might be argued against Lind that his proposal runs the risks of fueling right-wing nativism and chauvinism, and that the negative consequences of unlimited capital mobility and uncontrolled immigration would be better addressed by the development or deepening of an international labor movement. It is not that such a movement is neither desirable nor possible. But even if it were to be in place generally—so that one could contemplate work actions that extended across national boundaries—it would not do the job of constituting a *specifically political* opposition to capitalist hegemony, either locally, nationally, regionally, or internationally. It would simply transfer the endemic limitation of trade unionism noted by Lenin in *What Is to Be Done?*—that it is not as such a form of hegemonic political agency—into transnational space.

It is of course also true, as the Sandinistas discovered to their dismay and eventual defeat, that in a world economy dominated by GATT treaties and IMF and World Bank stabilization and adjustment programs, the economic limits of what any government in power in a given nation-state can accomplish are extremely narrow (this has made *all* socialist governments currently or recently in power essentially accomplices of neoliberal economic policies). In this sense, international trade unionism and related transnational projects to resist or limit the power of capital can broaden the space for maneuvering at the national or local level (as would a cultural-intellectual formation such as the New International that Derrida calls for in *Spectres of Marx*). To move beyond the nation-state as a point of reference for left politics, as Spivak suggests, however, seems "ultra-leftist." Unless it is possible to imagine a new form of hegemony which no longer depends on the territoriality of the nation, hegemony is still to be won, or lost, at the level of the nation-state and/or the local state. To put this another way: hegemony still has to *pass through* the nation-state at some point or another.

Of course, one may renounce the idea of hegemony as irrelevant to the new types of political-cultural dynamics generated in and around globalization: that, as I have suggested, is in effect the position argued by Canclini and the theorists of civil society and the new social movements. But the consequences of renouncing the struggle for hegemony are to leave in place the actual hegemony of neoliberalism, which even nominally progressive or social-democratic governments are now obliged to respect. Spivak may be right about the problem of "socialism in one country," but the transnational social movements she appeals to cannot become themselves hegemonic unless they articulate themselves somehow to a national context (that context could of course be a national community rather than a nation in the formal sense, or a perception of the need or desire to create a new nation or national community). Failing that, they remain movements of "resistance"—items on an ethical wish-list of middle-class or elite political correctness in the metropolitan centers of power and accumulation.

To avoid the perhaps inevitable misunderstanding: I am not saying that there should not be an international labor movement, or that NGO's, U.N. peacekeeping forces, International Women's Day, Greenpeace, Amnesty International, and so on are not important or worth struggling over (and in). Nor, as I detail below, do I think that an anti-immigration platform is a good "point of capture" for the left in the United States or anywhere else for that matter. But Lind's argument at least has the virtue of forcing us to think about the place of the nation-state in globalization. By contrast, the appeals to affirmative action, solidarity with the poor, and mobilization around single issues or single constituency groups bring in their wake the problems Fraser suggests. By distributing political energies along a line of proliferation of difference in an era of declining real incomes, structural unemployment, and downward social mobility even in the so-called advanced democracies, such appeals in effect do the work of capitalism, but ask the left to pay the price for the tensions and contradictions that accumulate.[26]

It is in trying to imagine an alternative that would unite a "politics of difference" with Mouffe and Laclau's "egalitarian imaginary" that I come to the most tentative, but also perhaps the most important part of my argument. Let me return to Gramsci's question about the relation of the nation-state as a legal-territorial entity and political-cultural hegemony. Generally, the articulation of the people/power bloc antagonism positions the people *against* the existing state, which is seen as the instrument of an oligarchy, a dominant class, foreign interests, or the like. A similar understanding is latent in the assumption in subaltern studies of the incommensurability between the subaltern and the nation-state. To construct the people/power bloc antagonism today, under the conditions of globalization and in the face of the neoliberal critique and privatization of state functions, requires, by contrast, a *relegitimization* of the state. That is, the project of the left, to the extent that it embodies subaltern will and agency, has to be posed paradoxically as a *defense* of the nation-state, rather than as something that is "against" or "beyond" the nation-state. Of course, what is entailed in this defense is also (to repeat) the need for a new kind of state.

What constitutes the unity of the national-popular for Gramsci is the putative identity between the interests of the people and the nation (which is why he sometimes uses the expression "people-nation" in place of national-popular). The relation between the terms national and popular is one of a moving equilibrium that can shift ideologically one way or another depending on who controls their representation. In the case of Italian history, Gramsci claims, the nation had been more a legal and rhetorical concept elaborated by intellectual and economic elites than a genuine cultural experience at the level of popular life: "people" and "nation" were disarticulated, in other words. But the disarticulation of the national and the popular or subaltern can also take the form of a disarticulation of the nation and the state.

Populist interpellation, as Laclau showed in a seminal essay,[27] involves picturing the integrity of the nation or national community as undermined in some way or another by the interests represented by the power bloc that controls (usually by an alleged act of usurpation) the machinery of the state. What the power bloc concretely is, in class or social identity terms—mandarinate, feudal aristocracy, oligarchy, colonial administration, capitalist class, comprador bourgeoisie, foreign interests, multinational finance capital and corporations, and so on—depends on the class-ideological character of the interpellation, which can range from religious fundamentalism, to fascism and various kinds of right-wing nationalism, to the New Deal Democratic Party in the United States, to social-democratic formations like British Labour, to Maoism or Sandinism.

In the case of Popular Front antifascist politics, the "people-nation" as such is interpellated as threatened in its collective and individual identities by the interests of certain (not all) capitalist or elite groups, both within the nation (the comprador bourgeoisie and landlords, "finance capital"), and outside it (foreign interests, military invasion, colonialism or imperialism). As we saw in the case of the Sandinistas, however, national-popular interpellation as such risks creating or reinforcing a narrative of national unity and identity that excludes or may exclude significant sectors of the population (and by excludes is implied for all practical purposes: makes them subaltern or resubalternizes them).

Stanley Aronowitz describes the resulting dilemma as follows:

> Gramsci's argument that the left must address itself to the national as an affirmative instance of what Benedict Anderson has called "imagined communities" seems, from the point of view of colonial subjects, an invitation to disaster. . . . The invocation of an affirmative national culture is ineluctably a category of *exclusion* . . . used . . . against immigrants, most recently from the south. . . . The validity of this critique from a subaltern standpoint seems undeniable. "Euro" or "national" communism signifies, ineluctably, the power of the nation and its culture as opposed to class, race, or gender identities, the other side of which is ethnocentrism. . . . Yet, Gramsci's question remains. If one of the crucial tasks on the road to social transformation is to gain moral and intellectual leadership within the boundaries of the nation-state, how can the left, in the broadest connotation, avoid the claim that they are the genuine legatees of both the democratic intellectual traditions and the best of its cultural achievements?[28]

Recalling Iris Young's idea, noted earlier, of a "heterogenous public," I think the best way to answer Aronowitz's question is to say that the "people-nation" should be understood as *essentially* heterogenous in character. In this way, multiculturalism—seen as one of the constitutive features of "the people" as such—can be detached from its subsumption as a form of liberal pluralism and made into a signifier for the potential anticorporate, anticapitalist unity of the popular subject-position. (In its initial formulations at least, the idea of multiculturalism incorporated explicitly the emphasis placed in subaltern studies on social inequality and disadvantage.)[29]

Positing "the people" as heterogenous and multicultural dispels the anxiety registered in Lind's argument about immigration, since there is no identity that is specifically and exclusively "national." This is *not* the same thing, however, as appealing to a liberal narrative of immigrant assimilation or toleration. That is because the bloc of the people—if it is to be defined by multiculturalism—is formed: (1) not only by non-national immigrants who have "become" national, but also by *non-immigrants* (in the Americas in general indigenous peoples and in the United States in particular many Hispanics are non-immigrants, and African Americans are involuntary immigrants—they didn't, on the whole, come here because they thought the Americas were better societies); (2) not only by legal residents, but also by undocumented subjects (that is, by citizens and non-citizens); and (3) not only by subject-positions formed in the dominant "national" culture and language, but also by those still tied to other territorialities, other languages, other value-systems, other—nonsynchronous—historicities.

Bonnie Honig argues that the idea of the United States as a "nation of immigrants"—that is, precisely the sort of "liberal" argument that might be used against Lind—ends up paradoxically also naturalizing the nativist belief that the country is a "special" society, based on choice, not inheritance, on civic not ethnic ties. Reviewing contrasting readings of the biblical story of Ruth by Cynthia Ozick and Julia Kristeva, Honig shows how for each writer, in a different way, Ruth becomes the "model immigrant."[30] To recall the essential details of the story: Ruth is from a gentile tribe, the Moabites. She marries into a Hebrew family that had itself immigrated out of Israel in search of work. On the death of her husband, Ruth pledges loyalty to her mother-in-law, Naomi, and decides to go back to Israel with her—a choice that, not incidentally, gives rise to the Davidic dynasty that founds the first Hebrew state. Her sister, Orpah, on the other hand, remains behind, faithful to her tribe and its gods.

Honig notes that, for Ozick, Ruth's choice "remarks the Israelites as the Chosen People, a people worthy of being chosen. Here the immigrant's choice of 'us' makes us feel good about who we are" (9). For Ozick, Ruth is the supplement—the non-Hebrew, the gentile—who nevertheless reinvigorates and completes the social-cultural order of the tribe, permitting it to become a nation. By contrast, for Kristeva (in a book significantly titled *Nations without Nationalism*), Ruth "unsettles the order she joins . . . because she disabuses [the Israelites'] fantasies of identity and makes them more open to difference and otherness" (7). Ruth does this by becoming an other herself, by converting and assimilating to Judaism. But she is never wholly that other. Her "foreignness" is not incidental to her role in rehabilitating the dynasty, and it remains as a troubling mark in the dynasty's future claims to legitimacy.

For Kristeva, the story of Ruth allegorizes a new kind of cosmopolitanism that transcends traditional boundaries of identity, whether these be "national," religious, or otherwise. As Honig notes, "Ruth is the model immigrant for Kristeva . . . because of Ruth's willingness to swear fidelity to Naomi, her people, and her god. Kristeva's cosmopolitanism depends on similar pledges of allegiance from French citizens and immigrants alike" (23), in a new framework of citizenship in which "the nation is still an important but not all-encompassing site of identity" (24). As such, Ruth serves Kristeva as a normative example "for those contemporary Moslem immigrants [to France] who tend to resist absorption into their receiving regimes"—for example, Moslem women who insist in wearing the veil and chador in French schools. Since Kristeva (herself an immigrant to France from Rumania) sees French national identity as centered not on *Volk* but on compact, Moslem women should accept the regulations of the society they are part of, and should not mark themselves off from it radically; vice versa, since "being French" is not a matter of ethnic or *volkish* identity, there should be no reason for the existing population of France not to accept the new immigrants as French. But, as Honig points out, this "cosmopolitanism" is attached by Kristeva specifically to the idea of a general spirit (*esprit general*) in Montesquieu and the Enlightenment: that is, it is a "French" form of cosmopolitanism, which paradoxically "works to shore up a uniquely French identity, even while claiming to overcome or transcend it."

Both Kristeva's and Ozick's readings of the story of Ruth are, Honig concludes, "part of a completion paradigm, in which the immigrant is judged in terms of what she will do for—or to—us." The completion paradigm works the other way too, in the sense that it also embodies a narrative of self-overcoming. For both Kristeva and Ozick, the story is a bildungsroman—a narrative allegory of the transition from gemeinschaft to gesellschaft, family to tribe, tribe to state, tradition to modernity (hence the importance for both of Ruth's conversion and assimilation to Judaism, as opposed to her sister Orpah's decision to remain faithful to her household gods). But, "the community that sees immigrants as a source of its own completion is the *same* community that—on a different day or with regard to different immigrants—will see the Other as a threat to the regime's completeness, a source of dilution and conflict. That is because it is the *same* feature, the immigrant's foreignness, that motivates each response" (10).

For Honig, by contrast, the story of Ruth "figures the deep undecidability of the immigrant" and therefore a radically different sense of national community and belonging, which she calls "democratic cosmopolitanism":

> A democratic cosmopolitanism must break with the completion paradigm that governs Ozick's and Kristeva's readings of Ruth and it must resist the re-enchantment of the nation-state (France) from which Kristeva's cosmopolitanism takes too much of its energy. It is not enough to replace *Volk* with compact, national identity with *esprit général*, for these replacements rework the binary of particularity versus universality. Instead, the binary must be broken and multiple sites of differentiated but perhaps compatible universalities must be explored and enacted from within and among the many particularities that constitute us. (27)

It goes without saying that what Honig calls the "perpetual public anxiety about national identity and unity" is, like multiculturalism itself, the consequence or superstructural effect of the contradictions of both colonialism and capitalist globalization. In other words, it is not enough to appeal, as Honig does, simply to an ethical-epistemological ideal and to the corresponding possibility of new legal arrangements (Honig supports, for example, the idea of alien suffrage and forms of institutional transnationalism like Sister City relationships that are associational and affective at the same time). It is not enough, but at the same time it is necessary.

I am suggesting here that what would be required beyond Honig's "democratic cosmopolitanism" is a hegemonic political-cultural project founded on the principle of multiculturalism and interclass equality *within* the territoriality of the nation as well as *between* national territorialities. Here my argument rejoins Bhabha's in "DissemiNation":

> The barred Nation It/*Self*, alienated from its eternal self-generation, becomes a liminal form of social representation, a space that is *internally* marked by cultural difference and the heterogeneous histories of contending peoples, antagonistic authorities, and tense cultural locations. . . . The nation reveals, in its own ambivalent and vacillating representation, the ethnography of its own historicity and opens up the possibility of other narratives of the people and difference. The

people turn *pagan* in that disseminatory act of social narrative that Lyotard defines, against the Platonic tradition, as the privileged pole of the *narrated*. . . . Once the liminality of the nation-space is established, and its "difference" is turned from a boundary "outside" to its finitude "within," the threat of cultural difference is no longer a problem of "other" people. It becomes a question of the otherness of the people-as-one. The national subject splits in the ethnographic perspective of culture's contemporaneity and provides both a theoretical position and a narrative authority for marginal voices of minority discourse. They no longer need to address their strategies of opposition to a horizon of "hegemony" that is envisaged as horizontal and homogenous.[31]

Why don't the "marginal voices of minority discourse" need to address themselves to a "horizon of 'hegemony' "? As he signals by referring to Lyotard's idea of the pagan, Bhabha is here trying to get at a sense of a collective social subject that is never completely totalizable as the people-as-one but nevertheless has effects on power. This subject is perhaps akin to what Paolo Virno calls the "multitude." In terms of the "multitude," hegemony is simply a screen onto which privileged groups—and intellectuals above all—project their anxiety about being displaced by a heterogenous, multiform popular subject.[32]

Where Bhabha/Virno see the constitution of the people/multitude as happening outside of formal politics—beyond hegemony, on the limits of the nation's narrative, and in "the incommensurable time of the subject of culture"—my concern here, by contrast, is whether it might be possible to create a counter-hegemonic "politics of the people" out of a cultural "politics of difference." Bhabha's argument—despite its claim to theorize a "non-pluralistic politics of difference" (305)—ends up theorizing in effect Laclau and Mouffe's democratic subject-position, where (to recall) "the proliferation of points of antagonism permits the multiplication of democratic struggles, but these struggles, given their diversity, do not tend to constitute a 'people.' " But there has to be an ultimate horizon that both identity politics and something like Honig's "democratic cosmopolitanism" have to address: that horizon is the hegemony of capitalism itself as a mode of production, to the degree that that hegemony implies necessarily the creation and perpetuation of the forms of social and cultural inequality that fuel identity politics.

The question of capitalist hegemony leaves me with the need to say something about the market. At one point in his autobiography, Althusser states that for him communism means essentially and necessarily a society in which all market relations have been transcended.[33] I am a follower of Althusser in many ways, but not in this. I share with Canclini and cultural studies the belief that in social formations characterized by combined and uneven development (and what social formation is not?), in which one form or another of precapitalist cultural stratification defined by a marked separation between intellectuals and the popular sectors of the sort Gramsci diagnosed in Italian history has prevailed, the commodification of cultural production through the operation of the market and the technologies of commercial mass culture can be a means of cultural democratization and redistribution of cultural use-values, allowing not only new modes of cultural consumption but also increased access to the means of cultural production by subaltern social subjects. By contrast, the cultural policies undertaken by both the Soviet model of state socialism and the various forms of populist nationalism in Latin America and elsewhere imply the perpetuation of a cultural ideology founded on the norms of literature and high culture—an ideology that maintains a close affinity with bourgeois humanism and, in the case of Latin America, with colonial or neocolonial cultural castes.

The work of subaltern studies on peasants abounds with cases where the market is a space in which subaltern territoriality is performatively enacted; where families and friends, peasants and artisans from different villages get together; where (as we saw in chapter 2) stories, rumor, and gossip pass from lip to lip; where agitators circulate among the crowd; where the exigencies of work give way to festive consumption and parodic debunking of authority. But, although a recognition of the democratic and even subversive function of the market may share certain elements with the neoliberal critique of state ownership and planning, it does not depend on an identification of the market with capitalism, nor is it a defense of the idea of civil society as the source of all that is good and valuable in our lives. As I argued in my critique of Canclini, the celebration of civil society and consumption-as-resistance, by making it seem that the key contradiction is the contradiction between civil society as such (seen as heterogenous, multitemporal, etc.) and the state (seen as unitary, monistic, etc.) is faulty in two ways: (1) it obscures the fact that control of the state is still ultimately what is at stake in power struggles between contending classes and social groups; and (2) it defers the need to think the logic of contradiction—of class, gender, race, ethnicity, religious identity—within what is being posited as civil society itself.

In taking up the question of the market, it is crucial to distinguish the market as *marketplace*—that is, as a liminal institution—from the market as something that under capitalism, as Hegel argued, becomes coextensive with society as such.[34] Guha and the subaltern studies historians mean, of course, the market as marketplace, not "market-society"—*burgerliche gesellschaft*. Nor is what I am trying to imagine here exactly the same thing as "market socialism."[35] The enterprises that would function as economic actors in market socialism would tend to bend to the law of value in their organization of labor productivity in order to survive competitively. But, if my argument is correct, a genuinely egalitarian society cannot be articulated hegemonically at the level of the economic by the capitalist law of value, because that would be to deny other forms of value that are not based on the commodification of socially necessary labor time and the hierarchical organization of work that it entails (similarly, the idea of "rational choice" Marxism that often accompanies the argument for market socialism likewise universalizes *one* form of rationality and subjectivity—that of "possessive individualism"—at the expense of others). Such a society must retain at its core a dominant area of social property and services, regulated by and through the state in favor of the diverse interests and values embedded in the popular bloc. This is not to say that those interests are or will be non-contradictory; but they are contradictory in a way that is different from the contradiction between the interests of "the people" and those of capitalist hegemony.

The question then is not the free market versus state planning, private versus collective ownership, consumption versus production, but rather whose interests are being hegemonically articulated in *both* the state and civil society: that is, it is a question of "politics in command." In particular, to say, as I do above, that market mechanisms can have in some cases a democratizing effect does not mean that everything must be ruled by the market (or that markets must be ruled by the law of value). It will be news to no one that, contrary to the claims of Milton Friedman and the Chicago School about the relationship between the free market and democracy, neoliberal political economy fits with some of the most reactionary and authoritarian regimes in the world today, in fact often requires such regimes for its effective implementation (this was, and to some extent still is, the lesson of Chile). That coincidence is one basis for the argument that capitalist hegemony in globalization is pushing in the direction of more repressive forms of social control and exploitation. Just as state-power is the political-legal precondition of neoliberalism—as Gramsci saw[36]—state-power is also the precondition of economic forms articulated by a multicultural, popular-democratic hegemony. Among other reasons, the state would have to exercise a redistributive-repressive function both to assure economic equality and to keep relations of production that depend on class or group inequality from reasserting themselves on the level of individual enterprises or of society as a whole.

The ability of the state to perform this function entails the need to nationalize (or "socialize") and democratize internally large areas of social production. But this is not the same thing as the abolition of the market. The market is not an institution exclusive to capitalism, nor do market relations as such define capitalism as a mode of production. Here I can do no more than mention the famous debate about whether it is changes in market relations or in the relations of production—that is, the special character of wage-labor as a commodity—that are decisive in the transition from feudalism to capitalism.[37] While capitalism passes through the market, indeed makes society itself coextensive with the market (this was the reason Marx himself, in the chapter on primitive accumulation in *Capital*, saw the modern nation-state as the necessary precondition of capitalism and vice versa), the market is not coextensive with capitalism or for that matter with regimes of class exploitation generally. There are relations of class exploitation that do not depend on market relations: for example, feudal relations. By the same token, there are market relations that do not depend on the law of value (at least, in the form it takes in capitalism), and that can be noncapitalist or even anticapitalist, as in the case of trade relations between (or within) so-called primitive communist societies. A generalized social regime of petty commodity production, such as existed in embryo in the North of the United States at the time of the American revolution, and, in principle at least, in the repressed plan of Radical Reconstruction after the Civil War (which aimed at making both ex-slaves and landless whites a self-reliant free peasantry in the South through confiscation and redistribution of the estates of the slave-owning oligarchy) is in a formal sense a classless society; but it entails a society that not only includes but in a sense depends on market-exchange relations. What is true in the case of a regime of intertribal exchange or petty commodity production is not that there are *no* market relations, but that an exchange-value logic *other* than that governing capitalist exploitation and accumulation is being expressed in them.[38]

One should not assume, therefore, an automatic relation among cultural commodification, the market, popular reception of mass culture, and democratization. The democratic character of the "national" culture will depend on the precise character of the articulation of the bloc of the people and its concrete incidence on the ideological apparatuses of the local and national state—including especially the education system, the cultural institutions and industries both inside and outside the state—and on the

effects of this incidence in the creation of popular festivals and entertain-
ments, social goals and values, and ultimately the narrative of national
identity and purpose itself.

By way of conclusion, and also as a way of bridging the North American
and Latin American dimensions of my concerns, I would like to ask what it
means today to articulate pedagogically the identity "American" in the
context of the rapid Hispanization—in both demographic and cultural-
linguistic terms—of U.S. society, a process I have alluded to several times in
the course of this book. I will use as reference points an op-ed article in the
Chronicle of Higher Education titled "Integrating Ethnicity into American Studies," by Sean Wilentz, the director of the program in American studies at
Princeton University, which might be said to embody a "hybrid" or neo-
Melting Pot idea of Americanism, and the syllabus for a team-taught
course called "American Identities" developed by Sacvan Bercovitch and
Doris Sommer at Harvard, which might be said to embody Honig's idea of
"democratic cosmopolitanism."[39] What underlies the anxiety about multiculturalism reflected in both documents is that the "liberal" narrative of
immigrant acculturation and assimilation that Honig critiques in fact does
not work for U.S. Latinos.[40]

Wilentz begins his piece with a pointed reference to the way in which
"with the arrival of record numbers of Latino and Asian American students
in the 80s interest in the study of ethnicity rose—with a harder separatist
edge than two decades earlier." Thus, "American studies programs have
become embroiled in the recent clashes over multiculturalism and diversity
in the curriculum." After a passing slap at the legacy of the New Left,
Wilentz notes that "[t]he study of ethnicity, like the study of race, in turn
became entangled in a postmodernist outlook that blamed Western rationality, universalism, and humanism for the subjugation of non-whites
(and for some writers, white women) by white men. This led students and
scholars to depict the United States chiefly in terms of ethnic (or racial)
identities and antagonisms."

Against the rise of ethnic studies, which seek to defend their cultures
"from assimilation into a hegemonic mainstream 'American' civilization,"
Wilentz declares:

> American studies at Princeton, while rejecting older parochial ideas
> about American culture, has moved in a different direction. . . . We
> fear, as the historian Arthur M. Schlesinger, Jr., has observed, that
> fixation on ethnic differences presents a distorted picture of the
> United States as a country that is all "pluribus" and no "unum." We

are equally convinced, however, that an ethnic or racial approach, narrowly conceived, does not do justice to the numerous ethnic and racial components of American culture. . . . And although the United States may not be a melting pot, neither its culture nor that of its ethnic groups is pristine. To paraphrase the writer Ralph Ellison, Americans are all "cultural mulattos."

Wilentz's appeal to "cultural mulattos" recalls the hybridity argument in Canclini and (perhaps less so) in Bhabha, because like the hybridity argument it subordinates the representation of social difference to a narrative of cultural assimilation and modernization in which previous antagonisms are sublated. It makes as a model for American culture the "crossover": almost inevitably, the cultural form Wilentz puts forward as a normative example is jazz. But the aesthetic-ideological force of "crossover" derives from the fact that two or more different, and sometimes antagonistic, cultural codes are being simultaneously enacted in the performance or artifact. This can suggest, rather than "fusion," the continuing pertinence of interethnic or interclass antagonisms, or the possibility of a cross-ethnic alliance politics in which differences are respected.

The course of American Identities taught by Doris Sommer and Sacvan Bercovitch at Harvard starts, by contrast, with the recognition that the Americas, including the United States, are a postcolonial space, subject to the same contradictory heterogeneity that characterizes other postcolonial territorialities.[41] Here is part of their preamble for the course syllabus:

American means different things, depending on the languages one speaks and the geographical or racial position of the speaker. It can mean a citizen of the United States or belonging to any part of the New World, center or periphery. The overlap and resulting competitions over the name and meaning of America is the subject of this course. Essays, poems, and narrative prose from Anglo-America and Ibero-America will suggest the terms of parallel or competing cultural constructions—as extensions of "old world" cultures, as subjects of indigenous developments, and as determined by mass displacements of Europeans, Africans and migrating Americans.

The course deploys along parallel lines readings and films in a more or less chronological sequence, from the era of discovery and conquest, the colonial period, the fight for independence, and the abolition of slavery, to the rise of capitalism, imperialism, and modernity. The colonial section pairs Puritan father John Winthrop's 1630 essay "A Model of Christian Charity" with selections from Bartolomé de las Casas's *Brief History of the Destruction* of the Indies (1542); the independence section pairs Thomas Jefferson's "Declaration of Independence" with Simón Bolívar's "Letter from Jamaica"; the nineteenth-century section Walt Whitman's "Song of Myself" with José Martí's essay on Whitman (one of the foundational texts of modern Latin American poetry), and Jorge Isaacs's romance María with James Fenimore Cooper's The Prairie (both as "foundational fictions" of creole nationalism); the modernity section William Faulkner's Absalom, Absalom! and Juan Rulfo's Pedro Paramo, both novels about how capitalist modernity displaces an earlier agrarian, village-based mode of production (Faulkner was a major influence on Latin American "boom" writers like Gabriel García Marquéz). I, Rigoberta Menchú is read against Richard Rodriguez's Hunger of Memory (as I have here). Other materials, including the Narrative of the Life of Frederick Douglass and the Disney film Pocahontas, explore the relation between the idea of America and the institution of slavery and the genocide and repression of the indigenous peoples.

I have no doubt that Wilentz would reply that this is just the sort of approach he has in mind, since Sommer and Bercovitch do not propose to look at ethnicity "in isolation."[42] But I would argue that in their vision of America as a site of multiple and sometimes competing discourses, Sommer and Bercovitch stress the antagonistic as well as the hybrid or transcultured character of American identity (and also issues of class, gender, and racial inequality and antagonism within both hegemonic North American and Latin American discourses of identity). In the design of their course, non-European indigenous, Latin American, Asian, African, Jewish identities are not just sublated into a larger, more all-embracing mixed or "mulatto" or creolized identity. They are not governed, in other words, by what Honig calls the "completion paradigm"; they have their own competing and continuing claims to historical, aesthetic, and epistemological authority. At the same time, they are all—as subaltern identities— connected in one way or another to something like what Mouffe and Laclau mean by the "egalitarian imaginary." They carry the implication (and the possibility), therefore, of a politics and ultimately a sense of the nation itself that would have to recognize and base itself on the principle of multicultural egalitarianism. By contrast, despite his own liberal credentials, Wilentz's defense of what he calls "hegemonic Americanism" seems a reactive if not reactionary response to the problem of multiculturalism which forestalls our ability, through our work, to make the academy, the media, and the arts environments where the possibility of a new historic bloc can emerge in American life.[43]

What is discouraging about Wilentz's position is also what is discouraging about the near unanimity of U.S. public intellectuals on the ebonics question. As in the neoconservative assault on bilingual education, it is forgotten that the point of such programs is to make the student eventually proficient in at least two languages, one of which is standard English (in other words, such programs establish bilingualism as a norm students should aspire to rather than a deficit they should overcome as soon as possible). The ebonics controversy highlights—and this was no doubt the intention of the Oakland school board in proposing the program—the fact that under the existing system of education, every Latino, every African America, every indigenous child, every child from a working-class or poor family, is made to feel disqualified and dysfunctional the minute he or she enters the classroom. For if to "become American" requires the suppression of a prior identity, language or dialect, and the corresponding values, it makes apprenticeship in European-based middle- or upper-class culture and values a de facto condition for citizenship: that is, it effectively (and for all practical purposes, permanently) disenfranchises significant sectors of the population. The sectors it disenfranchises are precisely the subaltern in U.S. terms.

This brings me back to the impasse in Gramsci's attempt to formulate the relation of subalternity, education, and hegemony: if the subaltern has to become us or like us to be hegemonic, what will have really changed? I have worked for thirty years at an urban public university in a city ravaged by deindustrialization. Despite my deep respect for what Sommer and Bercovitch are trying to do, I would not like to conclude this book with the idea that a course being taught at Harvard or Princeton can provide a good answer to this question. In this way, I inflect my own, admittedly relative, subalternity and ressentiment in my argument. Sommer and Bercovitch are willing to put "under erasure" many aspects of American identity in their course, but not the very ground of authority from which they speak. Their course cannot contain a critique of Harvard itself as an institution tied to the reproduction of class and other hierarchies of power in the United States, or of U.S. hegemony over the rest of the world, including Latin America and the Caribbean. Ultimately, their appeal, like Honig's, is an ethical rather than a political one: to become more aware of others, more tolerant and respectful of difference. (For Bercovitch in particular, the role of dissenting discourses in American life is to restore and renew its foundational liberalism.)[44]

I have tried to argue here that subaltern studies as a project within the academy is not so much preoccupied with the articulation of multiculturalism as a value in itself as with bringing to a critical point the antagonisms created by the social relations of inequality and exploitation inherent in multicultural difference. Institutions like Harvard are deeply involved in creating a new elite, which will look and think differently than the old elite. I do not mean to minimize the importance of this task; but I believe we will not have advanced very far if the concern with the subaltern results primarily in the creation of a new kind of multicultural yuppie, what in Miami is called (playing on the name of a root vegetable important in Caribbean cooking) a *yuca*: a young upwardly mobile Cuban American. The possibility of such an outcome is perhaps what the critics of subaltern studies I mentioned in the introduction have in mind when they see subaltern studies as an extension of the logic of U.S. identity politics. On the other hand, their own desire to reaffirm the integrity and authority of the existing Latin American tradition of critical thought against the authority of the North American academy seems to end up in the same place as Wilentz's "hegemonic Americanism": that is, in a reaffirmation of the authority of the "lettered city" and transculturation *over* the people.

The problem of the subaltern is not only ethical and epistemological, but also structural. Cross-cultural and cross-class dialogue cannot be simply something that happens *within* a course taught at an elite institution (or, for that matter, *inside* a given literary or artistic text). It must also happen *between* that course and something that is necessarily outside it and opposed to it. That is why, in the range of determinations expressed in Guha's definition of the subaltern ("class, caste, age, gender and office or in any other way"), I believe subaltern studies must return to the issue of class inequality and exploitation, because class is the form of subalternity that structures the others. In pedagogical terms, the articulation of multiculturalism is not only a matter of how to introduce Latin American or Asian or African or indigenous or women's or gay texts into the curriculum; it is also a matter of how, in Latin American, Asian, and African, as well as U.S. or European, schools, to introduce materials and ways of thinking that represent the interests, values, and hopes of working people as opposed to those that speak for the ruling classes, whose privilege, power, and wealth are founded on the perpetuation of inequality in all its—always interrelated—forms. In political terms, it is not only a matter of theorizing or legitimizing a "politics of difference"; it is also a matter of connecting a "politics of difference" to a new vision of socialism or communism.

I began this book with the question of the relation of the subaltern to the university as a knowledge center, because I believed that the project of subaltern studies was not just a question of representing (again, in the double sense of both "speaking about" and "speaking for") the subaltern, but of understanding how our own work in the academy functions actively to make or unmake subalternity. Let me end it with a final observation that has to do with this concern: Rather than lamenting the encapsulation of an important sector of the contemporary left in the academy, we should begin to think strategically about the possibilities of our location in higher education. There is no way of telling where the impulses that will revive the project of the left will come from, and there is no reason to suppose in advance that higher education today might not be what in the idiom of the Old Left was called a "key sector." But this also means assuming a new kind of responsibility for what we say and do.

That is perhaps the most important lesson subaltern studies teaches us.

Notes

Introduction

1 Gayatri Spivak, "Can the Subaltern Speak?" in *Marxism and the Interpretation of Culture*, ed. Cary Nelson and Lawrence Grossberg (Urbana: Univ. of Illinois Press, 1988).

2 José Rabasa, Javier Sanjinés, and Robert Carr, eds., *Subaltern Studies in the Americas*, a special issue of *Dispositio/n* 45–46 (1994/1996); Eve Cherniavsky, "Subaltern Studies in a U.S. Frame," *boundary 2* 23, no. 2 (1996): 85–110.

3 I owe this observation to Alberto Moreiras.

4 Following Spivak's elaboration in "Can the Subaltern Speak?" of the distinction between Vertretung and Darstellung in Marx, I understand by "speaking for" the act of political delegation and by "speaking about" mimetic representation or representing as an object of disciplinary knowledge.

5 Ileana Rodríguez, "Between Cynicism and Despair," in *New World [Dis]orders and Peripheral Strains*, ed. Michael Piazz and Marc Zimmerman (Chicago: MARCH/Abrazo, 1998), 232.

6 Austin: Univ. of Texas Press, 1990.

7   Roberto González Echevarría, *Myth and Archive: Towards a Theory of Latin American Narra-*
     tive (Cambridge: Cambridge Univ. Press, 1990); Homi Bhabha, ed., *Nation and Narration*
     (London: Routledge, 1990).

8   Doris Sommer, *Foundational Fictions: The National Romances of Latin America* (Berkeley:
     Univ. of California Press, 1991).

9   Latin American Subaltern Studies Group, "Founding Statement," in *The Postmodernism*
     Debate in Latin America, ed. John Beverley, José Oviedo, and Michael Aronna (Durham:
     Duke Univ. Press, 1995), 135–36.

10   Ranajit Guha, "On Some Aspects of the Historiography of Colonial India," in *Selected*
     Subaltern Studies, ed. Ranajit Guha and Gayatri Spivak (New York: Oxford Univ. Press,
     1988), 43 (emphasis added).

11   Angel Rama, *La ciudad letrada* (Hanover, N.H.: Ediciones del Norte, 1984); English
     version: *The Lettered City,* trans. Charles Casteen (Durham: Duke Univ. Press, 1995).

12   Rama's book was itself highly dependent on and derivative of work many people in
     literature had been doing in the 1970s on the relationship between literature, ideology,
     and power in Latin America, in particular in and around the University of Minnesota's
     Institute for the Study of Ideologies and Literature, headed by Hernán Vidal and Tony
     Zahareas, and Venezuela's Centro de Estudios Latinoamericanos "Rómulo Gallegos."

13   Patricia Seed, "Colonial and Post Colonial Discourse," *Latin American Research Review* 26,
     no. 3 (1991). See also the responses to Seed by Rolena Adorno, Walter Mignolo, and
     Hernán Vidal in the same journal 28, no. 3 (1993).

14   "The Italian bourgeoisie was incapable of uniting the people around itself, and this was
     the cause of its defeats and the interruption in its development." Antonio Gramsci,
     Selections from the Prison Notebooks, ed. and trans. Quintin Hoare and Geoffrey Nowell
     Smith (New York: International, 1971), 53.

15   Antonio Gramsci, *Selections from Cultural Writings,* ed. and trans. David Forgacs and
     Geoffrey Nowell Smith (London: Lawrence & Wishart, 1985), 206–8.

16   For a sense of the respective sides in this debate, see Roberto González Echevarría,
     Celestina's Brood: Continuities of the Baroque in Spanish and Latin American Literature (Durham:
     Duke Univ. Press, 1993); and my own *Una modernidad obsoleta: Estudios sobre el barroco* (Los
     Teques, Venezuela: Fondo Editorial ALEM, 1997).

17   David Forgacs, "National-Popular: Genealogy of a Concept," in *Formations of Nations and*
     Culture, ed. Tony Bennett (London: Routledge, 1984), 91.

18   José Joaquín Brunner, "Notes on Modernity and Postmodernity in Latin American
     Culture," in *Postmodernism Debate* 35.

19   "Yet to argue that culture is today no longer endowed with the relative autonomy it once
     enjoyed as one level among others in the early moments of capitalism (let alone in
     precapitalist societies) is not necessarily to imply its disappearance or extinction. Quite
     the contrary; we must go on to affirm that the dissolution of an autonomous sphere of
     culture is rather to be imagined in terms of an explosion: a prodigious expansion of
     culture throughout the social realm, to the point where everything in our social life—
     from economic value and state power to practices and to the very structure of the psyche
     itself—can be said to have become 'cultural' in some original and yet untheorized
     sense." Fredric Jameson, *Postmodernism, or the Cultural Logic of Late Capitalism* (Durham:
     Duke Univ. Press, 1991), 48.

20   The recent collection edited by Sonia Alvarez, Evelina Dagnino, and Arturo Escobar,
     Cultures of Politics/Politics of Cultures: Re-Visioning Latin American Social Movement (Boulder:
     Westview, 1998), is perhaps the most fully elaborated expression of the new paradigm

in Latin American studies. Its core argument is that "in Latin America today all social movements enact a cultural politics" (6). On the "turn to Gramsci" in Latin American studies, see José Aricó, *La cola del diablo: Itinerario de Gramsci en América Latina* (Buenos Aires: Puntosur, 1988), and Carlos Nelson Coutinho and Mario Aurelio Noguerira, eds., *Gramsci e a América Latina* (Sao Paulo: Paz y Tierra, 1988).

21 Ranajit Guha, "The Small Voice of History," *Subaltern Studies* 9 (1996): 1–8.

22 My friend Paul Bové calls this tendency "Left Conservatism." It might be defined as a conjunction of positivist epistemology with left-wing reformism.

23 "[T]he complex strategies of cultural identification and discursive address that function in the name of 'the people' or 'the nation' . . . [are] more hybrid in the articulation of cultural differences and identifications—gender, race or class—than can be represented in any hierarchical or binary structuring of social antagonism." Homi Bhabha, "DissemiNation," in *Nation and Narration* 292.

24 Hugo Achugar, "Leones, cazadores e historiadores: A propósito de las políticas de la memoria y del conocimiento," *Revista Iberoamericana* 180 (1997): 379–87; Mabel Moraña, "El boom del subalterno," *Revista de Crítica Cultural* 14 (1997): 48–53.

25 Expressing a similar concern, José Klor de Alva has argued that the conditions of coloniality were radically different in Latin America than in Asia or Africa—so much so as to challenge the viability of the very concept of colonial for Latin America.

26 Moraña charges subaltern studies with a critical neoexoticism that "keeps Latin America in the place of the Other, a pretheoretical, marginal, calibanesque site in relation to metropolitan discourse," thus unwittingly reinscribing center-periphery dynamics ("El boom" 50). Achugar writes similarly: "[L]a construcción que se propone de América Latina, dentro del marco teórico de los llamados estudios postcoloniales, parecería apuntar a que el lugar desde donde se habla no es o no debería ser el de la nación sino el del pasado colonial. . . . [El] lugar desde donde se lee América Latina parece ser, por un lado, el de la experiencia histórica del *Commonwealth* y por otro . . . el de la agenda de la academia norteamericana que está localizada en la historia de su sociedad civil" ("Leones" 381). Both authors echo without apparently being aware of it an earlier critique of subaltern studies as a kind of neo-Orientalism by Gareth Williams, "Fantasies of Cultural Exchange in Latin American Subaltern Studies," in *The Real Thing: Testimonial Discourse in Latin America*, ed. Georg Gugelberger (Durham: Duke Univ. Press, 1996), 225–53.

27 The question of what Walter Mignolo has called "the politics of location" of theory has been a major issue within the work of the Latin American Subaltern Studies Group itself, in a way that the critics fail to take into account sufficiently.

28 It is the signal virtue of Eve Cherniavsky's "Subaltern Studies in a U.S. Frame," noted earlier, to transfer the problematic of the subaltern to U.S. history, which it represents as essentially a postcolonial one: e.g., "to map the vectors of colonial power in the United States is to turn the spaces of Guha's postcolonial historiography inside out" (85–86).

29 Florencia Mallon, "The Promise and Dilemma of L A Subaltern Studies: Perspectives from Latin American History," *American Historical Review* 99, no. 5 (1994): 1491–1515.

30 On the relation of subaltern studies to the Naxalbari uprising, see Ranajit Guha, "Introduction," in *A Subaltern Studies Reader, 1986–1995*, ed. Guha (Minneapolis: Univ. of Minnesota Press, 1997), ix–xv. Guha himself was a functionary of the Indian Communist Party for many years before resuming his work as a historian.

31 Aijaz Ahmad, *In Theory* (London: Verso, 1992), 8.

32 I am sympathetic to the implications of Roger Bartra's remark that, "[f]ortunately, the moment has arrived for Marxism to disappear, to dissolve as it were. In fact, it is dissolving into the ocean of the left, but at the same time it's gaining a lot and so is everybody else." "An Interview with Roger Bartra," in *The Postmodern in Latin and Latino American Cultural Narratives*, ed. Claudia Ferman (New York: Garland, 1996), 88.

33 "[I]f the nationalisms with which we are in solidarity are to be radical or emancipatory, rather than fixed in the repressive apparatuses of state formations, it is their conjunctural relation to other social movements that needs to be emphasized and furthered, at both theoretical and practical levels. The possibility of nationalism against the state lies in the recognition of the excess of the people over the nation, and in the understanding that that is, beyond itself, the very logic of nationalism as a political phenomenon." David Lloyd, "Nationalisms against the State," in *The Politics of Culture in the Shadow of Capital*, ed. David Lloyd and Lisa Lowe (Durham: Duke Univ. Press, 1997), 192.

34 Ernesto Laclau, *Emancipation(s)* (London: Verso, 1996), 322.

35 "The storytelling that thrives for a long time in the milieu of work—the rural, the maritime, and the urban—is itself an artisan form of communication, as it were. It does not aim to convey the pure essence of the thing, like information or a report. It sinks the thing into the life of the storyteller, in order to bring it out of him again. Thus traces of the storyteller cling to the story the way the handprints of the potter cling to the clay vessel." Walter Benjamin, "The Storyteller," in *Illuminations*, trans. Harry Zohn (New York: Shocken, 1969), 91–92.

1 *Writing in Reverse: The Subaltern and the Limits of Academic Knowledge*

1 Jacques Lacan, *The Four Fundamental Concepts of Psycho-Analysis* (New York: Norton, 1981), 95–96. My thanks to Henry Krips for reminding me of this story.

2 Ranajit Guha, "Preface," *Selected Subaltern Studies*, ed. R. Guha and Gayatri Spivak (New York: Oxford Univ. Press, 1988), 35.

3 Ranajit Guha, *Elementary Aspects of Peasant Insurgency in Colonial India* (Delhi: Oxford Univ. Press, 1983), i.

4 "I do not think it is an exaggeration to say therefore that rewriting Indian history today is an extension of the struggle between subaltern and elite, and between the Indian masses and the British *raj*." Edward Said, "Foreword," *Selected Subaltern Studies*, vii.

5 Richard Rodriguez, *Hunger of Memory* (New York: Bantam, 1983), 137–38.

6 "Once upon a time I was a 'socially disadvantaged' child. An enchantedly happy child. Mine was a childhood of intense family closeness. And public alienation. Thirty years later I write this book as a middle-class American. Assimilated" (*Hunger* 3).

7 Rigoberta Menchú, with Elisabeth Burgos-Debray, *I, Rigoberta Menchú: An Indian Woman in Guatemala*, trans. Ann Wright (London: Verso, 1994), 1.

8 On the design of the course and the resulting controversy, see Mary Louise Pratt, "Humanities for the Future: Reflections on the Western Culture Debate at Stanford," in *The Politics of Liberal Education*, ed. Daryll Glass and Barbara Herrnstein Smith (Durham: Duke Univ. Press, 1992).

9 "When has history ever contradicted that practice norms theory, as subaltern practice norms official historiography in this case?" (*Selected Subaltern Studies* 16).

10 Gramsci notes: "They [the peasants] see the 'gentleman' [*signore*]—and for many, especially in the country, 'gentleman' means intellectual—complete, speedily and with ap-

parent ease, work which costs their sons tears and blood, and they think there is a 'trick.'" *Selections from the Prison Notebooks*, ed. and trans. Quintin Hoare and Geoffrey Nowell Smith (New York: International, 1971), 43.

11 Tomás Rivera's bildungsroman of Mexican farmworkers in collective, plural voice, . . . *y no se le tragó la tierra*—one of the masterpieces of the modern Chicano novel—is just such a narrative. Pilar Belver brought to my attention the testimonio of a migrant farm-worker, *Forged under the Sun: The Life of María Elena Lucas*, ed. Fran Buss (Ann Arbor: Univ. of Michigan Press, 1995).

12 Henry Staten, "Ethnic Authenticity, Class, and Autobiography: The Case of *Hunger of Memory*," PMLA 133 (1998): 111.

13 Doris Sommer has argued that it is not so much a question here of *real* secrets that Menchú needs to keep from us in the interests of protecting herself and her community, as of a *strategic* insistence that, despite Menchú's claim, proper to the generic conven-tion of testimonio, that she is telling us "toda la verdad de mi pueblo" (which the English edition mistranslates as "the reality of a whole people"), there is something she will in fact *not* tell, that we cannot know. Doris Sommer, "No Secrets," in *The Real Thing. Testimonial Discourse in Latin America*, ed. Georg Gugelberger (Durham: Duke Univ. Press, 1996), 130–60.

14 In her talk at the conference "Cross-Genealogies and Subaltern Knowledges," at Duke University, 15–18 October 1998, the dean for interdisciplinary studies at Duke, Cathy Davidson, noted that she saw subaltern studies as the model for future work in the humanities and social sciences. But, that idea is itself a measure of the problem: How can subaltern studies become part of an institution dedicated to producing the ruling elite? For a more radical perspective, see, for example, J. Elspeth Stuckey's eloquent critique of adult literacy programs, *The Violence of Literacy* (Portsmouth, N.H.: Heine-mann, 1991).

15 Dipesh Chakrabarty, "Postcoloniality and the Artifice of History: Who Speaks for the 'Indian' Past?" In *A Subaltern Studies Reader, 1986–1995*, ed. Ranajit Guha (Minneapolis: Univ. of Minnesota Press, 1997), 263–94.

16 Florencia Mallon, *Peasant and Nation: The Making of Postcolonial Mexico and Peru* (Berkeley: Univ. of California Press, 1995).

17 In particular, "the more radical forms of local communal discourse in central Peru remained more isolated than those in Mexico and potentially less available for connec-tion to alternative national coalitions" (Mallon 315). I will come back to the question of the relation between territoriality and hegemony in chapter 6.

18 That is exactly what Shahid Amin does in *Event, Metaphor, Memory: Chauri Chaura, 1922–1992* (Berkeley: Univ. of California Press, 1995), or in the long essay that preceded it, "Remembering Chauri Chaura," reprinted in *Subaltern Studies Reader*, 179–239. Like Mallon, Amin is concerned with retrieving peasants' "local memory"—in this case of a "riot" in 1922 in the course of which peasants in a small town in northern India burned down a police station, killing twenty-three policemen; but he is also concerned with finding a way formally to incorporate the narratives about the event textually. Recent ethnographic work provides examples of polyphonic texts in which the narrative voice and authority of the ethnographer is counterpointed against the voice and authority of the subaltern subjects the ethnographer is concerned with representing: for exam-ple, Ruth Behar's *Translated Woman: Crossing the Border with Esperanza's Story* (Boston: Beacon, 1993); or Phillipe Bourgois, *In Search of Respect: Selling Crack in the Barrio* (Cam-bridge: Cambridge Univ. Press, 1995). Malin herself has been working on what she

calls "an experimental" testimonio with a Chilean Mapuche feminist activist, Isolde Reuque.

19 "The formative layers of the developing state were ruptured again and again by these seismic upheavals until it was to learn to adjust to its unfamiliar site by trial and error and consolidate itself by the increasing sophistication of legislative, administrative and cultural controls" (Guha, Aspects 2).

20 Dipesh Chakrabarty, "A Small History of Subaltern Studies," paper presented at the conference "Cross-Genealogies and Subaltern Knowledges," Duke University, 15– 18 October 1998.

21 The phrase is from a series of lectures Gutiérrez delivered on "The New Evangelism" at the Pittsburgh Theological Seminary in May 1993.

22 Richard Rorty, "Solidarity or Objectivity?" in Post-Analytic Philosophy, ed. John Rajchman and Cornel West (New York: Columbia Univ. Press, 1985), 3.

23 "[W]hen Rorty argues for the desirability of 'conversation' in place of rational episte-mology, he does not take seriously the asymmetrical situation of the other, the concrete empirical impossibility that the 'excluded,' 'dominated,' or 'compelled' can intervene effectively in such a discussion. He takes as his starting point 'we liberal Americans,' not 'we Aztecs in relation to Cortés,' or 'we Latin Americans in relation to a North American in 1992.' In such cases, not even conversation is possible." Enrique Dussel, "Eurocentrism and Modernity," in The Postmodernism Debate in Latin America, ed. John Beverley, José Oviedo, and Michael Aronna (Durham: Duke Univ. Press, 1995), 75 n. 15.

2 Transculturation and Subalternity: The "Lettered City" and the Túpac Amaru Rebellion

1 Said, in Selected Subaltern Studies, ed. Ranajit Guha and Gayatri Spivak (New York: Oxford Univ. Press, 1988), ix–x. David Lloyd makes a similar point about the form of agency of the intellectual in the colonial world: "Nationalism is generated as an oppositional discourse by intellectuals who appear, by virtue of their formation in imperial state institutions, as in the first place subjected to rather than the subjects of assimilation. Their assimilation is, furthermore, inevitably an uneven process: by the very logic of assimilation, either the assimilated must entirely abandon their culture of origin, sup-posing it to have existed in anything like a pure form, or persist in a perpetually split consciousness, perceiving the original cultural elements as a residue resistant to the subject formed as a citizen of the empire." David Lloyd, Anomalous States: Irish Writing and the Post-Colonial Moment (Durham: Duke Univ. Press, 1992), 112. See also Paul Gilroy's take on W. E. B. DuBois's idea of the "double-consciousness" of Afro-Atlantic intellectuals in The Black Atlantic: Modernity and Double Consciousness (Cambridge: Harvard Univ. Press, 1993).

2 As Tim Brennan has noted, a figure like Rushdie is not even representative of the culture of the South Asian or Caribbean immigrant communities in England: "Despite [Rushdie's] fresh thinking about national form, about a new homelessness that is also a worldliness, about a double-edged post-colonial responsibility, The Satanic Verses shows how strangely detached and insensitive the logic of cosmopolitan 'universality' can be. It may be, as he [Rushdie] says, that 'bigotry is not only a function of power,' but it does not seem adequate to argue in the particular immigration/acculturation complex of contemporary Britain that the central issue is one of 'human evil.' The means of distributing that evil are obviously very unequal, and the violence that comes

from defending one's identity or livelihood as opposed to one's privileges is not the same." Timothy Brennan, *Salman Rushdie and the Third World* (New York: St. Martin's, 1989), 165.

3 "For if subaltern history is construed to be only a separatist enterprise—much as early feminist writing was based on the notion that women had a voice or a room of their own, entirely separate from the masculine domain—then it runs the risk of just being a mirror opposite the writing whose tyranny it disputes" (Said, *Selected Subaltern Studies* viii).

4 "There was hardly a peasant uprising on any significant scale in colonial India that did not cause the destruction of large quantities of written and printed material including rent rolls, deeds and bonds, and public records of all kinds. . . . Writing was [to the peasant] a sign of his enemy." Ranajit Guha, *Elementary Aspects of Peasant Insurgency in Colonial India* (Delhi: Oxford Univ. Press, 1983), 52.

5 Angel Rama, *Transculturación narrativa en América Latina* (Mexico: Siglo XXI, 1982).

6 Fernando Ortiz, *Cuban Counterpoint: Tobacco and Sugar*, trans. Harriet de Onís (Durham: Duke Univ. Press, 1995), xlvii.

7 "Las obras literarias no están fuera de las culturas sino que las coronan y en la medida en que estas culturas son invenciones seculares y multitudinarias hacen del escritor un productor que trabaja con las obras de innumerables hombres. Un compilador, hubiera dicho Roa Bastos. El genial tejedor, en el vasto taller histórico de la sociedad americana." Rama, *Transculturación narrativa*, quoted in Oritz, *Cuban Counterpoint*, ix n. 2.

8 "The author has become reintegrated with the linguistic community and speaks from within it, with unimpeded use of its idiomatic resources. If that community is, as often occurs, of rural type, or borders on an indigenous speech group, then it is starting from this linguistic system that the writer works, no longer attempting to imitate a regional speech from without but, rather, to elaborate it from within, with an artistic goal" (Rama, *Transculturación* 42).

9 Ortiz, *Cuban Counterpoint* 98, 99, 100. I owe this observation to Hugo Achugar, who adds, "La insistencia en la especifidad cubana y en segundo término latinoamericana de la transculturación no impiden observar, como el mismo Ortiz lo sostiene, que la diferencia con otros procesos similares—también vividos por Europa—radica sólo en la concentración temporal del proceso; lo que en un lugar tomó cuatro milenios en el otro, sólo cuatro siglos." Hugo Achugar, "Repensando la heterogeneidad latinoamericana: a propósito de lugares, paisajes y territorios," *Revista Iberoamericana* 176–77 (July–December 1996). For useful discussions of Ortiz's idea of transculturation, see Gustavo Pérez Firmat, *The Cuban Condition* (New York: Cambridge Univ. Press 1989); and Alberto Moreiras, "Transculturación y pérdida del sentido," *Nuevo Texto Crítico* 3, no. 6 (1990): 105–19.

10 I owe this observation to Luis Duno.

11 "Sin duda, pero no de la cultura indígena sino de la cultura mestiza, porque la cultura india ya no tenía sentido. Lo que él [Arguedas] comprendió es que efectivamente la salida era esa barrosa salida del mestizaje. Ese zigzagueante, y muchas veces sucio, camino, como la vida misma, pero que era mucho más rico en posibilidades." Angel Rama, in Jesús Díaz, *Angel Rama o la crítica de la transculturación (Ultima entrevista)* (Lima: Lluvia Editores, 1991), 32 (my translation). It is interesting to compare Rama's remarks with the more recent observations on the same subject by Mario Vargas Llosa, who in other respects is situated at the other end of the political spectrum: "The price they [Indian peasants] must pay for integration is high—renunciation of their culture, their

language, their beliefs, their traditions and customs, and the adoption of the culture of their ancient masters. . . . . If forced to choose between the preservation of Indian cultures and their complete assimilation, with great sadness I would choose modernization of the Indian population, because there are priorities. . . . [M]odernization is possible only with the sacrifice of the Indian cultures." Mario Vargas Llosa, cited in *Harper's Magazine* (December 1990), 52–53.

12 Neil Larsen, *Modernism and Hegemony* (Minneapolis: Univ. of Minnesota Press, 1992), 64.

13 On the relation between "boom" narrative, the idea of transculturation, and dependency theory, see Tulio Halperin Donghi, "Nueva narrativa y ciencias sociales hispanoamericanas en la década del sesenta," *Hispamérica* 27 (1980): 3–18.

14 Antonio Cándido, "Literatura e subdesenvolvimento," *Argumento* 1 (1973). I am grateful to Vicente Lecuna for bringing Cándido's essay to my attention.

15 There exists in fact a perhaps apocryphal letter of Juan Bautista Túpac Amaru to Bolívar, in which he writes among other things that the blood of "mi tierno y venerado hermano . . . fue el ruego que había preparado aquella tierra para fructificar los mejores frutos que el gran Bolivar habrá de recoger con su mano valerosa y llena de la mayor generosidad." Several historians have suggested a link between the *Memorias* and the program advanced by the party of Manuel Belgrano in the Wars of Independence, which included the idea of restoring the Inca empire.

16 "Just as any other reader, he [Rousseau] is bound to misread his text as the promise of political change. The error is not within the reader; language itself dissociates the cognition from the act. *Die Sprache verspricht (sich)*; to the extent that it is necessarily misleading, language just as necessarily conveys the promise of its own truth. This is also why textual allegories on this level of rhetorical complexity generate history." Paul de Man, *Allegories of Reading* (New Haven: Yale Univ. Press, 1979), 277.

17 *Antiliterary* because writing was one of the symbols of colonial power itself. Leon Campbell, "The Influence of Books and Literature on the Túpac Amaru Rebellion," paper presented at the Brown University conference on The Book in the Americas, 1987. Copy of author's typescript.

18 See, on this point, Bruce Mannheim, *The Language of the Inka Since the European Invasion* (Austin: Univ. of Texas Press, 1991).

19 "Si la aristocracia neoinca, que carecía de un poder político real, pretendía crear las condiciones para una restauración incaica, no le convenía, por cierto, insistir en las perrogativas discrecionales de los Incas históricos. Para recuperar el poder en la situación política del siglo XVIII, necesitaba al menos la alianza con los demás sustratos indígenas, probablemente también con los criollos liberales. No podía permitirse el lujo de alarmar a sus hipotéticos aliados con la perspectiva de un gobierno inca totalmente inflexible. Si el *Ollantay* pertenece a este contexto neoinca, es lógico pensar que el o los autores del drama prefirieran ofrecer una imagen más adecuada para apoyar la lucha revindicativa de los 'Incas' contemporáneos. Una imagen más humana, pero no devirtuada: el drama ilustra precisamente la capacidad de la sociedad inca para restablecer, en una época de crisis, un poder supremo 'justo.' " Martin Lienhard, *La voz y su huella* (Havana: Casa de las Américas, 1990), 248.

20 Steve Stern, *Resistance, Rebellion, and Consciousness in the Andean Peasant World* (Madison: Univ. of Wisconsin Press, 1987), 76 (emphasis added). In similar terms, Aníbal Quijano has argued that the Túpac Amaru rebellion displays an "Andean rationality" that parallels the project of the Enlightenment and the bourgeois revolutions, but on a different, and sometimes antagonistic historical track. Aníbal Quijano, "Modernity, Identity, and

Utopia in Latin America," in *The Postmodernism Debate in Latin America*, ed. John Beverley, José Oviedo, and Michael Aronna (Durham: Duke Univ. Press, 1995), 210–16. On the "hybrid" concepts of nation and nationality held by the Andean elite, José Mazzotti's *El coro mestizo del Inca Garcilaso* (Lima: Fondo de Cultura Económica, 1996), is informative.

21 Juan de Espinosa Medrano, *Apologético en favor de don Luis de Góngora* (Caracas: Biblioteca Ayacucho, 1982), 25.

22 "But the game of associations [in the *Apology*] culminates with the comparison between the moon [in Spanish, luna], which establishes a cosmico-metaphoric connection between the Cordobesan poet and the Indianos. . . . The moon is the heavenly body known for its reflected light, for its secondariness, like silver in relation to gold, like baroque conceits, dependent on the blinding glare of tradition. *Lunarejo* [Espinosa's pen name, which means covered with moles and which referred to a physical deformity he suffered] inscribes himself as emblem at the beginning of his own text through his nickname, a sign that sets him apart as an enigmatic figure, in the very foundations of his own art. . . . [T]he modernity of *Lunarejo's* poetics is that combination of resentment, alienation, and self-acceptance as a being that, if it is true, enjoys the status of the new, suffers a congenital belatedness that condemns him to an anxious rummaging through the given in search for that which shapes him, for the source of the strangeness that he is and embodies." Roberto González Echevarría, *Celestina's Brood: Continuities of the Baroque in Spanish and Latin American Literature* (Durham: Duke Univ. Press, 1993), 169.

23 "The Christian Fathers in the Andes had the supremely difficult task of supplanting pagan views of nature with Church-derived doctrine. They had to effect a revolution in the moral basis of cognition itself. . . . A new semiotic had to be written, as large and all-encompassing as the universe itself. . . . The Christian Fathers sought to demonstrate to the Indians that phenomena could not be gods because of their regularity. . . . A conception of a self-organized system of mutually supportive things was transformed into a conception of a different sort of organic unity that was dominated and orchestrated by a single leader, God—the celestial engineer, the unmoved mover. Christianity sought to supplant the system of mutually conditioning parts with one that wrote the master-slave relationship into nature." Michael Taussig, *The Devil and Commodity Fetishism in South America* (Chapel Hill: Univ. of North Carolina Press, 1980), 174–75.

24 Raquel Chang-Rodríguez, "La subversión del Barroco en *Amar su propia muerte* de Juan Espinosa Medrano," in *Relecturas del Barroco de Indias*, ed. Mabel Moraña (Hanover, N.H.: Ediciones del Norte, 1994), 117–47.

25 Faría had repeated the charge of the Spanish critics of Gongorism that Góngora was the "Mohammed of Spanish poetry." Espinosa replies in kind: "[S]epa Faría que no supo lo que se dijo: que a Mahoma por la largura del apetito y por lo licencioso de la sensualidad bestial, le siguen hombres ignorantes, brutos, ciegos, bárbaros, selváticos, y bestiales; pero a Góngora, que no escribió para todos, penétranle los discretos, sondéanle los eruditos y apláudenle los doctos. Pues de aclamar bárbaros y de clasificar doctos, véase la diferencia que hay" (*Apologético* 70–71).

26 "[L]os escritores criollos, condicionados ya por un deseo de perfil nativista de representar la tierra cada vez con mayor complejidad . . . fueron impulsados a escribir por motivaciones tanto de orden interno como externo. O si se quiere, de manera más concreta: por el deseo de legitimarse en la naturaleza autóctona y en el color local y, a la vez, por el de imitar desde posiciones utilitarias las instituciones de la Europa moderna. Es precisamente este deseo bifurcado, imposible de ser resumido dialécticamente por una síntesis, lo que define en Hispanoamérica lo Nacional y lo que caracteriza su

discurso *paradójico y excesivo*, comenzando por la problemática del lenguaje mismo."
Antonio Benítez-Rojo, "Nacionalismo y nacionalización en la novela hispanoameri-
cana del siglo XIX," *Revista de Crítica Literaria Latinoamericana* 38 (1993): 188.

27   It seems in particular an instance of what Judith Butler means by "performance" as an
act which at once deconstructs the binaries that constitute identity but also posits or
"plays out" identity in terms of the values inscribed in those binaries. Judith Butler,
Gender Trouble: Feminism and the Subversion of Identity (New York: Routledge, 1990).

28   Shahid Amin, "Gandhi as Mahatma," in *Selected Subaltern Studies* 288–350.

29   Antonio Cornejo Polar, "Una heterogeneidad no dialéctica: Sujeto y discurso migrante
en el Perú moderno," in *Crítica cultural y teoría literaria latinoamericanas*, a special issue, ed.
Mabel Moraña, of *Revista Iberoamericana* 176–77 (1996): 837–44.

30   In Juan Biondi and Eduardo Zapata, *Representación oral en las calles de Lima* (Lima: Universidad de Lima, 1994).

3   Our Rigoberta? I, Rigoberta Menchú, Cultural Authority, and the Problem of Subaltern Agency

1   John Beverley, "The Margin at the Center: On *Testimonio*," in *The Real Thing: Testimonial
Discourse and Latin America*, ed. Georg Gugelberger (Durham: Duke Univ. Press, 1996),
24, 26.

2   David Stoll, *Rigoberta Menchú and the Story of All Poor Guatemalans* (Boulder: Westview,
1999).

3   Gayatri Spivak, *The Post-Colonial Critic: Interview, Strategies, Dialogues*, ed. Sarah Harasym
(New York: Routledge, 1990), 33. My thanks to Therese Tardio for this citation.

4   "[T]he anonymity of the counterautobiography, which is among other things the testimonial novel, is then in that sense not the loss of a name, but—quite paradoxically—the
multiplication of proper names." Fredric Jameson, "On Literary and Cultural Import-
Substitution in the Third World: The Case of Testimonio," in *The Real Thing*, 185.
"Master subject" is from Jameson's earlier interview with Anders Stephanson: "I always insist on a third possibility beyond the old bourgeois ego and the schizophrenic
subject of our organization society today: a *collective subject*, decentered but not schizophrenic. It emerges in certain forms of storytelling that can be found in third-world
literature, in testimonial literature, in gossip and rumors and things of this kind. . . . It
is decentered since the stories you tell there as an individual subject don't belong to
you; you don't control them in the way the master subject of modernism would. But you
don't just suffer them in the schizophrenic isolation of the first-world subject of today." Anders Stephanson, "Regarding Postmodernism—A Conversation with Fredric
Jameson," *Social Text* 17 (1987): 45.

5   Alice Britten and Kenya Dworkin, "Rigoberta Menchú: 'Los indígenas no nos queda-
mos como bichos aislados,' " *Nuevo Texto Crítico* 6, no. 11 (1993): 214 (my translation).
Ironically, the reverse of what Menchú is complaining about happens in the recent
English translation of her new book, *Crossing Borders*, which continues the story begun
in *I, Rigoberta Menchú* up to the present (London: Verso, 1998). Though Menchú prepared the book in close collaboration with an Italian editor, Giani Mina, and the
Guatemalan literary scholar Dante Liano, both Mina and Liano are eliminated entirely
from the English edition, which appears as the sole product of Menchú, transcribed
and edited by the translator, Ann Wright. Elisabeth Burgos has continued to insist in
various interviews that she is the "sole" author of *I, Rigoberta Menchú*, even as she has

sought to distance herself from Menchú's politics. In one way or another, the issue of authorship in testimonio is often a point of conflict between the parties involved in its production. For example, in the first edition of *Biografía de un cimarrón*, published in Cuba, Miguel Barnet appeared as the author, even though the text itself is a first-person narrative by his subaltern informant, Esteban Montejo. In the subsequent English translation (London: Bodley Head, 1968; New York: Meridian, 1969), now out of print, the work was retitled, more accurately in my opinion, *Autobiography of a Runaway Slave*, and the author was designated as Esteban Montejo, with Barnet appearing as the editor. In a new English translation recently published by Curbstone Press (1995), prepared with Barnet's approval, the book is again titled *Biography of a Runaway Slave* and Barnet again appears as the author (I owe this information to Goffredo Diana).

6   "There is nothing that commends a story to memory more effectively than that chaste compactness which precludes psychological analysis. And the more natural the process by which the storyteller foregoes psychological shading, the greater becomes the story's claim to a place in the memory of the listener, the more completely is it integrated into his own experience, the greater will be his inclination to repeat it to someone else someday, sooner or later." Walter Benjamin, *Illuminations*, trans. Harry Zohn (New York: Shocken, 1969), 91.

7   "Figures like the goddess Athena—'father's daughters self-professedly uncontaminated by the womb'—are useful for establishing women's ideological self-debasement, which is to be distinguished from a deconstructive attitude toward the essentialist subject." Gayatri Spivak, "Can the Subaltern Speak?" in *Marxism and the Interpretation of Culture*, ed. Cary Nelson and Lawrence Grossberg (Urbana: Univ. of Illinois Press, 1988), 308.

8   I often return to Walter Mignolo's observation that the violence of the Spanish practice of segregating the children of the indian aristocracy from their families in order to teach them literacy and Christianity "is not located in the fact that the youngsters have been assembled and enclosed day and night. It comes, rather, from the interdiction of having conversations with their parents, particularly with their mothers. In a primary oral society, in which virtually all knowledge is transmitted by means of conversation, the preservation of oral contact was contradictory with the effort to teach how to read and write. Forbidding conversations with the mother meant, basically, depriving the children of the living culture imbedded in the language and preserved and transmitted in speech." Walter Mignolo, "Literacy and Colonization: The New World Experience," in *1482–1992: Re/Discovering Colonial Writing*, ed. René Jara and Nicholas Spadaccini (Minneapolis: Prisma Institute, 1989), 67.

9   "No representa una reacción genuina y espontánea del 'sujeto-pueblo multiforme' frente a la condición postcolonial, sino que sigue siendo un discurso de las élites comprometidas a la causa de la democratización." Elzbieta Sklodowska, "Hacia una tipología del testimonio hispanoamericano," *Siglo XX/Twentieth Century* 8, nos. 1–2 (1990–1991): 113. The concept of "sujeto-pueblo multiforme" Sklodowska alludes to comes from the Chilean critic Jorge Narvaéz.

10   Gayatri Spivak, *In Other Worlds* (New York: Methuen, 1987), 95.

11   Dinesh D'Souza, *Illiberal Education* (New York: Free Press, 1991), 87.

12   Mary Louise Pratt tells me that a poll of undergraduates at Stanford shows that *I, Rigoberta Menchú* was the book that had the greatest impact on them. A similar poll at the University of Pittsburgh would, I think, yield a very different result, in part because many of the students here are themselves from working-class or lower-middle-class

backgrounds, and (on the whole) are destined for middle-management or low-level professional jobs, rather than the elite. On the contradictions of teaching *I, Rigoberta Menchú* in U.S. classrooms, see the essays in Allen Carey-Webb and Stephen Benz, *Teaching and Testimony* (New York: SUNY Press, 1996).

13 For example, "They have tried to take our things away and impose others on us, be it through religion, through dividing up the land, through schools, through books, through radio, through all things modern." Rigoberta Menchú, with Elisabeth Burgos-Debray, *I, Rigoberta Menchú: An Indian Woman in Guatemala*, trans. Ann Wright (London: Verso, 1994), 170–71. Or: "When teachers come into the villages, they bring with them the ideas of capitalism and getting on in life. They try and impose these ideas on us. I remember that in my village there were two teachers for awhile and they began teaching the people, but the children told their parents everything they were being taught in school and the parents said: 'We don't want our children to become like *ladinos*.' And they made the teachers leave. . . . For the indian, it is better not to study than to become like *ladinos*" (*Menchú* 205).

14 Gareth Williams, "Fantasies of Cultural Exchange in Latin American Subaltern Studies," in *The Real Thing*, 225–53.

15 René Jara, "Prólogo," in *Testimonio y literatura*, ed. René Jara and Hernán Vidal (Minneapolis: Institute for the Study of Ideologies and Literature, 1986), 2.

16 I owe this observation to Pat Seed. Romanticizing victimization was the strategy of the anti-slave narrative produced by liberal elites or would-be elites in the nineteenth century in both Latin America and the United States. It is also a problem in *Schindler's List*, as the emerging critical discussion of the film has begun to register. Steven Spielberg's use of the Schindler story personalizes the Holocaust and brings it closer to the viewer: it differentiates his film from a modernist film treatment of the Holocaust such as Alain Resnais's *Night and Fog*. The price, however, is that the Jews (as a group) can be represented in the film only as victims, dependent on Schindler and on the character played by Ben Kingsley, who symbolizes the role of the traditional Jewish leadership of the Judenrats, for their salvation. A Zionist or Communist representation would have critiqued the role of the Judenrats and stressed the possibility of Jewish self-organization from below and armed struggle against the Nazi system, instead of their reliance on the benevolence of both Jewish and non-Jewish elites. Even the representation of the Holocaust, in other words, is taken away in *Schindler's List* from the actual victims or participants. The film as a capitalist enterprise mirrors Schindler's business venture (arms manufacture) as the *necessary* vehicle for Jewish salvation. It is instructive to contrast Spielberg's narrative strategy in the film with the collective montage of direct testimonios by Holocaust survivors presented in the Holocaust Museum in Washington or with the similar video produced under his auspices, *Voices of the Holocaust*.

17 See the text of her interview with Juan Jesús Aznárez, "Los que me atacan humillan a las víctimas," for the Spanish newspaper El País. A translation of the interview, together with documents, journalistic articles, interviews, and essays representing a variety of positions in the Stoll/Menchú debate, including Stoll's own response to his critics, are forthcoming in *The Properties of Words: Rigoberta Menchú, David Stoll, and Identity Politics in Central America*, ed. Arturo Arias (Minneapolis: Univ. of Minnesota Press, 2000). A balanced general account of the controversy may be found in Peter Canby, "The Truth about Rigoberta Menchú," *The New York Review of Books*, April 8, 1999: 28–34.

18 David Stoll, *Between Two Armies in the Ixil Towns of Guatemala* (New York: Columbia Univ. Press, 1993).

19 For the counter-case to Stoll, see, for example, Carol Smith, "Why Write an Exposé of Rigoberta Menchú," in Arias, *The Properties*, and Canby, "The Truth."

20 Shoshana Felman and Dori Laub, *Testimony: Crises of Witnessing in Literature, Psychoanalysis, and History* (New York: Routledge, 1992), 59.

21 "Any statement of authority has no other guarantee than its very enunciation, and it is pointless for it to seek another signifier, which could not appear outside this locus in any way. Which is what I mean when I say that no metalanguage can be spoken, or, more aphoristically, that there is no Other of the Other. And when the Legislator (he who claims to lay down the Law) presents himself to fill the gap, he does so as an imposter." Jacques Lacan, *Ecrits: A Selection* (New York: Norton, 1977), 310–11.

22 See Beth and Steve Cagan's meticulous account of one such community, *This Promised Land, El Salvador* (New Brunswick: Rutgers Univ. Press, 1991).

23 Menchú notes that, "[i]n the eyes of the community, the fact that anyone should even change the way they dress shows a lack of dignity. Anyone who doesn't dress as our grandfathers, our ancestors, dressed, is on the road to ruin" (*Menchú* 37). But I have been told by the Guatemalan writer Arturo Arias, who has worked with her, that outside the public eye Menchú has been known to wear blue jeans and T-shirts. Guha has several lucid passages on the semiotics of dress as a form of subaltern negativity in *Elementary Aspects of Peasant Insurgency in Colonial India* (Delhi: Oxford Univ. Press, 1983); see, e.g., 65–66.

24 I noted in the last chapter some examples of the work of the subaltern studies historians on orality in South Asian peasant cultures. What is relevant to *I, Rigoberta Menchú* is that the mode of transmission of oral culture is dependent on the highly socialized character of everyday community life, in which women play a key role.

25 Mary Louise Pratt's idea of testimonio as "ethnobiography" is pertinent here. Where in oral history or ethnographic "life history" it is the intentionality of the interlocutor which is paramount, in ethnobiography a subaltern subject *finds* an interlocutor from the hegemony who is in a position to make her story known to a wider, "lettered" audience. In the "life history" the text is the product of a form of hegemonic agency; in ethnobiography it is the product of subaltern agency. Menchú's *Nuevo Texto Crítico* of the transcript of *I, Rigoberta Menchú* was done not only by Elisabeth Burgos but also by a team of Menchú's *compañeros* from the military-political organization she was associated with in Guatemala, the ERP, including the historian Arturo Taracena, working together with her after the sessions with Burgos in Paris. *I, Rigoberta Menchú* is, in this sense, the proverbial text written by a committee (and a central committee at that!).

26 On this point, see Mario Roberto Morales, *La articulación de las diferencias: Los discursos literarios y políticos del debate interétnico en Guatemala* (Guatemala City: FLACSO, 1999). I should note, however, that I disagree with Morales's polemic against Mayan identity politics in Guatemala. The reasons for my disagreement are at the core of my argument about multiculturalism in chapter 6.

4 Hybrid or Binary? On the Category of "the People" in Subaltern and Cultural Studies

1 Ranajit Guha, "On Some Aspects of the Historiography of Colonial India," *Selected Subaltern Studies*, ed. R. Guha and Gayatri Spivak (New York: Oxford Univ. Press, 1988), 35.

2   "[C]oncepts are purely differential and defined not by their positive content but nega-
    tively by their relations with the other terms of the system. Their most precise charac-
    teristic is in being what others are not." Ferdinand de Saussure, *Course in General Linguis-
    tics*, trans. Wade Baskin (New York: McGraw-Hill, 1966), 117. The idea of negation as
    constitutive of identity in Western philosophy comes, of course, from Spinoza. Guha
    locates an anticipation of Saussure's idea in the idea of the *lopa* or grammatical blank in
    classical Sanskrit literature: see *Elementary Aspects of Peasant Insurgency in Colonial India*
    (Delhi: Oxford Univ. Press, 1983), 46 n. 81.

3   Homi Bhabha, "DisseminNation," in *Nation and Narration*, ed. Bhabha (London: Rout-
    ledge, 1990), 292.

4   They are from, respectively, Sara Suleri, *The Rhetoric of English India* (Chicago: Univ. of
    Chicago Press, 1992); Ann Stoler, *Race and the Education of Desire: Foucault's History of
    Sexuality and the Colonial Order of Things* (Durham: Duke Univ. Press, 1995), 199; and
    Patricia Seed, "Subaltern Studies in the Postcolonial Americas," in *Subaltern Studies in the
    Americas*, a special issue, ed. José Rabasa, Javier Sanjinés, and Robert Carr, of *Dispositio/n*
    45–46 (1994/1996): 220.

5   Ranajit Guha, "A note on the terms 'elite,' 'people,' 'subaltern,' etc. as used above,"
    Selected Subaltern Studies 44.

6   Aijaz Ahmad finds this passage "remarkable in its contortions as he [Guha] undertakes
    to reconcile a language taken partly from Gramsci and partly from American sociology
    with the Maoism of New Democracy and 'contradictions among the people.'" *In Theory*
    (London: Verso, 1992) 321 n. 7. Spivak notes similarly that "[t]he object of the group's
    investigation, in the case not even of the people as such but of the floating buffer zone
    of the regional elite-subaltern, is a *deviation* from an *ideal*—the people or the subaltern—
    which is itself defined as difference from the elite. . . . Whether or not they themselves
    perceive it—in fact Guha sees his definition of 'the people' within the master-slave
    dialectic—their text articulates the difficult task of rewriting its own conditions of
    impossibility as the conditions of its possibility." Spivak, "Can the Subaltern Speak?" in
    Marxism and the Interpretation of Culture, ed. Cary Nelson and Lawrence Grossberg (Ur-
    bana: Univ. of Illinois Press, 1988), 304.

7   Spivak notes the "counterpointing" in Guha's definition "between the ostensible lan-
    guage of quantification—*demographic* difference—which is positivistic, and the dis-
    course of a definitive difference—demographic *difference*—which opens the door to
    deconstructive gestures" ("Can the Subaltern Speak?" 297).

8   Georgi Dimitrov, "The Fascist Offensive and the Tasks of the Communist Interna-
    tional," in *The United Front: The Struggle against Fascisim and War* (New York: International,
    1938), 9–93.

9   "We prefer not to use the 'worker's governments,' and *speak of a united front government*,
    which in political character is something absolutely different, *different in principle*, from
    all Social-Democratic governments which usually call themselves 'workers' (or labor)
    governments.' While the Social-Democratic government is an instrument of class col-
    laboration with the bourgeoisie in the interests of the preservation of the capitalist
    order, *a united front government* is an instrument of the collaboration of the revolutionary
    vanguard of the proletariat with other anti-fascist parties, in the interests of the entire
    toiling population" (Dimitrov 73).

10 "Fascism is able to attract the masses because it demagogically appeals to their *most
    urgent needs and demands*. Fascism not only inflames prejudices that are deeply ingrained

in the masses, but also plays on the better sentiments of the masses, on their sense of justice, and sometimes even on their revolutionary traditions" (Dimitrov 13).

11 The slogan propounded by Earl Browder, the head of the CP-USA during the Popular Front period, was "Communism Is Twentieth-Century Americanism."

12 Ernesto Laclau and Chantal Mouffe, Hegemony and Socialist Strategy (London: Verso, 1985), 131.

13 "For some reason, after class and subject are withered away as stable signs, equally 'fictional' terms such as Third World or the people remain." Doris Sommer, "No Secrets," in The Real Thing: Testimonial Discourse in Latin America, ed. Georg Gugelberger (Durham: Duke Univ. Press, 1996), 156.

14 Ernesto Laclau, "Why Do Empty Signifiers Matter to Politics?" in Emancipation(s) (London: Verso, 1996), 36–46. If I understand Laclau's argument correctly, the figure of José Martí in Cuban politics would be an "empty signifier," since it is capable of being mobilized both by the revolution and the cultural politics of the Cuban émigré community.

15 For a concise account of the evolution of Sandinista policy for ethnic minorities on the Atlantic Coast see Carlos Vilas, State, Class, and Ethnicity in Nicaragua (Boulder: Lynne Rienner, 1989). Ironically, the Atlantic coast, which had at one point been the main target of CIA destabilization, ended up voting for the Sandinistas in the 1990 elections.

16 Charles Hale, Resistance and Contradiction: Miskitu Indians and the Nicaraguan State, 1894–1987 (Stanford: Stanford Univ. Press, 1994), 35–36. There is a new book on this topic by Jeffrey Gould, To Die in This Way: Nicaraguan Indians and the Myth of Mestizaje, 1880–1965 (Durham: Duke Univ. Press, 1998), but I have not had a chance to see it as of this writing.

17 María Josefina Saldaña-Portillo, "Developmentalism's Irresistible Seduction—Rural Subjectivity under Sandinista Agricultural Policy," in The Politics of Culture in the Shadow of Capital, ed. Lisa Lowe and David Lloyd (Durham: Duke Univ. Press, 1997), 164–66.

18 Alberto Moreiras, "Populism in a Double Register," paper presented at the Latin American Subaltern Studies meeting, College of William and Mary, 2–4 May 1997.

19 For example: "The people are neither the beginning or the end of the national narrative; they represent the cutting edge between the totalizing powers of the social and the forces that signify the more specific address to contentious, unequal interests and identities within the population" (297). Or: "Hybridity is the perplexity of the living as it interrupts the representation of the fullness of life; it is an instance of iteration, in minority discourse, of the time of the arbitrary sign—the 'minus in the origin'— through which all forms of cultural meaning are open to translation because their enunciation resists totalization. Interdisciplinary is the acknowledgement of the emergent moment of culture produced in the ambivalent movement between the pedagogical and performative address. . . . Cultural difference arises from the borderline moment of translation" (314).

20 As John Kraniauskas puts it incisively, "we are dealing here [in Bhabha] with something like transculturation in a psychoanalytic mode." John Kraniauskas, "On Hybridity," in From Miscegenation to Hybridity? ed. Avtar Brah and Annie Coombes (forthcoming). Bhabha would reply that hybridity is "at once very cultural and very savage" (The Location of Culture [New York: Routledge, 1994], 158). Savage because hybridity marks the subject of culture as abyssal, always/already split, founded on lack, and therefore not representable or recuperable by a "cultural" politics of hybridity and "difference"

that itself is bidding to become hegemonic in globalization—that is, liberal multi-culturalism.

21 In her introduction, titled "Deconstructing Historiography," to *Selected Subaltern Studies*. My citations here are from the version of this introduction in Spivak's *In Other Worlds: Essays in Cultural Politics* (New York: Methuen, 1987).

22 Spivak, *In Other Worlds* 246, 244–45. Also: "Especially in a critique of metropolitan culture, the event of political independence can be automatically assumed to stand between colony and decolonization as an unexamined good that operates a reversal. But the political goals of the new nation are supposedly determined by a regulative logic derived from the old colony, with its interests reversed: secularism, democracy, social-ism, national identity, and capitalist development. Whatever the face of this supposi-tion, it must be admitted that there is always a space in the new nation that cannot share in the energy of this reversal. This space has no established agency of traffic with the culture of imperialism. Paradoxically, this space is also outside of organized labor, below the attempted reversals of capital logic. Conventionally, this space is described as the habitat of the *subproletariat* or the *subaltern*." Spivak, *Outside in the Teaching Machine* (New York: Routledge, 1993), 78.

23 I am indebted to Mario Caro for this observation.

24 Spivak, "Politics of the Subaltern," *Socialist Review* 20, no. 3 (1990): 91. In Spivak's own "Can the Subaltern Speak?" the role of the abjected subaltern woman is assumed by Bhubaneswari Bhaduri, the nationalist activist whose suicide is "misread" even by her closest family.

25 "Does it follow that cultural studies is not a policed disciplinary area? That it is whatever people do, if they choose to call or locate themselves within the project and practice of cultural studies? I am not happy with that formulation either. Although cultural studies as a project is open-ended, it can't be simply pluralist in that way. Yes, it refuses to be a master discourse or a meta-discourse of any kind. Yes, it is a project that is always open to that which it doesn't yet know, to that which it can't yet name. But it does have some will to connect; it does have some stake in the choices it makes. It does matter whether cultural studies is this or that. It can't be just any old thing which chooses to march under a particular banner. It is a serious enterprise, or project, and that is inscribed in what is sometimes called the 'political' aspect of cultural studies." Stuart Hall, "Cul-tural Studies and Its Theoretical Legacies," in *Cultural Studies*, ed. Lawrence Grossberg, Cary Nelson, and Paula Treichler (New York: Routledge, 1992), 278.

26 "The Frankfurt scholars argued that the transformation of art into commodity inevita-bly sapped imagination and withered hope—now all that could be imagined was what was. But the artistic impulse is not destroyed by capital; it is transformed by it. As utopi-anism is mediated through the new processes of cultural production and consumption, new sorts of struggles over community and leisure begin." Simon Frith, *Sound Effects: Youth, Leisure and the Politics of Rock 'n' Roll* (New York: Pantheon, 1981), 264–68.

27 Stanley Aronowitz retraces some of the lines of this connection: "The popular front counterculture never wished to contest the space of high art. Rather, its intervention in American culture was to insist on the *plurality* of legitimate expressive forms. . . . [It] fought what proved to be an opening battle in the still-unfinished culture wars: the struggle for a democratic conception of national culture, and the battle to obliterate high culture's designation of popular culture as 'low.' " Stanley Aronowitz, *Roll over Beethoven: The Return of Cultural Strife* (Hanover, N.H.: Wesleyan Univ. Press, 1993), 166. On the cultural policy of the Popular Front in the United States and the very rich and varied

production it gave rise to, see Michael Denning's encyclopedic *The Cultural Front: The Laboring of American Culture in the Twentieth Century* (London: Verso, 1996), esp. 423–63.

28 It should come as no surprise then that many of the very intellectuals who defended in journals like the *Partisan Review* or *Tel Quel* the leftist political credentials of modernism against socialist realism and populism have mutated into the neoconservatives of today.

29 As John Kraniauskas puts it, "[cultural studies] extends the democratizing gesture of the anthropological concept of culture as a 'whole way of life' *into ideology*, whilst—at its non-populist best—recognizing the power of existing structures, including the intellectual elitism of the ideology of 'ideology': culture, now, as a 'whole way of struggle.' Rather than the mere valorization of popular or mass cultural forms as such, it is this cultural work of recovery that constitutes the populism that Cultural Studies must—perhaps rightly—risk and pass through." John Kraniauskas, "Globalization Is Ordinary: The Transnationalization of Cultural Studies," *Radical Philosophy* 90 (1998): 11.

30 Paul Willis, *Learning to Labour* (Ashgate: Aldershot, 1993). Willis himself saw working-class youth culture as contradictory: on the one hand, it constituted a sharp critique of the values of the class society these young people were being absorbed into; on the other, it lacked—in his view—a power of counter-hegemonic agency. For a recent Birmingham-style restatement of the problem of youth culture which is also a compelling manifesto for a re-politicized practice of cultural studies, see Phil Cohen, *Rethinking the Youth Question: Education, Labour, and Cultural Studies* (London: Macmillan, 1997).

31 For me the locus classicus of reception-oriented cultural studies is Jane Feuer's essay "Reading Dynasty: Television and Reception Theory," *South Atlantic Quarterly* 88, no. 2 (spring 1989). Michel de Certeau's work on everyday forms of resistance has also been extremely influential in this regard.

32 "[T]he temporary contract is in practice supplanting permanent institutions in the professional, emotional, sexual, cultural, family, and international domains, as well as in political affairs. This evolution is of course ambiguous: the temporary contract is favored by the system due to its greater flexibility, lower cost, and the creative turmoil of its accompanying motivations—all of these factors contribute to increased operativity. In any case, there is no question here of proposing a 'pure' alternative to the system: we all now know, as the 1970s come to a close, that an attempt at an alternative of that kind would end up resembling the system it was meant to replace. We should be happy that the tendency toward the temporary contract is ambiguous: it is not totally subordinated to the goal of the system, yet the system tolerates it." Jean-François Lyotard, *The Postmodern Condition*, trans. Brian Massumi (Minneapolis: Univ. of Minnesota Press, 1985).

33 See, for example, Meaghan Morris, "Banality in Cultural Studies," *Discourse* 10, no. 2 (1988): 3–29; and Fredric Jameson, "On 'Cultural Studies,'" *Social Text* 34 (1993): 17–52.

34 Beatriz Sarlo, *Escenas de la vida posmoderna* (Buenos Aires: Ariel, 1994). Many of the themes of this book are present in Sarlo's essay "Aesthetics and Post-Politics: From Fujimori to the Gulf War," in *The Postmodernism Debate in Latin America*, ed. John Beverley, José Oviedo, and Michael Aronna (Durham: Duke Univ. Press, 1995), 241–63.

35 Sarlo's critique of "media neopopulists" dovetails with James Petras's sense that the hegemony of neoliberalism has created a new type of intellectual in Latin America, the "institutional intellectual," "ostensible critic of the neoliberal economic model, but just as deeply embedded in dependent relations with overseas networks as their adversaries among the export-oriented and financial elites. . . . The ascendancy of the institutional intellectuals has banished the key concepts which illuminate popular struggles: imperi-

alism, socialism, popular power, and class struggle have disappeared down the memory hole—they are unfashionable." James Petras, "The Metamorphosis of Latin America's Intellectuals," *Latin American Perspectives* 65 (1990): 106, 108.

36 Silviano Santiago, "Meaning and Discursive Intensities: On the Situation of Postmodern Reception in Brazil," in *Postmodernism Debate* 249.

37 Daniel Bell, *The Cultural Contradictions of Capitalism* (New York: Basic, 1976).

38 A re-reading of Marcuse in this light, particularly his *Eros and Civilization*, might be warranted. María Milagros López's work on "post-work subjectivity" and the new strategies of public policy and cultural interpellation it entails is extremely suggestive: see, for example, her "Postwork Society and Postmodern Subjectivities," in *Postmodernism Debate* 165–91.

5 Civil Society, Hybridity, and the " 'Political' Aspect of Cultural Studies" (on Canclini)

1 The student of Spanish literature will recognize certain similarities between this incident and Lope de Vega's famous play, *Fuenteovejuna*, about a peasant rebellion—and its relation to the formation of the absolutist state—in the times of Ferdinand and Isabella.

2 See, for example, Ricardo Salvatore, "Stories of Proletarianization in Rural Argentina, 1820–1860," in *Subaltern Studies in the Americas*, a special issue of *Dispositio/n* 45–46 (1994/1996): 197–216.

3 Mahmood Mamdani, *Citizen and Subject: Contemporary Africa and the Legacy of Late Colonialism* (Princeton: Princeton Univ. Press, 1996), 13–23.

4 The key text is Anthony Arato and Jean Cohen, *Civil Society* (Cambridge: MIT Press, 1993). For a useful genealogy of the concept of civil society see Dominique Colas, "Civil Society: From Utopia to Management, from Marxism to Anti-Marxism," in *Nations, Identities, Cultures*, ed. V. Y. Mudime (Durham: Duke Univ. Press, 1997), 29–44.

5 Antonio Gramsci, *Selections from the Prison Notebooks*, ed. and trans. Quintin Hoare and Geoffrey Nowell Smith (New York: International, 1971), 52.

6 Partha Chatterjee, *The Nation and Its Fragments: Colonial and Postcolonial Histories* (Princeton: Princeton Univ. Press, 1993), 235.

7 Enrique Dussel, "Eurocentrism and Modernity," in *The Postmodernism Debate in Latin America*, ed. John Beverley, José Oviedo, and Michael Aronna (Durham: Duke Univ. Press, 1995), 73.

8 The idea that the state should displace its internal contradictions onto the colonies goes back in European political thought at least to Machiavelli. Dominique Colas explains the filiation between class rule by the bourgeoisie and colonialism-imperialism in Hegel's concept of civil society as follows: "[T]he term used by Hegel as the German equivalent of 'koinonia politiké,' or 'civil society,' is *burgerliche Gesellschaft*. 'Burger' is a polysemic term, and Hegel made good use of this polysemy. A burger was, first, an inhabitant of a city, that is, someone that enjoyed civic rights, a citizen. But a burger was also someone who enjoyed an elevated social status—a master of a corporation, for example—and, according to Hegel, the typical member of civil society was just such a 'bourgeois,' in the French sense of that word. However, at the same time that civil society was engendering a bourgeoisie at one of its poles, it was creating what Hegel called a 'rabble' as its other pole—with a gap between the two that could only increase. One way to regulate civil society, according to Hegel, was to encourage what he considered surplus members of the rabble to go off and found colonies elsewhere" (Colas, "Civil Society" 36–37).

9   This is the basis of Guha's idea that the colonial state involved "dominance without hegemony": "The consent which empowered the bourgeoisie to speak for all citizens in the hegemonic states of Europe was also the license used by the latter to assimilate the respective [native] civil societies to themselves. But no such assimilation was feasible under colonial conditions where an alien power ruled over a state without citizens, where the right of conquest rather than the consent of its citizens constituted its charter, and where, therefore, dominance would never gain the hegemony it coveted so much. So it made no sense to equate the colonial state with India as constituted by its own civil society. The history of the latter would always exceed that of the Raj." Ranajit Guha, "The Small Voice of History," *Subaltern Studies* (1996): 3. On this point, see also Guha's early monograph, *A Rule of Property* (1963; Durham: Duke Univ. Press, 1995).

10 For example: "The Mexican Civil Society has called for a 'marcha virtual' [virtual march] to show International support for including the Zapatistas in national dialogues towards peaceful solutions to Mexico's crisis. Given the fact that the members of the EZLN travelling to Mexico City are Mexican citizens, and are thus guaranteed by the Mexican constitution the freedom to travel unencumbered anywhere in the Republic, and given the fact that the Mexican government does not consider them criminals or terrorists . . . it is extremely important to pressure the Mexican Government into . . . guaranteeing the free travel of the Zapatista Delegation to the National Indigenous Congress which will take place on October 7." Zapatista e-mail ACTION ALERT, "Cyberspace Demonstration. Support Zapatista Delegation to Indigenous Congress," 7 October 1996.

11 Arturo Escobar, *Encountering Development* (Princeton: Princeton Univ. Press, 1995), 170–71.

12 Silvia Rivera Cusicanqui's work on *ayllu* communities in present-day Bolivia is both a model for such an intervention and a caution about some of the complexities involved in it. Rivera maintains that "attempts by liberals, populists, and leftists to impose liberal democratic models on the *ayllus* have actually hindered the emergence and consolidation of democratic practices and institutions." She argues instead for a non-integrationist concept of citizenship, founded on a "recognition of the right to be different as a fundamental human right." At the same time, however, she notes that conflicts within the *ayllus*—for example, between men and women, or young people and elders—are frequent, and produce complex articulations between economic individualism and market forces, formal civil society based on individual "rights," the activity of NGOs, and the logic of collective production and control of the *ayllu* itself. These conflicts also involve inequalities of power and prestige; one should conclude, then, that the problem of the subaltern cannot be essentialized as "community" versus state or civil society either, but rather appears *within* both civil society and community, as well as in the relationship between them. Silvia Rivera Cusicanqui, "Liberal Democracy and Ayllu Democracy in Bolivia," in *The Challenge of Rural Democratization: Perspectives from Latin America and the Philippines*, ed. Jonathan Fox (London: Cass, 1990), 97–121. I owe this reference to Alberto Moreiras. To the same end, see Guha's magisterial reconstruction of a botched abortion and the women's self-help network that is articulated around it among poor peasants in nineteenth-century Bengal: "Chandra's Death," in *A Subaltern Studies Reader*, ed. Ranajit Guha (Minneapolis: Univ. of Minnesota Press, 1997): 34–63.

13 Néstor García Canclini, *Hybrid Cultures: Strategies for Entering and Leaving Modernity*, trans. Christopher Chiappari and Silvia López (Minneapolis: Univ. of Minnesota Press, 1995; first Spanish edition: Mexico: Grijalbo, 1990).

14 "[S]e require que las políticas culturales, los partidos que critican el neoliberalismo, y los movimientos sociales, superen su concepción gutemberguiana de la cultura y elaboren estrategias consistentes de actuación en los medios" Néstor García Canclini, *Consumidores y ciudadanos* (Mexico: Grijalbo, 1995), 190.

15 "Una cuestión cardinal para la redefinición de la sociedad civil . . . es la crisis de la nación. . . . Las sociedades civiles parecen cada vez menos como comunidades nacionales, entendidas como unidades territoriales, lingüísticas y políticas. Se manifiestan más bien como *comunidades interpretativas de consumidores*, es decir, conjuntos de personas que comparten gustos y pactos de lectura respecto de ciertos bienes (gastronómicos, deportivos, musicales) que les dan identidades compatidas" (*Consumidores* 194–95).

16 See in particular Canclini's critique of the way in which the Mexican National Museum of Anthropology stages the Mexican patrimony by "*monumentalization and nationalist ritualization* of culture" (*Hybrid Cultures* 120).

17 For example: "The neo-Gramscians see culture as part of a struggle for hegemony rather than as a space of distinction and political conflict between classes. Therefore, this model is utilized by those who emphasize autonomy and the capacity for initiative and opposition by subaltern sectors. . . . [This] has stimulated unilateral and utopian views. . . . The difficulties become more acute . . . when their models are used as superparadigms and generate popular strategies to which they attempt to subordinate the totality of all facts: all that is not hegemonic is subaltern, or the inverse. The descriptions then omit ambiguous processes of interpretation and mixing in which the symbolic movements of different classes engender other processes that cannot be ordered under the classifications of hegemonic and subaltern, modern and traditional" (*Hybrid Cultures* 199; see also 180–81).

18 Canclini's double articulation of the idea of hybridity is represented on the cover of the first Mexican edition of *Hybrid Cultures* by a double image: a photo of the frontier between the United States and Mexico, at the place where the border fence comes to an end on a beach. Because the legal limit of territoriality is the high tide line, at low tide it is possible to cross unobstructed between Mexico and the United States (the picture shows families normally separated by the border carrying picnic coolers from one side to the other). Superimposed over this black and white photo is a picture in color of an ordinary window frame painted over à la Rauschenberg, which embodies the collapse of the distinction between the aesthetic and the utilitarian, the auratic and the postauratic. By the same token, the relation between the photograph of the beach and the painting-assemblage suggests also a crossing of the boundary between high culture and popular culture, enacting thus one of the features of pastiche: the combination in a single art object—in this case the book cover—of dissimilar or contradictory aesthetic or cultural sign systems.

19 Although he does not mention transculturation explicitly, Canclini explains the filiation of the concept of the hybrid as follows: "Occasional mention will be made of the terms *syncretism, mestizaje,* and others used to designate processes of *hybridization.* I prefer this last term because it includes diverse intercultural mixtures—not only racial ones to which *mestizaje* seems to be limited—and because it permits the inclusion of the modern forms of hybridization better than does 'syncretism,' a term that almost always refers to religious fusions or traditional symbolic movements" (*Hybrid Cultures* 11 n. 1).

20 "A diferencia de la época en que se enfrentaban quienes colocaban todas sus ilusiones en alguna transformación mágica del estado y quienes confiaban todo el cambio al proletariado o a las clases populares, ahora se trata de ver cómo podemos rehacer conjuntamente el papel del Estado y de la sociedad civil" (*Consumidores* 189).

21 López, "Postwork Society and Postmodern Subjectivities," in *The Postmodernism Debate*, ed. John Beverley, José Oviedo, and Michael Aronna (Durham: Duke Univ. Press, 1995), 189.

22 For example: "In these exchanges of traditional symbols with international communications circuits, culture industries, and migrations, questions about identity and the national, the defense of sovereignty, and the unequal appropriation of knowledge and art do not disappear. The conflicts are not erased, as a neoconservative postmodernism claims. They are placed in a different register, one that is multifocal and more tolerant, and the autonomy of each culture is rethought—sometimes—with smaller fundamentalist risks" (*Hybrid Cultures* 240–41).

23 "Veo en las actuales polémicas europeas un intento de desfatalizar el paradigma neoliberal" (*Consumidores* 88).

24 George Yúdice, in "Civil Society, Consumption, and Governmentality in an Age of Global Restructuring," *Social Text* 14, no. 4 (1995): 1–25, argues that "societies may have reached a historical threshold in which it is no longer possible to think such ideas as citizenship and democracy in the absence of consumption" (20).

25 Alberto Moreiras, "A Wind Storm from Paradise: Negative Globality and Latin American Cultural Studies," cited from ms.

26 I am indebted to Hugo Achugar for this observation.

27 Jameson, "On 'Cultural Studies,' " *Social Text* 34 (1993): 17–52.

6 Territoriality, Multiculturalism, and Hegemony: The Question of the Nation

1 Antonio Gramsci, *Selections from the Prison Notebooks*, ed. and trans. Quintin Hoare and Geoffrey Nowell Smith (New York: International, 1971), 57.

2 Ranajit Guha, *Elementary Aspects of Peasant Insurgency in Colonial India* (Delhi: Oxford Univ. Press, 1983), 166.

3 Guha notes that "[a] correlate of the category of space [in peasant insurgency] was a sense of time. . . . Expressed in its most generalized form as a contrasted pair of times (then/now), a good past negated by a bad present, its function was to endow the struggle against the alien with the mission of recovering the past as a future" (*Aspects* 291).

4 See, for example, David Slater, "Rethinking the Spatialities of Social Movements," in *Cultures of Politics/Politics of Culture: Revisioning Latin American Social Movement*, ed. Sonia Alvarez, Evelina Dagnino, and Arturo Escobar (Boulder: Westview, 1998), 380–401.

5 That is, the nation or nation-state is not a "thing," but a concept or—in Benedict Anderson's phrase—an "imagined community."

6 Gyan Prakash, "Subaltern Studies as Postcolonial Criticism," *American Historical Review* 99 (1994): 1480.

7 "That the mechanicist conception has been a religion of the subaltern is shown by an analysis of the development of Christianity" (*Notebooks* 337). Gramsci has a similar problem with syndicalism: "Here we are dealing with a subaltern group [organized labor] which is prevented by this theory from ever becoming dominant, or from developing beyond the economic-corporate stage and rising to the plane of ethical-political hegemony in civil society, and of domination of the State. . . . The transformation of the subordinate group into a dominant one is excluded" (*Notebooks* 160).

8 Anderson's hypothesis in *Imagined Communities* (London: Verso, 1991) is that the modern nation-state requires the prior existence of and indoctrination into literary-scientific

print culture or (as Anderson himself prefers) "print capitalism." As I noted in my discussion of the Túpac Amaru rebellion in chapter 2, however, what is at stake here is not so much the inability of the subaltern to "imagine" a nation as such as the fact that it tends to produce a *different* sense of national territoriality and history.

9   De Man ended up as a collaborator with the Fascist regime in Belgium, a fact that may help explain his nephew's early protofascist sympathies.

10 "Even if one admits that other cultures have had an importance and a significance in the process of 'hierarchical' unification of world civilisation (and this should be admitted without question), they have a universal value only in so far as they have become constituent elements of European culture, which is the only historically and concretely universal culture—in so far, that is, as they have contributed to the process of European thought and have been assimilated by it" (*Notebooks* 416). I am grateful to José Rabasa for bringing to my attention David Lloyd's critique of Gramsci's idea that the history of subaltern groups is episodic or fragmentary, in *Anomalous States: Irish Writing and the Post-Colonial Moment* (Durham: Duke Univ. Press, 1992), 127ff.

11 Linda Singer, "Recalling a Community at Loose Ends," in *Community at Loose Ends*, ed. Miami Theory Collective (Minneapolis: Univ. of Minnesota Press, 1991), 128.

12 Nancy Fraser, "From Redistribution to Recognition? Dilemmas of Justice in a 'Post-Socialist' Age," *New Left Review* 212 (1995): 68–93.

13 Laclau and Mouffe put it this way: "[W]hereas political leadership can be grounded upon a conjunctural coincidence of interests in which the participating sectors retain their separate identity, moral and intellectual leadership requires that an ensemble of 'ideas' and 'values' be shared by a number of sectors—or, to use our own terminology, that certain subject positions traverse a number of class sectors. Intellectual and moral leadership constitutes, according to Gramsci, in a higher synthesis, a 'collective will,' which, through ideology, becomes the organic concept unifying a historic bloc." Thus, "a class does not *take State power, it becomes* the State, transforming its own identity by articulating to itself a plurality of struggles and democratic demands." Ernesto Laclau and Chantal Mouffe, *Hegemony and Socialist Strategy* (London: Verso, 1985), 66–67, 70.

14 This was, of course, the major lesson of Althusser and his school. As we say in chapter 3, David Stoll's appeal to "verification," like Sokal's prank, implies the identification of the left with "science."

15 Todd Gitlin, *The Twilight of Common Dreams: Why America Is Wracked by Culture Wars* (New York: Metropolitan, 1995); Richard Rorty, *Achieving Our Country: Leftist Thought in Twentieth-Century America* (Cambridge: Harvard Univ. Press, 1998). As I noted earlier, Jorge Castañeda's *Utopia Disarmed* makes a similar case for the (dissimilar) situation of the failure of the Latin American revolutionary left.

16 Iris Marion Young, *Justice and the Politics of Difference* (Princeton: Princeton Univ. Press, 1990).

17 In the aftermath of the Simpson trial, in an ABC *Nightline* special forum, a representative of Los Angeles NOW gave an eloquent and bitter denunciation of the verdict as injurious to women's rights, while representatives of the black community and of various left sects argued in favor of the verdict as a victory in the community struggle to control a racist police force. The NOW spokesperson was subsequently rebuked by the national leadership for seeming to polarize women's issues against issues of racial injustice and prejudice. But the damage was done.

18 Charles Taylor, "The Politics of Recognition," in *Multiculturalism*, ed. Amy Gutman (Princeton: Princeton Univ. Press, 1994).

19 Homi Bhabha, "Editor's Introduction," *Front Lines/Border Posts*, a special issue of *Critical Inquiry* 23, no. 3 (1997): 458–60. Given my remarks in chapter four on Bhabha's articulation of cultural difference, I wonder if this characterization of Taylor might not also apply to his own work (or, alternatively, if perhaps I have misunderstood what Bhabha was trying to get at).

21 Chantal Mouffe, "Feminism, Citizenship, and Radical Democratic Politics," in *Feminists Theorize the Political*, ed. Judith Butler and Joan Scott (New York: Routledge, 1992), 369–84.

22 López, "Postwork Society and Postmodern Subjectivities," in *The Postmodernism Debate*, ed. John Beverley, José Oviedo, and Michael Aronna (Durham: Duke Univ. Press, 1995), 190. The specific reference is to Iris Young's essay "Polity and Group Difference: A Critique of the Ideal of Universal Citizenship," *Ethics* 99 (1989): 250–74.

23 Gayatri Spivak, "More on 'Imperialism Today,'" *Against the Current* 63 (July/August 1996): 20, 21.

24 Lisa Lowe, "Work, Immigration, Gender: New Subjects of Cultural Politics," in *The Politics of Culture in the Shadow of Capital*, ed. David Lloyd and Lisa Lowe (Durham: Duke Univ. Press, 1997), 370.

25 Michael Lind, *The Next American Nation: The New Nationalism and the Fourth American Revolution* (New York: Free Press, 1996).

26 As Todd Gitlin puts it succinctly, in the United States "[t]he Republican tilt of white men is the most potent form of identity politics in our time" (*Twilight* 253).

27 Ernesto Laclau, "Towards a Theory of Populism," in *Politics and Ideology in Marxist Theory* (London: New Left, 1977), 143–98.

28 Aronowitz, *Roll over Beethoven: The Return of Cultural Strife* (Hanover, N.H.: Wesleyan Univ. Press, 1993), 116–17.

29 For example: "Multiculturalism is not a tourist's eye view of 'ethnicity,' nor is it a paean to the American mythology defining the nation as a collection of diverse and plural groups living happily together and united by their knowledge of, and proper respect for, something called 'Western Culture.' Multiculturalism, as an organizing principle to which universities are increasingly paying at least lip service, is understood at its most simplistic to mean exposure to different cultures. Simple exposure, however, is absolutely meaningless without a reconsideration and restructuring of the ways in which knowledge is organized, disseminated, and used to support inequitable power differentials." Ted Gordon and Wahneema Lubianao, "The Statement of the Black Faculty Caucus," in *Debating P.C.*, ed. Paul Berman (New York: Dell-Laurel, 1992), 249–50.

30 Bonnie Honig, "Ruth, the Model Emigree: Mourning and the Symbolic Politics of Immigration," in *Cosmopolitics*, ed. Pheng Cheah and Bruce Robbins (Minneapolis: Univ. of Minnesota Press, 1998). Quotations are from the typescript.

31 Homi Bhabha, "DissemiNation," in *Nation and Narration*, ed. Bhabha (London: Routledge, 1990), 299–301.

32 For the "multitude" as versus the "people," see Virno's essay on Exodus in *Radical Thought in Italy: A Potential Politics*, ed. Paolo Virno and Michael Hardt (Minneapolis: Univ. of Minnesota Press, 1996); and Michael Hardt and Toni Negri, *Empire* (Cambridge: Harvard Univ. Press, forthcoming). I owe this suggestion and a great deal else to Jon Beaseley-Murray. "The great contribution of Foucault's last published work," Bhabha observes, "is to suggest that people emerge in the modern state as a perpetual movement of the 'marginal integration of individuals'" ("DissemiNation" 301).

33 Louis Althusser, *The Future Lasts Forever* (New York: New Press, 1993). Jameson echoes

this rejection of the market in his essay on "actually-existing" Marxism, which at the same time is his effort to come to terms with the challenge of subaltern studies for Marxism: "[I]n this essay I presuppose the systemic incompatibility between the market and socialism, something demonstrated by the destructive power of the market in Eastern Europe, not only in terms of the disintegration of social relations after the downfall of the Communist state, but also in terms of the superstructural corruption produced by the fantasies of consumption and western mass culture that preceded and prepared the way for this downfall." Fredric Jameson, "El marxismo realmente existente," *Casa de las Américas* 211 (1998): 17 (my re-translation).

34   I owe this crucial distinction to Jean-Christophe Agnew.

35   For a contemporary statement, see, e.g., John Roemer, *A Future for Socialism* (London: Verso, 1994).

36   See my remarks on this in chapter 4.

37   The key documents are collected in *The Transition from Feudalism to Capitalism*, ed. Rodney Hilton (London: New Left, 1976).

38   As Marx noted in *Capital*, petty commodity production is characterized by a different formula for the production and circulation of commodities than capitalism; it is thus literally a different mode of production. That is what permitted Bukharin to argue, against Stalin's policy of forced collectivization, that a land-owning peasantry was not necessarily incompatible with communism. Marx's formula for the circuit of petty commodity production in *Capital* is C-M-C, that is, commodity-money-commodity, where the aim of market exchange is to assure the possession of use-values produced by others; thus all producers in such a mode of production are nominally "equal." By contrast, the formula for the circuit of capitalist production is M-C-M, money-commodity-money, where the aim is to produce an M larger than the initial M. This requires, however, according to the labor theory of value, the exploitation of labor power: that is, a class society. Marx's distinction between petty commodity production and capitalist production corresponds, more or less, to the Aristotelian distinction between *oikonomike* (the activity to procure the use-values necessary to the "household") and *krematistike* (economic activity directed by the desire to accumulate wealth as such). Subaltern political economy tends to be *oikonomike*: that is, "home economics" as versus Economics.

39   Sean Wilentz, "Integrating Ethnicity into American Studies," *Chronicle of Higher Education* (November 1996); Doris Sommer and Sacvan Bercovitch, course syllabus, "American Identities," Harvard Univ., spring 1997.

40   To begin with, it is far from being the case that all Latinos are immigrants, since many of them are descendants of people who lived in the continental United States before its formation as a nation. Those that are immigrants have not in general lost the use of Spanish beyond the first generation or their sense of connection to Spanish and Latin American culture. This is reflected in the proliferation of Spanish-language newspapers, radio stations, advertising, music, bookstores, and so on. In fact a city like Miami shows what Alejandro Portes calls "acculturation in reverse": Anglos, Jews, and African Americans have had to adjust to the language and cultural forms of the new population—learn about Latin American foods like yuca or frijoles, for example, or listen to Gloria Estefan in Spanish. Though most Latino intellectuals write in English (because, like Richard Rodriguez in *Hunger of Memory*, they see English as the dominant language in academic and literary terms), actual Latino culture in the United States is bilingual and characterized by code-switching. If recent Latino novels like *Dreaming in*

Cuban or *How the García Girls Lost Their Accents* (both of which were published in separate Spanish and English editions) were actually to reflect in their dialogue the speech forms of the communities their characters belong to, they would be at least *bilingual* and would require therefore a reader with a reading knowledge of both Spanish and English (leaving aside the question of national, regional, and/or class dialects of Spanish). For all practical purposes, the United States is now as much a bilingual society as Canada, and will become more so.

41   It is perhaps appropriate that the Americanism of both Bercovitch and Sommer is itself aporetic. Bercovitch is a Canadian Jew; Sommer is the child of Jewish parents from Eastern Europe who came to the United States after escaping the Holocaust.

42   According to an article in the *Princeton Alumni Weekly*, Wilentz's own course, "American Democracy and the Atlantic World," "breaks from customary frameworks, which tend to emphasize the United States's unique role in history; instead, it emphasizes the idea of the country as an Atlantic nation, one whose relationships to Europe, Latin America, the Caribbean, and Africa are central to its past and present. The syllabus frames a comparative and cross-regional perspective." "University Revamps American Studies Program," *Princeton Alumni Weekly* (17 December 1997): 4.

43   Likewise, in its stress on individual achievement—e.g., "America may be a multicultural society, but it is also a society of multicultural individuals; and the most gifted of them have turned their multicultural visions into art"—Wilentz's argument, perhaps inadvertently, echoes the very language of neoliberal hegemony. If there is a model for a politics of the left bound up with Wilentz's argument, it might be something like Rorty's attempt to revive Deweyan Progressivism in *Achieving Our Country*. But, like Kristeva's "cosmopolitanism," Rorty's proposals for the American left turn out to be yet another case of "hegemonic Americanism": in effect, an "americanized" version of Fabian socialism, celebratory of the goals and values the United States claims to represent as the dominant world power, and therefore like Fabian socialism in its heyday a kind of "social imperialism."

44   I am indebted to Jo Tavener for this observation.

Index

Academy, the, 1–24 passim, 28–32, 38–40, 70–72, 76–79, 103, 104, 108–109, 161, 166–167, 180 n.13; critique of academic knowledge, 31; and cultural studies, 112–116, 127–132; debate over American studies, 162–66, 193 n.42; Gramsci on education, 138–140; Western Culture debate (Stanford) 29, 70–71, 82, 172 n.8. *See also* Anthropology; Deconstruction; Ebonics; History/historiography; Humanities; Intellectuals; Literature; Lyotard, Jean-François; Multiculturalism; Subaltern studies

Acculturation, 43–44, 79, 83, 128, 162; "acculturation in reverse," 192 n.40

Achugar, Hugo: critique of postcolonial and subaltern studies, 17–19, 166, 171 n.26

Adorno, Theodor, 104, 109

African-American, 9, 19, 45, 143–144, 151, 155, 164–166, 190 n.12, 191 n.29

Agency, 4, 11–12, 13, 27, 31, 36, 71, 75, 79–80, 82, 102–103, 105–107, 113, 123, 129, 131, 135–136, 142, 147, 148, 173 n.13, 181 n.25, 185 n.30

Ahmad, Aijaz: critique of subaltern studies, 20–21, 182 n.6

Althusser, Louis, 4, 17, 22, 70, 99, 100, 107, 131, 150, 158–159, 190 n.14

American studies. *See* Academy

Amin, Shahid: on orality and peasant
resistance, 61–62, 173 n.18
Anderson, Benedict: "imagined commu-
nity," 5, 10, 55, 137, 154, 189 n.3, 189–
190 n.8
Anthropology, 2, 3, 9–10, 11, 13, 30–31, 43–
45, 68–69, 73, 77, 79–82, 104, 107, 115,
116, 128, 137–138, 157–158, 185 n.29;
new ethnography, 173–174 n.18
Antonio the Counsellor: Canudos rebellion,
117
Anzaldúa, Gloria, 80
Apartheid: as model for Latin American culture, 59
Arguedas, José María, 43, 62–64
Arielism, 18–19
Armed struggle/guerrilla struggle. See
Guatemala; Mao Tse Tung/Maoism; Sandinism; Zapatistas
Aronowitz, Stanley: on Gramsci and hegemony, 154; on Popular Front cultural politics, 184 n.27

Balibar, Etienne, 22
Barnet, Miguel: Autobiography of a Runaway
Slave. See Testimonio
Baroque, 12; as colonial cultural form, 56–
59, 170 n.16, 177 n.24
Bartra, Roger: on crisis of Marxism,
172 n.32
Baudrillard, Jean, 108
Bell, Daniel: The Cultural Contradictions of Cap-
italism, 112–13
Benítez-Rojo, Antonio: "bifurcated desire"
in Latin American nationalism, 58–59,
177–178 n.26
Benjamin, Walter, 44, 79, 109; Arcades Proj-
ect and cultural studies, 107; concept of
Jetzeit, 37; "The Storyteller," 24, 68–69,
172 n.35, 179 n.6
Bennett, William, 111
Bercovitch, Sacvan: course on "American
Identities," 162–165. See also Sommer,
Doris; Wilentz, Sean
Beverley, John: Literature and Politics, 3–5, 8;
on testimonio, 65; on the Baroque,
170 n.16
Bhabha, Homi, 5, 13, 16–17, 85–87, 106,

123–126, 133, 163; on Charles Taylor,
145–146; critique of, 98–100, 102–103,
171 n.23, 183 n.19; on national subject,
157–158; and savage hybridity, 183–
184 n.20
Bilingualism, 29–30, 55, 62, 69, 164–165,
192–193 n.40
Binary, 61, 85–87, 103, 106, 126–130, 157
Birmingham Centre, 104, 107
Blair, Tony: and Third Way, 99
"Boom," the, 45, 176 n.13
Borges, Jorge Luis, 24
Bové, Paul: on "Left Conservatism," 171 n.22
Brecht, Bertolt: plumpen Denken, 136
Brennan, Tim: critique of Rushdie, 174–
175 n.2
Brunner, José Joaquín, 13, 14, 17, 122
Burgos, Elisabeth, 68, 79–82, 178–179 n.5,
181 n.25
Butler, Judith, 22; "performance," 178 n.27

Campbell, Leon: on role of books and writing in Túpac Amaru rebellion, 51–53, 59.
See also Túpac Amaru; Writing
Candido, Antonio: on literature and underdevelopment, 48–49, 110
Castañeda, Jorge: Utopia Disarmed, 129,
190 n.15
Chakrabarty, Dipesh: on history, 34, 36–38,
42
Chatterjee, Partha, 21, 41, 120
Cherniavsky, Eve: "Subaltern Studies in a
U.S. Frame," 2, 171 n.28
Citizenship, 18, 34, 36, 48–49, 71, 90, 95,
110–112, 116–122, 125–131, 139, 146–
148, 149, 155–157, 163, 165, 174 n.2,
184 n.22, 186 n.38, 186 n.8, 187 nn. 9–12,
189 nn. 22 and 24. See also Civil society
Civil society, 107, 113, 115–132 passim,
143, 151–152, 159–160, 186 nn. 4, 8,
187 nn. 9–12
Class, 6, 9–12, 19, 24, 26, 28–30, 35, 38–
40, 43, 45–47, 50, 53–55, 70, 76, 80, 83,
86–96, 101–102, 104, 107, 109, 110, 113,
119–120, 126–127, 129, 132, 135–140,
143–144, 147, 148, 151, 154, 159, 160–161,
163, 164, 165–166, 182 n.9, 188 n.20,
190 n.13

Clifford, James: on ethnographic writing, 11

Communism, 3, 20–24, 72, 88–91, 123, 158–159, 166, 180 n.16, 183 n.11, 191–192 n.33

"Contradictions among the people," 24, 76, 90, 182 n.6. *See also* Heterogeneity; Identity politics; Mao Tse Tung/Maoism; Multiculturalism

Cornejo-Polar, Antonio: on Andean immigration and heterogeneity, 62–64

Coronil, Fernando: on transculturation, 43–45

Cosmopolitanism: and globalization, 149–157; and Rushdie, 174–175 n.2. *See also* Honig, Bonnie; Kristeva, Julia

Critical regionalism. *See* Moreiras, Alberto

Cultural studies, 7, 15, 18, 21, 84, 104–113, 115, 122–132, 159, 184 n.25, 185 nn. 29–33

da Cunha, Euclides: *Rebellion in the Backlands*, 117. *See also* Antonio the Counsellor; Vargas Llosa, Mario

Deconstruction, 16, 19, 22, 37, 70, 86, 97–104, 123–127, 135, 142

Deleuze, Gilles, 126

de Man, Henri: polemic with Gramsci, 137–138

de Man, Paul, 18, 51, 137, 176 n.16

Democracy/democratization, 4–6, 8, 11, 14, 18, 34–35, 40, 54–55, 70, 80–81, 89–91, 93–94, 104, 106, 108, 111, 118, 122, 128–129, 140, 143, 145–146, 148, 151, 154, 157, 158–161, 184 n.22, 185 n.29, 189 n.24, 190 n.13; Gramsci on, 138–139; Rivera Cusicanqui on *ayllu* democracy, 187 n.12

"Democratic cosmopolitanism." *See* Honig, Bonnie

"Democratic subject position." *See* Laclau, Ernesto; Mouffe, Chantal

Dependency theory, 14, 47, 91–93, 176 n.13

Derrida, Jacques, 19, 37, 125; on New International, 152

Devi, Mahasweta: relation with Spivak, 101–102

Diccionario Enciclopédico de Literatura Latinoamericana, 48–49. *See also* Osorio, Nelson

Dimitrov, Georgi: on the Popular Front, 88–91, 103, 182 nn. 9–10

Disciplinarity. *See* Academy

D'Souza, Dinesh: on *I, Rigoberta Menchú*, 29, 70–71, 82

Dussel, Enrique: on modernity and civil society, 120–122; on Rorty, 174 n.23

Dylan, Bob, 105

Ebonics, 164–165

Education. *See* Academy; Gramsci, Antonio

"Egalitarian imaginary." *See* Laclau, Ernesto; Mouffe, Chantal

Equality, 23–24, 40, 44, 54, 73, 77, 131, 144–166 passim. *See also* Democracy/democratization

Escobar, Arturo: on globalization and cultural affirmation, 122

Espinosa Medrano, Juan de: *Apology*, 50, 56–59, 177 n.25

Ethnography/ethnographers. *See* Anthropology

Fascism, 9, 89–91, 104

Felman, Shoshana: on testimonio, 78–79

Feminism. *See* Women/Women's movement

Feuerbach, Ludwig: on Negation, 31–32

Foucault, Michel, 7, 8, 16, 20, 37–39, 113, 118, 145

Frankfurt School, 103–107, 109, 110, 184 n.26

Fraser, Nancy: on the left, 141–142, 144, 153

Fukuyama, Francis: "end of history" thesis, 107

Gandhi, Mahatma: and Indian nationalism, 61–62. *See also* Amin, Shahid; Chatterjee, Partha; Guha, Ranajit

García Canclini, Néstor, 16, 63, 113, 115, 133, 152, 159, 163, 188 nn. 14–20, 189 nn. 22–23; *Hybrid Cultures*, critique of, 122–132, 137, 142; "mixed times," 131

Garcilaso the Inca: *Comentarios reales*, 50, 52

Giddens, Anthony: and the Third Way, 99

Gitlin, Todd: *The Twilight of Common Dreams*, 143, 147

Globalization, 3, 7, 14, 15, 17, 28, 79–80, 83–84, 141–142, 148–153; and cultural studies, 108–113, 122–132

Goméz Peña, Guillermo, 80

González Echevarría, Roberto, 5; on Espinosa and colonial Baroque, 57–58, 170 n.16, 177 n.22

Gordon, Ted. See Lubiano, Wahneema

Gramsci, Antonio, 2, 11–15, 19, 20, 23, 32, 35, 37–38, 71, 102, 105–106, 123–125, 128–129, 133, 135, 143, 147, 154, 160, 189 n.7; on civil society and the state, 118–119; on education, 135–141, 165; Eurocentrism of, 138, 190 n.10; on the national-popular, 4, 56, 142, 153–155; "people-nation," 153–155; on *signore*, 172–173 n.10

Guatemala: armed struggle in, 65–84 passim

Guha, Ranajit, ix, 6, 15, 17, 21, 26–40, 41–42, 47, 59–61, 67, 85, 91–92, 99, 100–104, 136, 140, 144, 160, 171 nn. 28, 30, 174 n.19, 175 n.4, 182 nn. 6–7, 187 n.9; "Chandra's Death," 187 n.12; on colonial civil society, 121–122; definition of the subaltern, 26, 65, 91, 135, 166; on "the people," 87–88; on territoriality, 134–135, 189 n.3; on writing and Santal rebellion, 60–61

Gutiérrez, Gustavo: definition of "the poor," 38–40

Habermas, Jürgen, 16, 18, 46, 109–111, 121, 143–144

Hale, Charles: on Sandinista/Miskitu conflict, 95

Hall, Stuart: on the " 'political' aspect of cultural studies," 104, 107, 122, 184 n.25

Harrington, Michael, 23

Hegel, G. W. F., 31–32, 45, 138; concept of civil society, 121, 186 n.8; on market, 159–160

Hegemony, 1–7, 10–18, 28, 30, 34–35, 53–56, 67, 74, 76, 80, 82–84, 90–97, 100, 103, 104, 106, 108, 109–112, 119, 124, 128–129, 132, 133–168 passim; posthegemony, 97–98, 157–158

Heidegger, Martin, 110

Heterogeneity, 28, 62–64, 76, 87, 90–91, 101, 103, 112, 125, 131, 138, 147–148, 154–159, 163

History/historiography, 7–10, 19–22, 25–40 passim, 78–79, 81–82, 88; critique of Mallon, *Peasant and Nation*, 34–38; and Gramsci on subaltern history, 136–138; Guha on, 26–27; Spivak on, 100–101; Túpac Amaru rebellion, 52–56. *See also* Chakrabarty, Dipesh

Hobsbawm, Eric, 21, 134

Hoggart, Richard, 104, 107

Holocaust: representation of, 79–80; and *Schindler's List*, 180 n.16

Honig, Bonnie: on "democratic cosmopolitanism," 155–158, 162, 164, 165. *See also* Cosmopolitanism; Immigration

Humanities, 1, 6, 8, 11–16, 18–19, 28–31, 34, 41–42, 46–49, 56–58, 70–71, 76–77, 82, 100, 108–109, 112, 132, 137–139; and American studies, 162–164; subaltern studies as new model for, 31, 164–167, 173 n.14. *See also* Literature

Huntington, Samuel: "clash of civilizations," 24

Hybridity, 16, 17, 42, 62–64, 162–164; in Bhabha, 86–87, 98–100, 183 n.19; in García Canclini, 123–132. *See also* Bhabha, Homi

Identity politics, 14, 16–17, 24, 77, 83–84, 93–96, 113, 122, 135, 141–148, 158–159, 162–167, 181 n.26. *See also* Laclau, Ernesto; Mouffe, Chantal; Multiculturalism

"Imagined community." *See* Anderson, Benedict

Immigration, 62–64, 148–157, 174–175 n.2

Indigenous peoples/Indians, 19, 155, 165–166; and armed struggle in Guatemala, 65–84 passim, 181 n.26; and Ecuadoran civil society, 116–120, 187 n.12; in Peru, 49–64; and transculturation, 175–176 n.11

Institute for the Study of Ideologies and Literature, 170 n.12

Intellectuals, 12, 17–19, 35–36, 42, 56–58, 71, 79–84, 92, 110–112, 128–129, 158, 174 n.1, 174–175 n.2; Gramsci on, 138–140, 154, 159; Latin American, 185–186 n.35

Jackson, Jesse: and Rainbow Coalition, 143
James, C. L. R., 9
Jameson, Fredric, 5, 14, 23, 67, 109, 130; on cultural studies, 131–132, 170 n.19; on markets, 191–192 n.33; "national allegory," 53–54, 93, 101, 111–112; on testimonio, 178 n.4
Jara, René: on testimonio, 72
Jetzeit. See Benjamin, Walter

Kant, Immanuel: aesthetics, 56–57
Kraniauskas, John: on Bhabha, 183–184 n.20; populism of cultural studies, 185 n.29
Kristeva, Julia: idea of the abject and the subaltern, 102; on immigration and cosmopolitanism, 155–157, 193 n.43. See also Honig, Bonnie; Lind, Michael

Lacan, Jacques, 2, 25–28, 36, 39, 69, 73, 102, 147, 181 n.21
Laclau, Ernesto, 22, 23; and Chantal Mouffe's distinction of "democratic" and "popular" subject position, 93–94, 113, 143–148, 158; "egalitarian imaginary," 145, 147, 153, 164; on intellectual and moral leadership, 190 n.13; on populism, 154
Latin American Subaltern Studies Group, ix–x, 5–8, 19–20, 22, 37, 48, 97
Latinos (in the U.S.), 17, 28–29, 48, 162–166, 192–193 n.40
Laub, Dori: on testimonio, 78–79
Law, 27, 45, 90–91, 123, 127, 134, 139, 153, 156–157, 173 n.18, 181 n.21, 186 n.8, 187 n.9, 188 n.18; and indigenous communities, 116–120; and O. J. Simpson trial, 144, 190 n.17; and Túpac Amaru rebellion, 50–55. See also Citizenship; Civil society
Left, the, 3, 14, 20–24, 47–48, 74–75, 103–104, 113, 151–154, 166–167; and cultural studies, 123, 128–132, 141–166 passim
Lenin, V. I., 103, 139–140, 148, 149, 152
"Lettered city," the, 8, 18–19, 37, 48, 50, 54, 58–59, 70, 123, 166. See also Literature; Rama, Angel; Writing
Liberation theology, 38–40; and Sandinism, 95

Lienhard, Martin: on Ollantay and neo-Inca nationalism, 55, 176 n.19
Lind, Michael: on immigration, 151–153, 155
Literature, 1–24 passim, 28, 41–64 passim, 70–71, 170 n.12, 176 n.17; literary canon, 49, 51–56, 58, 71, 82. See also "Lettered city"; Writing
Lloyd, David: on Gramsci, 190 n.10; "nationalism against the state," 23, 172 n.33; nationalism and intellectuals, 174 n.1
López, María Milagros, ii–iii, 128; on citizenship, 148; "post-work subjectivity," 186 n.38
Lubiano, Wahneema: on multiculturalism, 191 n.29
Lukács, Georg, 49, 106
Lyotard, Jean-François, 15; notion of differend, 70; on "the pagan," 158; The Postmodern Condition, 108–109, 127; "temporary contract," 185 n.32

Malinowski, Bronislaw: on concept of transculturation, 43–44
Mallon, Florencia, 8, 19–20, 55, 74, 79, 82, 133, 173 n.17; Peasant and Nation, critique of, 34–42
Mamdani, Mahmood: on civil society and third world, 117–118
Mao Tse Tung/Maoism, 21, 90, 160, 182 n.6; and Naxalites and subaltern studies, 20, 171 n.30
Marcus, George: on ethnographic writing, 11
Marcuse, Herbert, 103, 104, 186 n.38
Market: and democratization, 107–198, 151, 158–161; market socialism, 160. See also Neoliberalism
Martí, José, 3
Marxism/Marx, 6, 12, 20–24, 49, 89, 101, 104, 113, 161, 191–192 n.33; Gramsci on, 136–140; on petty commodity production, 161, 192 n.38; and rational choice Marxism, 160
Mass culture, 48–49, 104–113, 123–132, 159, 161, 185 n.29, 192 n.33
Master/slave dialectic, 25–28, 99–100, 147, 177 n.23, 182 n.6

Menchú, Rigoberta: conflict with Elisabeth Burgos, 67–68, 178–179 n.5, 181 n.25; *Crossing Borders*, 178 n.5; *I, Rigoberta Menchú*, 29–31, 51, 65–84 passim, 99, 139, 164, 173 n.13, 179–180 n.12, 180 nn. 13, 17, 181 nn. 23–25

Mignolo, Walter: colonial language policy, 179 n.8; "politics of location" theory, 171 n.27

"Mixed times." *See* García Canclini, Néstor

Modernity/modernism, 7, 14, 23, 34, 36, 67, 69, 156, 164; and civil society, 117–132; and the Frankfurt School, 104, 106, 111; in Gramsci, 138; and hybridity, 126–127; and literary transculturation, 45–49, 57–59; and Sandinism, 96–97

Morales, Mario Roberto: critique of Mayan identity politics, 181 n.26

Moraña, Mabel: critique of subaltern studies, 17–19, 166, 171 n.26

Moreiras, Alberto: on critical regionalism, 130–131; on hegemony, 97, 104

Morris, Meaghan: on cultural studies, 109

Morrison, Toni, 42

Mouffe, Chantal: on citizenship, 147–148; "egalitarian imaginary," 145, 147, 153, 164; and Ernesto Laclau on "popular subject position," 93–94, 113, 143–147

Multiculturalism, 3, 17, 18, 28–29, 31, 62–64, 76–77, 83, 97, 108, 144–167 passim, 181 n.26, 191 n.29, 193 n.43. *See also* Heterogeneity; Identity politics; Laclau, Ernesto; Mouffe, Chantal; Taylor, Charles

Narrative transculturation. *See* Rama, Angel

Nation/nation-state, 3–11, 17–24, 33–40, 46–49, 61–64, 89–91, 98, 101, 103–104, 123–127, 133–167 passim, 172 n.33, 183–184 n.20; and multiculturalism, 62–64; Sandinista nationalism, 94–96; in Túpac Amaru rebellion, 53–56

"National allegory." *See* Jameson, Fredric

National-popular. *See* Gramsci, Antonio

Native informant, 74, 79

Negation, 26, 31–34, 36, 59–60, 64, 85, 99, 106, 122, 130–131, 136–137, 140, 147, 182 n.2

Neoconservatism, 108, 111, 113, 165; and modernism, 185 n.28

Neoliberalism, 7, 84, 110, 118–119, 129–132, 150–153, 159–160

New social movements, 14, 103, 104, 118, 129, 143–148, 152, 170–171 n.20

Nietzsche, Friedrich: on slave morality, 32, 137

"Non-dialectical heterogeneity." *See* Cornejo-Polar, Antonio

Nugent, Daniel, 9

Ollantay, 50–56, 59, 62, 176 n.19

Orality, 24, 44, 49, 52–69, 71, 81–82, 179 n.8, 181 n.24; rumor as a form of orality, 59–62. *See also* Amin, Shahid; Benjamin, Walter and "The Storyteller"; Guha, Ranajit; Testimonio; Writing

Ortiz, Fernando: concept of transculturation, 43–45, 47, 126. *See also* Rama, Angel; Transculturation

Osorio, Nelson. See *Diccionario Enciclopédico de Literatura Latinoamericana*

Ozick, Cynthia: on immigration, 155–156. *See also* Honig, Bonnie; Kristeva, Julia; Lind, Michael

Paglia, Camille, 107

People, the, 76, 85–113 passim, 117, 135, 143, 151, 153–161, 164. *See also* Dimitrov, Georgi; Gramsci, Antonio; National-popular

"People-nation." *See* Gramsci, Antonio

Petty commodity production, 161, 192 n.38

Popular Front, 88–96, 103, 112, 148, 154, 183 n.11; cultural politics of, 105–106, 184–185 n.27. *See also* Dimitrov, Georgi; Mao Tse Tung/Maoism

"Popular subject position." *See* Laclau, Ernesto; Mouffe, Chantal

Populism, 9, 97, 154, 159–160; of cultural studies, 109–113, 123, 185 n.29; *narodniks*, 38–40. *See also* Laclau, Ernesto; Moreiras, Alberto

Postcoloniality, 16–18, 20–24, 34–35, 41, 163

Postmodernism, 3, 14–15, 22–24, 67, 76–83, 108–113, 118, 148, 162; and hybridity, 123–127

Poststructuralism, 7–8, 20–22
Poulantzas, Nikos, 22
Power, 1, 10, 11, 13, 33, 37–39, 79, 87, 99–
100, 106, 119, 134, 142, 145; "biopower"
(Foucault), 16. See also Agency; Hegemony
Prakash, Gayan: on failure of subaltern
agency, 135
Pratt, Mary Louise: on "ethnobiography,"
181 n.25; on Stanford Western Culture
Debate, 172 n.8, 179–180 n.12

Quijano, Aníbal: on "Andean rationality,"
176–177 n.20

Rainbow Coalition, 142–143
Rama, Angel, 8, 10–11, 170 n.12; concept of
"narrative transculturation," 10, 43–49,
51, 58–59, 123, 126, 133, 175 nn. 7–9,
175–176 n.11. See also "Lettered city";
Ortiz, Fernando; Transculturation
Reception theory, 107, 111–112, 185 n.31
Regional federalism, 130–131. See also
García Canclini, Néstor; Moreiras,
Alberto
Representation, 1–40 passim, 43, 51–58, 91,
98–99, 100–103, 107, 109, 112, 113, 126,
131, 140, 142, 147, 150, 154, 157, 163, 166,
180 n.16, 183 n.19; in testimonio, 66–67,
70–83
Rivera Cusicanqui, Silvia: on ayllu democ-
racy in Bolivia, 187 n.12
Rodríguez, Ileana: on crisis of revolutionary
left, 3
Rodriguez, Richard: Hunger of Memory, 28–
30, 69, 139, 164, 172 n.6, 192 n.40
Rorty, Richard: on solidarity, 39, 174 n.23;
Achieving Our Country, 143, 147, 193 n.43
Rousseau, Jean-Jacques: Confessions, 51; Paul
de Man on, 176 n.16
Rushdie, Salman, 42; critique of, 174–
175 n.2

Said, Edward, 2, 27, 33, 41–43, 45, 62,
172 n.4, 175 n.3
Saldaña, María Josefina: critique of Sandinism, 96–97
Sandinism, 3–4, 8, 23, 75, 94–97, 152, 154,
183 nn. 15–17

Santiago, Silviano: on popular reception,
111–112
Sarlo, Beatriz, 18, 123, 185 n.35; Escenas de la
vida posmoderna, critique of, 109–113; on
"media populism," 109, 185 n.35
Sartre, Jean-Paul: "serialization," 144
Saussure, Ferdinand de: on negation, 85,
182 n.2
Schmitt, Carl: category of "the enemy," 90
Seed, Patricia, 10, 22; on hybridity, 86
Serialization. See Sartre, Jean-Paul
Singer, Linda: critique of Marxism, 140–
141
Sklodowska, Elzbieta: on testimonio, 70–
72, 82–83, 179 n.9
Socialism, 3, 14, 23–24, 89–90, 104, 97,
137–138, 140, 149–150, 159–161, 166,
193 n.43; and "socialism in one country,"
149, 152. See also Communism; Left, the
Sokal affair, 16, 190 n.14
Solidarity, 3–4, 38–39, 66, 69, 73, 77, 81–
84, 153
Sommer, Doris, 5, 8, 93, 173; course on
"American Identities," 162–165 (see also
Bercovitch, Sacvan; Wilentz, Sean); on
I, Rigoberta Menchú, 173 n.13
South Asian Subaltern Studies Group, 5–8,
11, 17, 20–22, 27, 30, 160, 181 n.24
Soviet Union, 21, 89, 118, 120, 137, 149–150,
159
Spivak, Gayatri, ix, 2, 7, 16, 29, 31, 37, 66–
67, 69–71, 75, 82–83, 87–88, 106, 122,
135, 142, 148–149, 152, 169 n.1, 172 n.9,
179 n.7, 182 nn. 6–7, 184 nn. 22, 24; critique of, 100–104, 152
State, 23, 27, 36–37, 83, 107, 110, 113, 117–
123, 141–145, 150–154, 159–161, 190 n.13;
and cultural studies, 128–129; Hebrew,
155–156; neo-Inca, 50, 53–56, 176 n.19,
176–177 n.20; and "people-state"/
"people-nation," 151, 153–155; and territoriality, 133–167 passim. See also
Nation/nation-state
Stern, Steve: on Andean subaltern nationalisms, 8, 55
Stoler, Ann: on hybridity, 86
Stoll, David: Rigoberta Menchú and the Story of
All Poor Guatemalans, 66–83 passim

Subaltern studies, 1–24 passim, 28–31, 38–40, 41–42, 100–104, 122–123, 134, 141, 153, 159, 165–167, 171 n.28. See also Guha, Ranajit; Latin American Subaltern Studies Group; South Asian Subaltern Studies Group; Spivak, Gayatri

Suleri, Sara: on hybridity, 86

Taussig, Michael: on Christianization of New World, 177 n.23; on the "devil contract," 9

Taylor, Charles: on the "presumption of equal worth," 141, 145–146

Territoriality, 2, 7, 63, 142, 148–153, 173 n.17; borders, 125, 188 n.18. See also Cornejo-Polar, Antonió; Globalization; Guha, Ranajit

Testimonio (testimonial narrative), 4, 37, 48, 51, 65–84 passim, 135; and conflict over authorship, 178–179 n.5; and Holocaust testimonio, 79–80, 180 n.16. See also Beverley, John; Jameson, Fredric; Menchú, Rigoberta; Orality; Sklodowska, Elzbieta

Thompson, E. P., 104, 107

Transculturation, 41–64 passim, 69, 127–128, 131, 164–166, 183 n.20. See also Hybridity; Ortiz, Fernando; Rama, Angel

Túpac Amaru: and José Gabriel, Genealogía, 49–56, 63; and Juan Bautista, Memorias, 49–51; letter to Bolivar, 176

Túpac Amaru rebellion, 49–56, 59, 62

University. See Academy

Vanguard party, 97, 139–140. See also Lenin, V. I.; Sandinism

Vargas Llosa, Mario: on Indians and modernity, 175–176 n.11; The War at the End of the World, 117, 122. See also Antonio the Counsellor

Virno, Paolo: concept of "the multitude," 158

Weber, Max: concept of modernity, 14, 57–58

Western Culture debate. See Academy

Wilentz, Sean: on American studies, 162–166, 193 nn. 42–43

Williams, Gareth: critique of subaltern studies, 71, 171 n.26

Williams, Raymond, 63, 104

Willis, Paul: Learning to Labour, 107, 185 n.30

Wittgenstein, Ludwig, 33

Women/women's movement, 19, 41, 42, 47, 62, 68, 89, 93, 97, 104, 116–117, 129, 140, 143, 149, 151, 152, 162, 187 n.12, 190 n.12; Guha, "Chandra's Death," 187 n.12; and orality, 179 n.8; Rigoberta Menchú, 65–84 passim; Said on, 175 n.3; Sandinism, 96–97, 103; Spivak on, 179 n.7, 184 n.24

Writing, 25–40 passim, 48–49, 59–61, 175 nn. 3–4, 176 n.17

Young, Iris Marion: critique of Mouffe, 147–148; on the politics of new social movements, 144, 154

Yúdice, George: on citizenship and consumption, 189 n.27

Zapatistas, 42–43, 74, 122

Zimmerman, Marc: Literature and Politics, 3–5, 8

John Beverley is Professor of Hispanic Languages and
Literatures at the University of Pittsburgh. He is the author of
Against Literature, *Del Lazarillo al Sandinismo: Una modernidad
obsoleta: Estudios sobre el barroco*, and *Aspects of Gongora's
"Soledades."* He coauthored, along with Marc Zimmerman,
Literature and Politics in the Central American Revolutions. He has
coedited a number of books, including *The Postmodernism Debate
in Latin America* with Michael Aronna and José Oviedo, *La voz del
otro: Testimonio, subalternidad, y verdad narrativa* with Hugo
Achugar, and *Texto y sociedad: Problemas de historia literaria* with
Bridget Aldaraca and Edward Baker.

Library of Congress Cataloging-in-Publication Data
Beverley, John.
Subalternity and representation : arguments in cultural theory
/ John Beverley.
p.   cm. — (Post-contemporary interventions)
Includes index.
ISBN 0-8223-2382-6 (cloth : alk. paper). —
ISBN 0-8223-2416-4 (pbk. : alk. paper)
1. Marginality, Social.   2. Marginality, Social—Political
aspects—Latin America.   3. Learning and scholarship—
Political aspects.   4. Knowledge, Theory of—Political
aspects.   5. Postcolonialism.   6. Culture conflict.
I. Title.   II. Series.
HM1136.B48   1999
305.5'6—dc21   99-31551